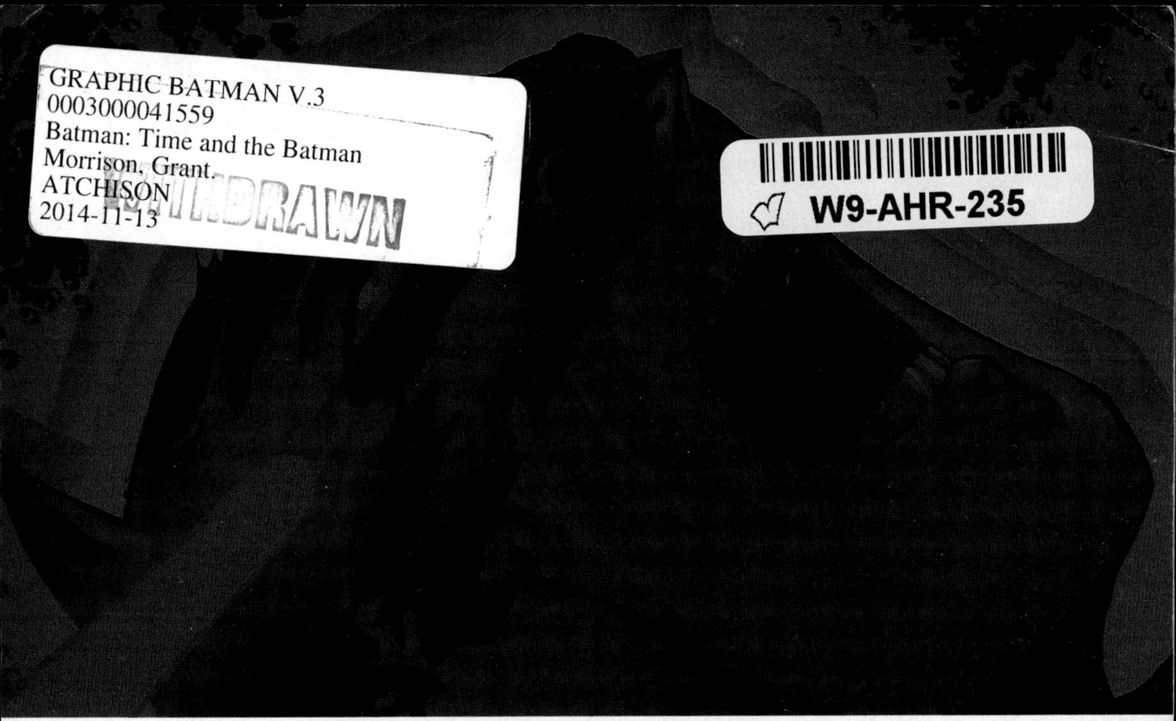

BATMAN
TIME AND THE BATMAN

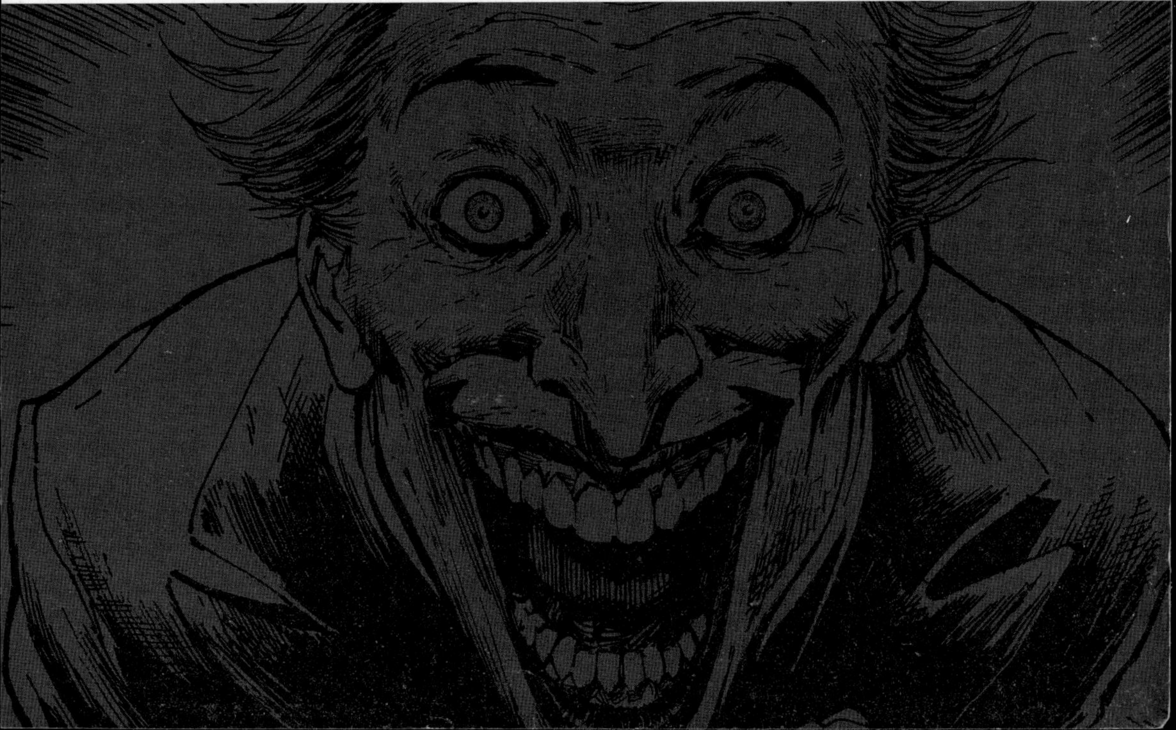

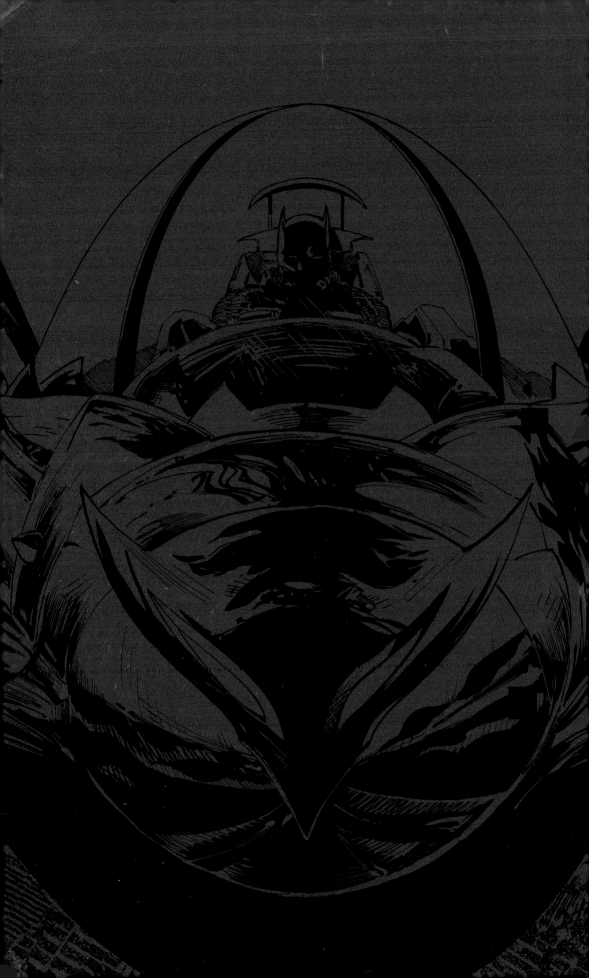

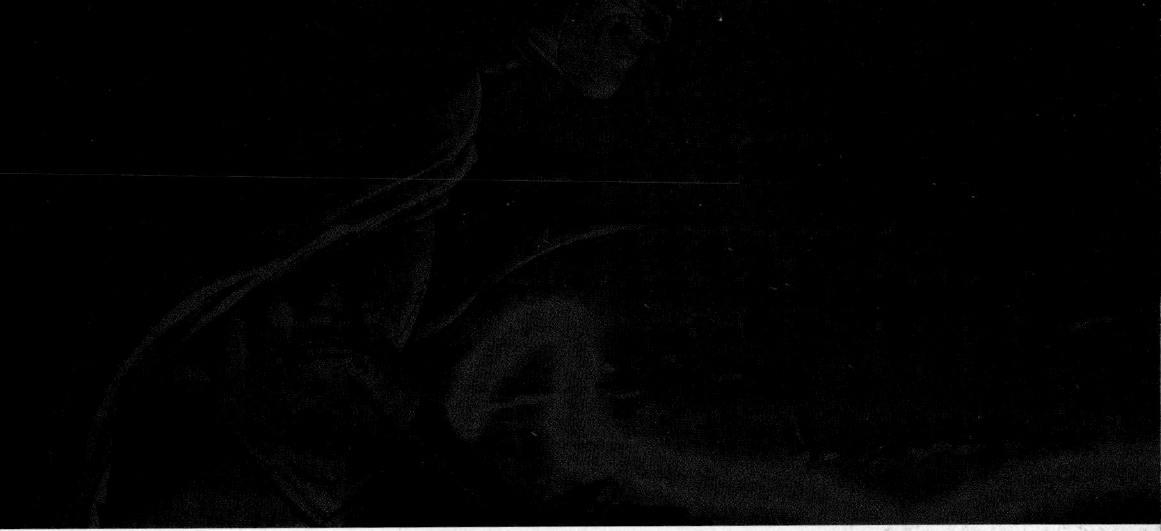

BATMAN
TIME AND THE BATMAN

WRITTEN BY GRANT MORRISON FABIAN NICIEZA

ART BY TONY S. DANIEL CLIFF RICHARDS ANDY KUBERT FRANK QUITELY DAVID FINCH RICHARD FRIEND SCOTT KOLINS

COLORED BY IAN HANNIN ALEX SINCLAIR TONY AVIÑA BRAD ANDERSON PETER STEIGERWALD

LETTERED BY JARED K. FLETCHER TRAVIS LANHAM

COVER ART BY DAVID FINCH AND SCOTT WILLIAMS

ORIGINAL SERIES COVERS BY TONY S. DANIEL DAVID FINCH SCOTT WILLIAMS ANDY KUBERT MIKE MIGNOLA KEVIN NOWLAN

BATMAN CREATED BY BOB KANE

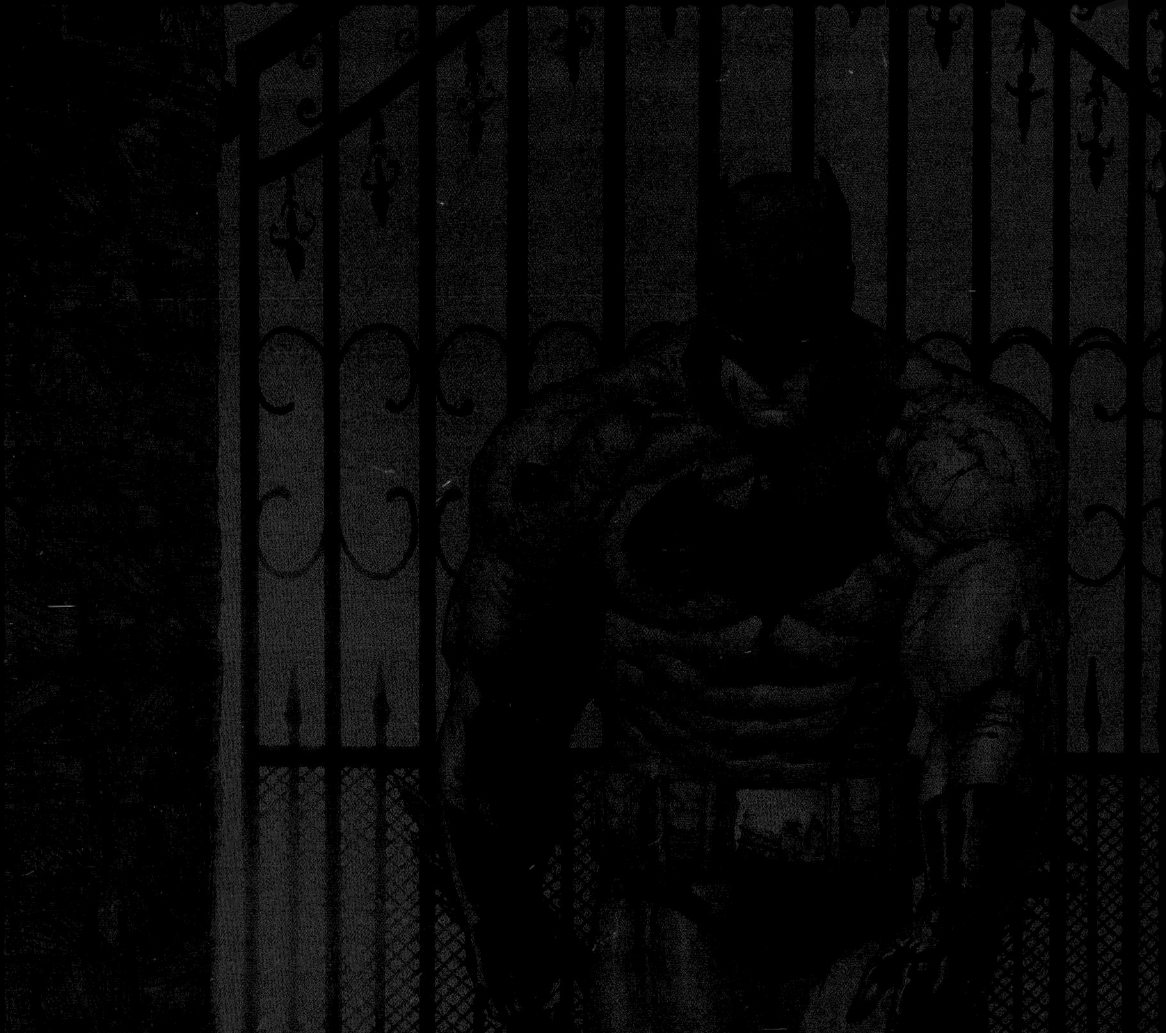

Mike Marts Editor - Original Series **Janelle Siegel** Associate Editor - Original Series
Scott Nybakken Editor **Robbin Brosterman** Design Director - Books

Bob Harras Senior VP - Editor-in-Chief, DC Comics

Diane Nelson President **Dan DiDio and Jim Lee** Co-Publishers **Geoff Johns** Chief Creative Officer
John Rood Executive VP - Sales, Marketing and Business Development **Amy Genkins** Senior VP - Business and Legal Affairs
Nairi Gardiner Senior VP - Finance **Jeff Boison** VP - Publishing Planning **Mark Chiarello** VP - Art Direction and Design **John Cunningham** VP - Marketing
Terri Cunningham VP - Editorial Administration **Alison Gill** Senior VP - Manufacturing and Operations
Hank Kanalz Senior VP - Vertigo and Integrated Publishing **Jay Kogan** VP - Business and Legal Affairs, Publishing **Jack Mahan** VP - Business Affairs, Talent
Nick Napolitano VP - Manufacturing Administration **Sue Pohja** VP - Book Sales **Courtney Simmons** Senior VP - Publicity **Bob Wayne** Senior VP - Sales

Cover color by Peter Steigerwald.

BATMAN: TIME AND THE BATMAN

DC Comics
1700 Broadway, New York, NY 10019
A Warner Bros. Entertainment Company.
Printed by RR Donnelley, Salem, VA. 11/29/13. Third Printing.
ISBN: 978-1-4012-2990-0

SUSTAINABLE FORESTRY INITIATIVE Certified Chain of Custod
At Least 20% Certified Forest Co
www.sfiprogram.org
SFI-01042
APPLIES TO TEXT STOCK ONLY

Library of Congress Cataloging-in-Publication Data

Morrison, Grant.
Batman : time and the Batman / Grant Morrison, Fabian Nicieza, Tony S. Daniel, Cliff Richards, Andy Kubert, Frank Quitely, David Finch.
p. cm.
"Originally published as Batman 700-703."
ISBN 978-1-4012-2990-0
1. Graphic novels. I. Nicieza, Fabian. II. Daniel, Tony S. (Antonio Salvador) III. Richards, Cliff. IV. Kubert, Andy. V. Quitely, Frank, 1968- VI. Finch, David, 1972- VII. Title.
PN6728.B36M76 2012
741.5'973--dc23

2012025234

TABLE OF CONTENTS

TIME AND THE BATMAN 7

Written by Grant Morrison

YESTERDAY 10
Art by Tony S. Daniel / Colors by Ian Hannin / Letters by Jared K. Fletcher

TODAY 18
Art by Frank Quitely (pages 18-22) and Scott Kolins (pages 23-25)
Colors by Alex Sinclair (pages 18-22) and Tony Aviña (pages 23-25)
Letters by Jared K. Fletcher

TOMORROW 26
Art by Adam Kubert / Colors by Brad Anderson / Letters by Jared K. Fletcher

AND TOMORROW... 35
Pencils by David Finch / Inks by Richard Friend / Colors by Peter Steigerwald
Letters by Jared K. Fletcher

R.I.P — THE MISSING CHAPTER 41

Written by Grant Morrison

PART ONE: THE HOLE IN THINGS 43
Art by Tony S. Daniel / Colors by Ian Hannin / Letters by Jared K. Fletcher

PART TWO: BATMAN'S LAST CASE 67
Art by Tony S. Daniel / Colors by Ian Hannin / Letters by Travis Lanham

THE GREAT ESCAPE 91

Written by Fabian Nicieza / Art by Cliff Richards / Colors by Ian Hannin
Letters by Jared K. Fletcher

CREATURES OF THE NIGHT: A BATMAN GALLERY 113

OPERATIONAL FILES: THE BATCAVE 122

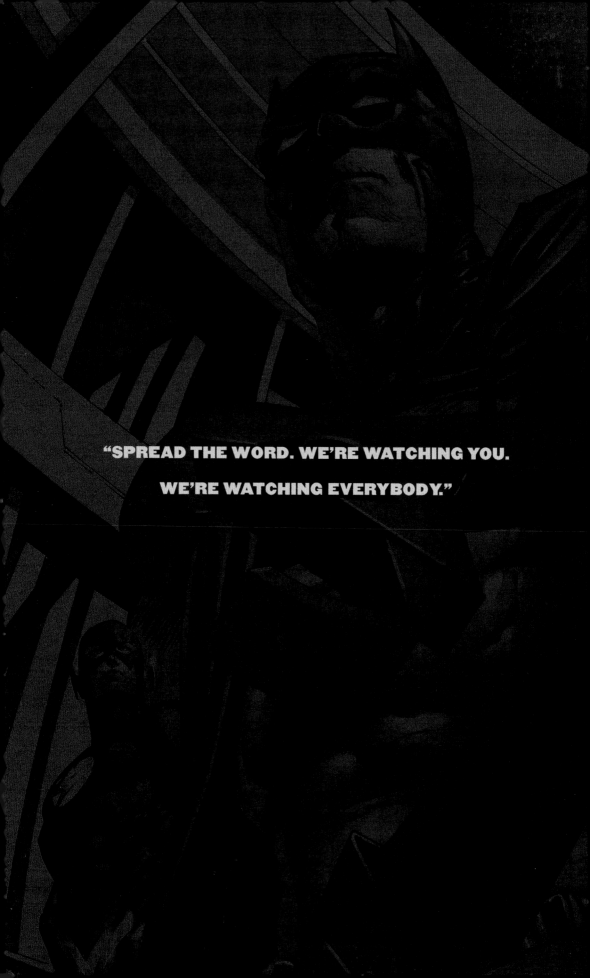

"SPREAD THE WORD. WE'RE WATCHING YOU.

WE'RE WATCHING EVERYBODY."

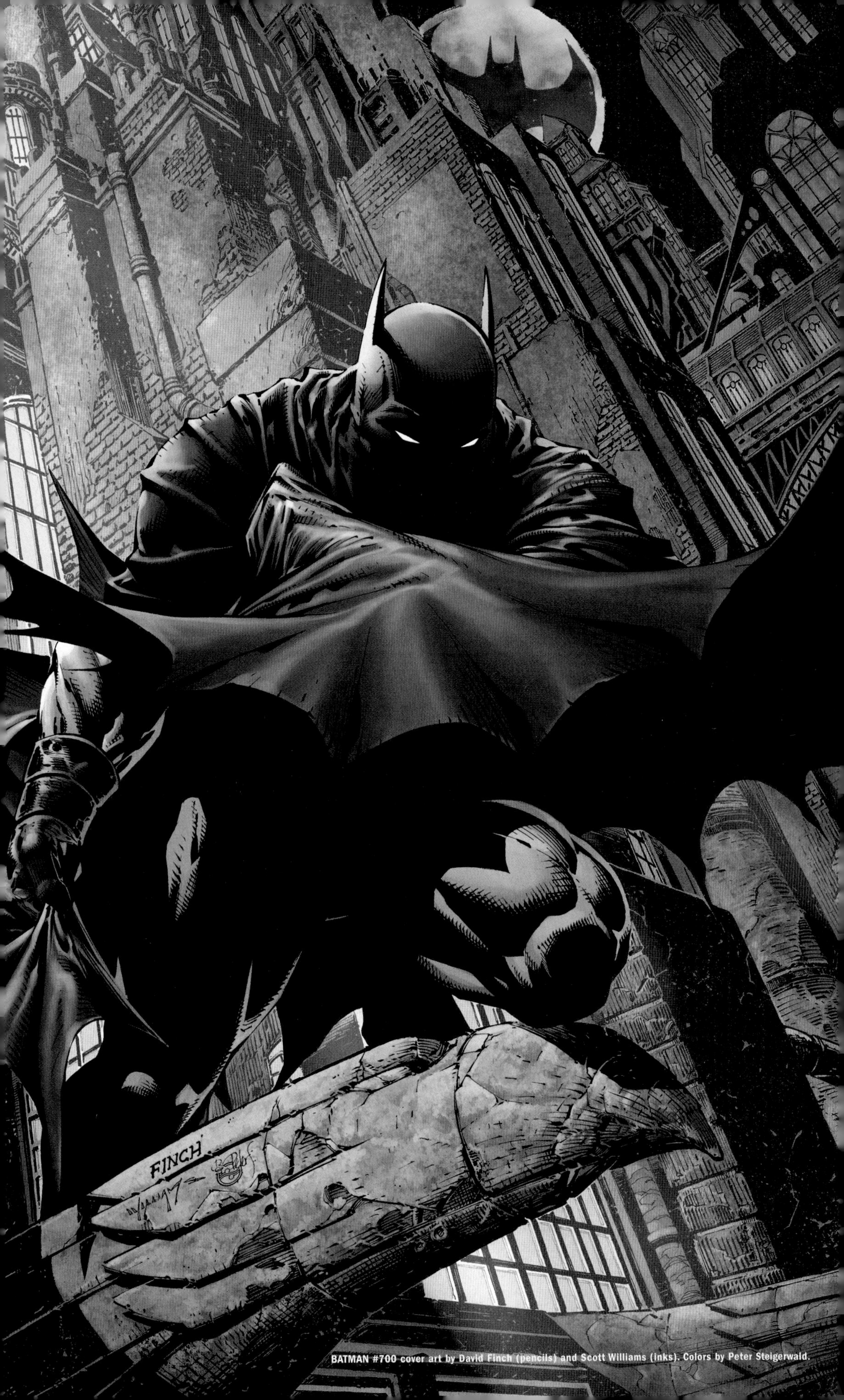
FINCH

BATMAN #700 cover art by David Finch (pencils) and Scott Williams (inks). Colors by Peter Steigerwald.

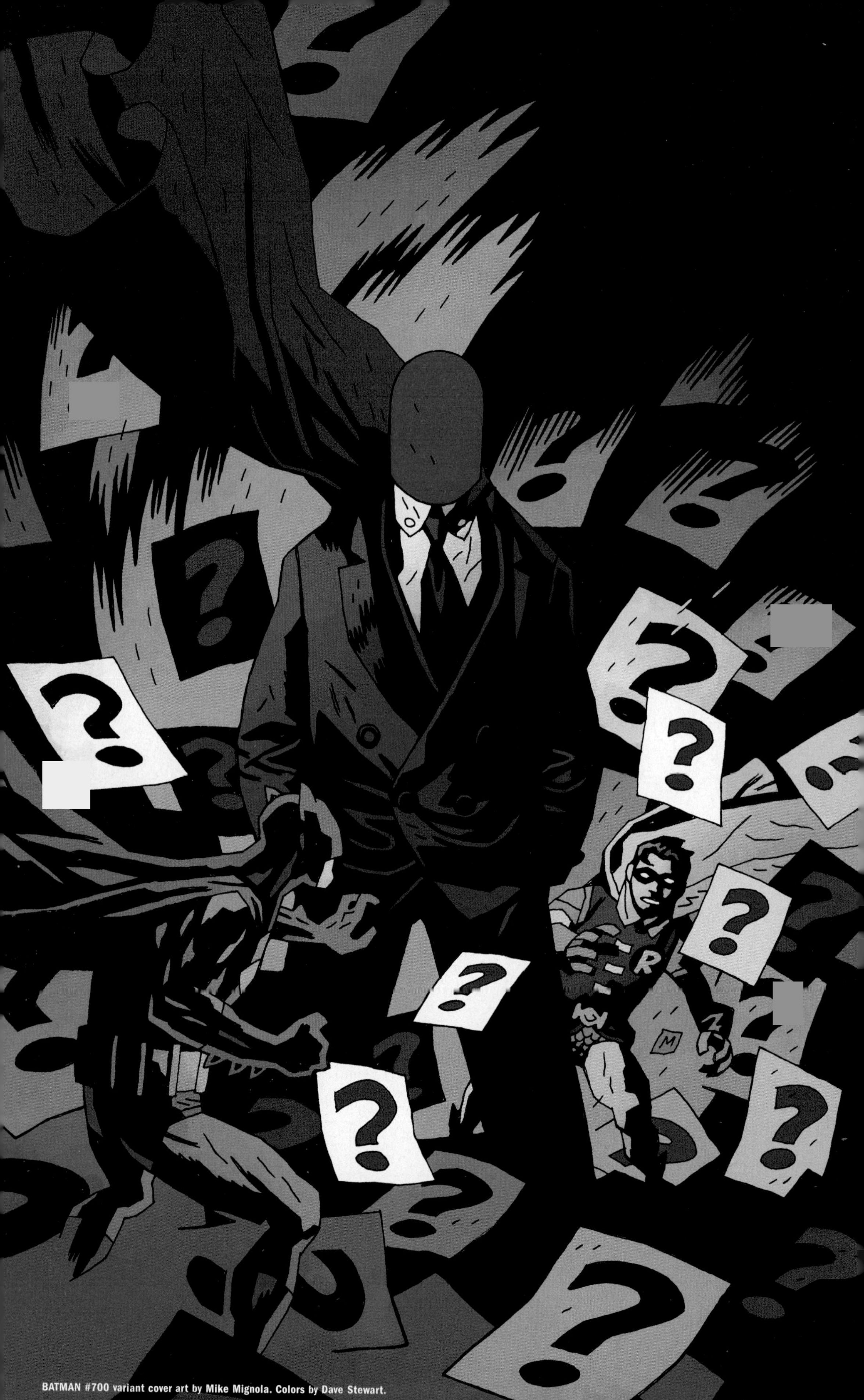

BATMAN #700 variant cover art by Mike Mignola. Colors by Dave Stewart.

THREE BATMEN

BRUCE WAYNE DICK GRAYSON DAMIAN WAYNE

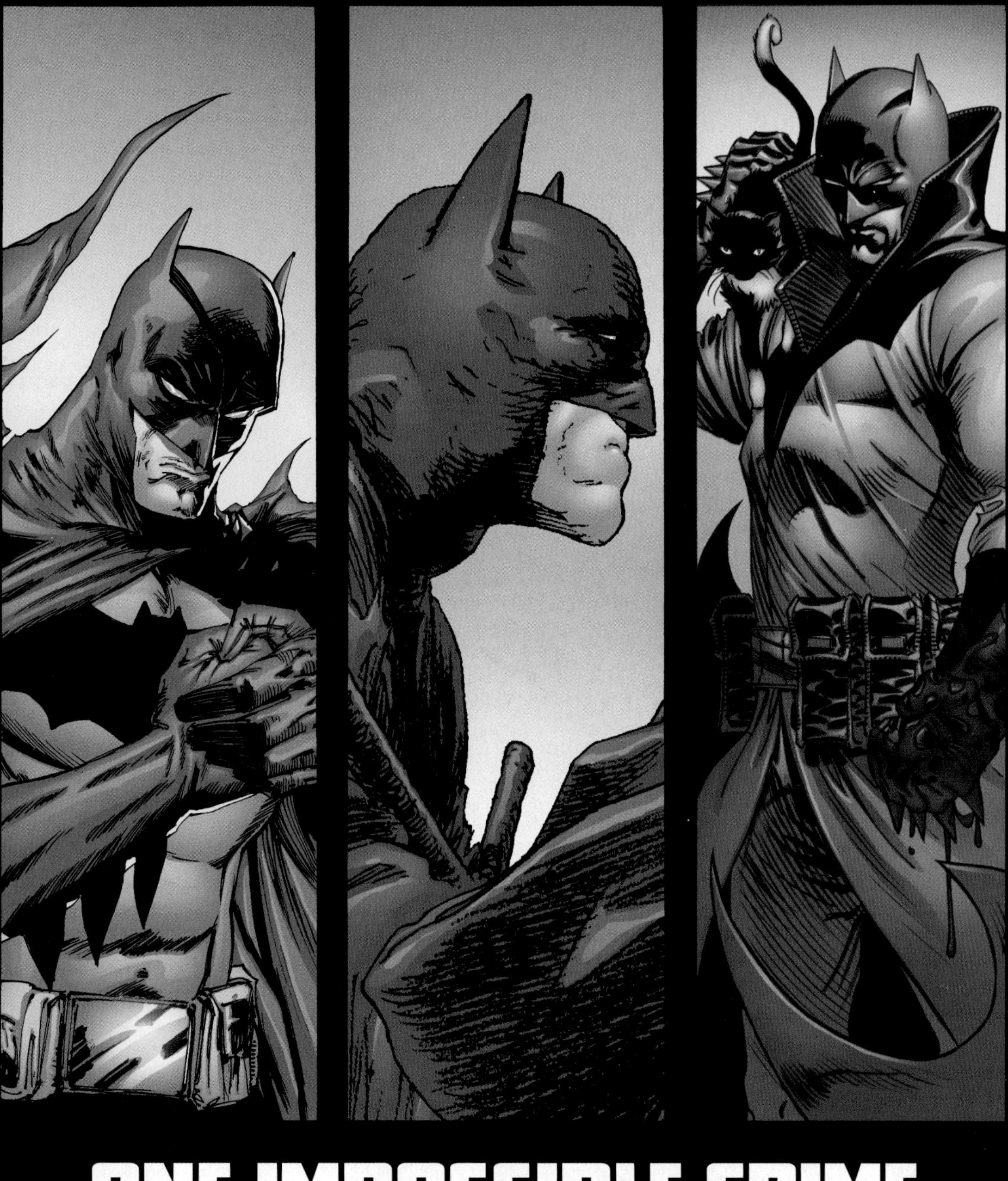

ONE IMPOSSIBLE CRIME

CAN YOU CRACK THE CASE?

"TIME AND THE BATMAN"

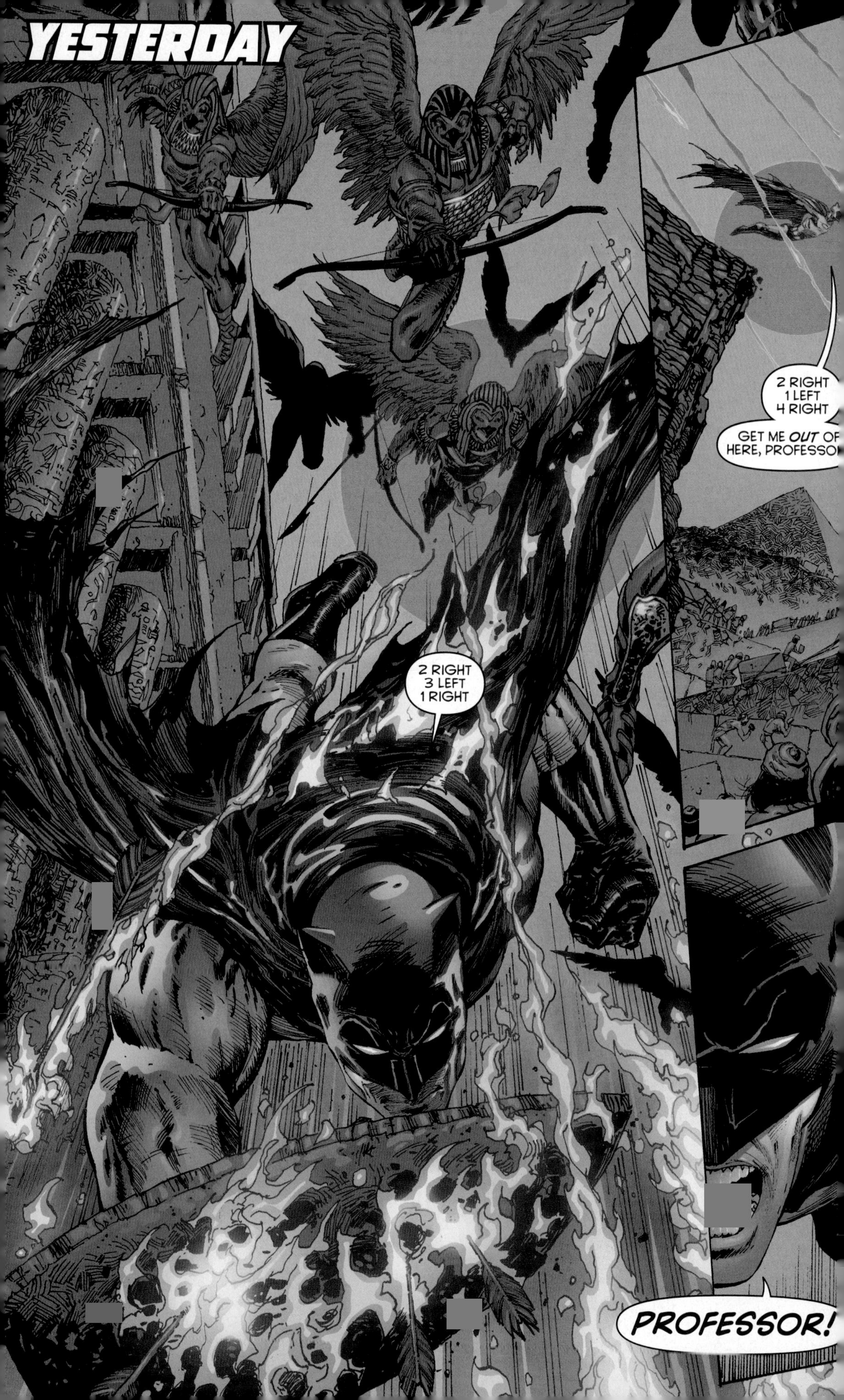
YESTERDAY
2 RIGHT 3 LEFT 1 RIGHT
2 RIGHT 1 LEFT 4 RIGHT
GET ME OUT OF HERE, PROFESSO
PROFESSOR!

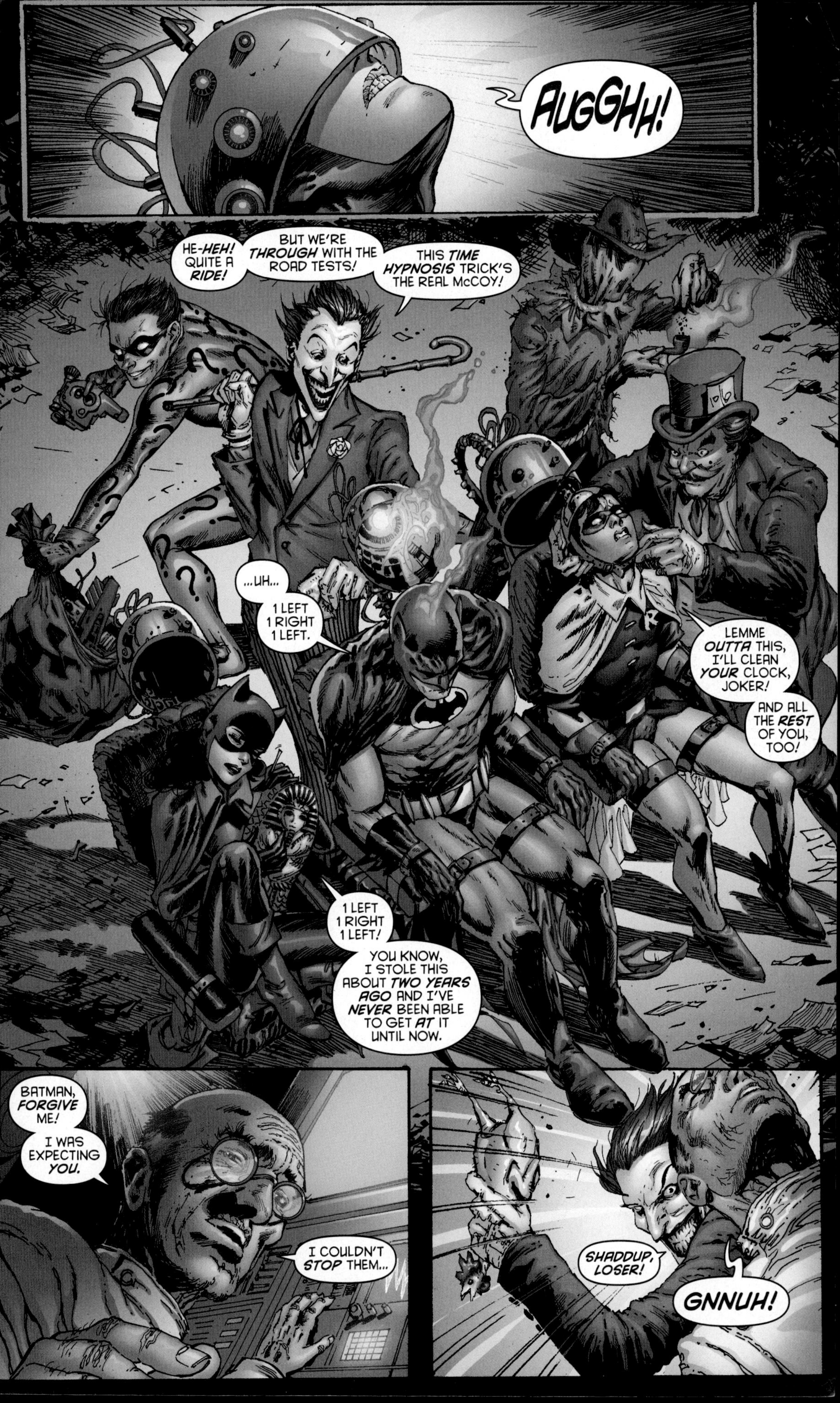
AUGGHH!
HE-HEH! QUITE A RIDE!
BUT WE'RE THROUGH WITH THE ROAD TESTS!
THIS TIME HYPNOSIS TRICK'S THE REAL McCOY!
...UH...
1 LEFT 1 RIGHT 1 LEFT.
LEMME OUTTA THIS, I'LL CLEAN YOUR CLOCK, JOKER!
AND ALL THE REST OF YOU, TOO!
1 LEFT 1 RIGHT 1 LEFT!
YOU KNOW, I STOLE THIS ABOUT TWO YEARS AGO AND I'VE NEVER BEEN ABLE TO GET AT IT UNTIL NOW.
BATMAN, FORGIVE ME!
I WAS EXPECTING YOU.
I COULDN'T STOP THEM...
SHADDUP, LOSER!
GNNUH!

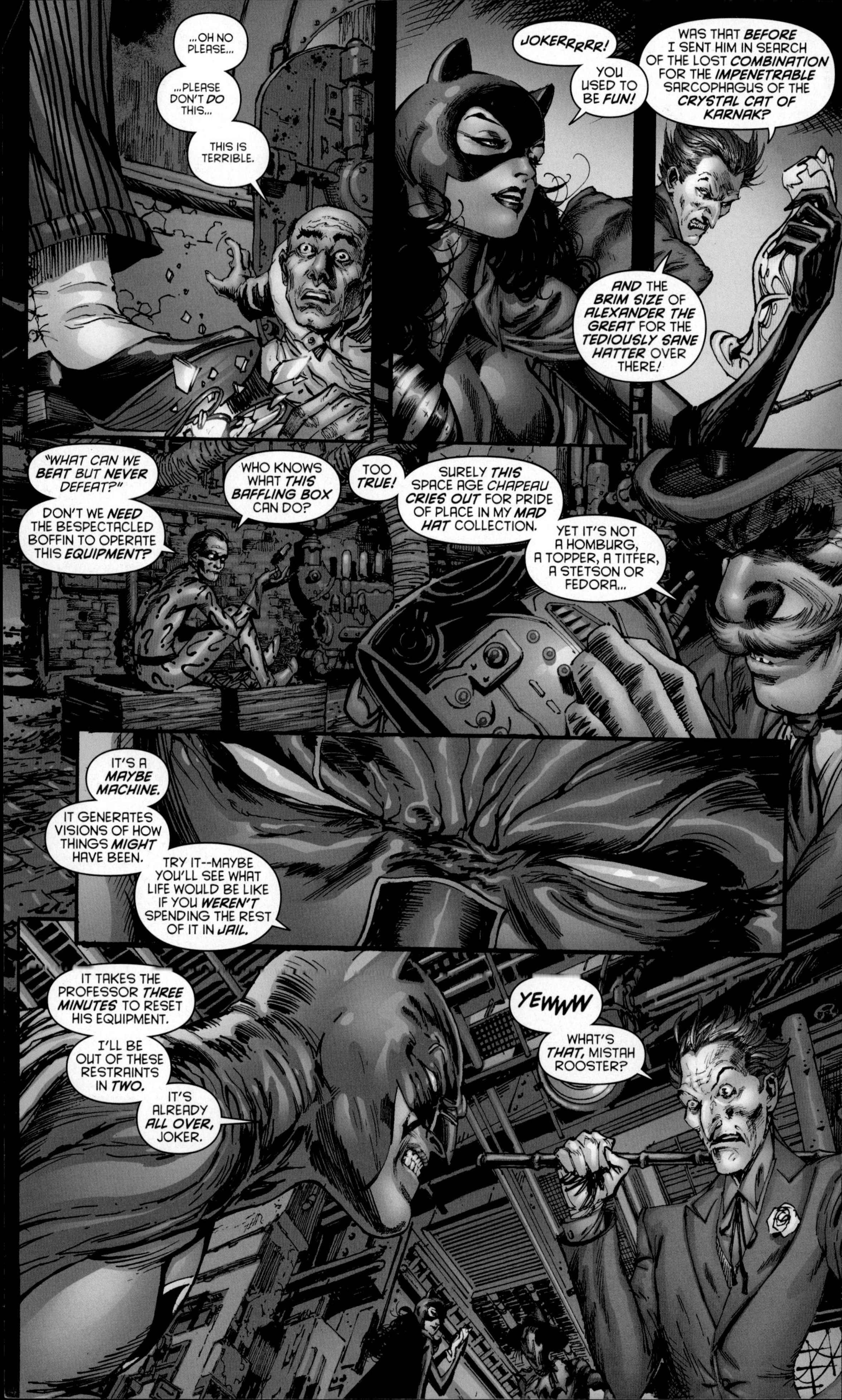
...OH NO PLEASE...
...PLEASE DON'T DO THIS...
THIS IS TERRIBLE.
JOKERRRRR!
YOU USED TO BE FUN!
WAS THAT BEFORE I SENT HIM IN SEARCH OF THE LOST COMBINATION FOR THE IMPENETRABLE SARCOPHAGUS OF THE CRYSTAL CAT OF KARNAK?
AND THE BRIM SIZE OF ALEXANDER THE GREAT FOR THE TEDIOUSLY SANE HATTER OVER THERE!
"WHAT CAN WE BEAT BUT NEVER DEFEAT?"
DON'T WE NEED THE BESPECTACLED BOFFIN TO OPERATE THIS EQUIPMENT?
WHO KNOWS WHAT THIS BAFFLING BOX CAN DO?
TOO TRUE!
SURELY THIS SPACE AGE CHAPEAU CRIES OUT FOR PRIDE OF PLACE IN MY MAD HAT COLLECTION.
YET IT'S NOT A HOMBURG, A TOPPER, A TITFER, A STETSON OR FEDORA...
IT'S A MAYBE MACHINE.
IT GENERATES VISIONS OF HOW THINGS MIGHT HAVE BEEN.
TRY IT--MAYBE YOU'LL SEE WHAT LIFE WOULD BE LIKE IF YOU WEREN'T SPENDING THE REST OF IT IN JAIL.
IT TAKES THE PROFESSOR THREE MINUTES TO RESET HIS EQUIPMENT.
I'LL BE OUT OF THESE RESTRAINTS IN TWO.
IT'S ALREADY ALL OVER, JOKER.
YEWWW
WHAT'S THAT, MISTAH ROOSTER?

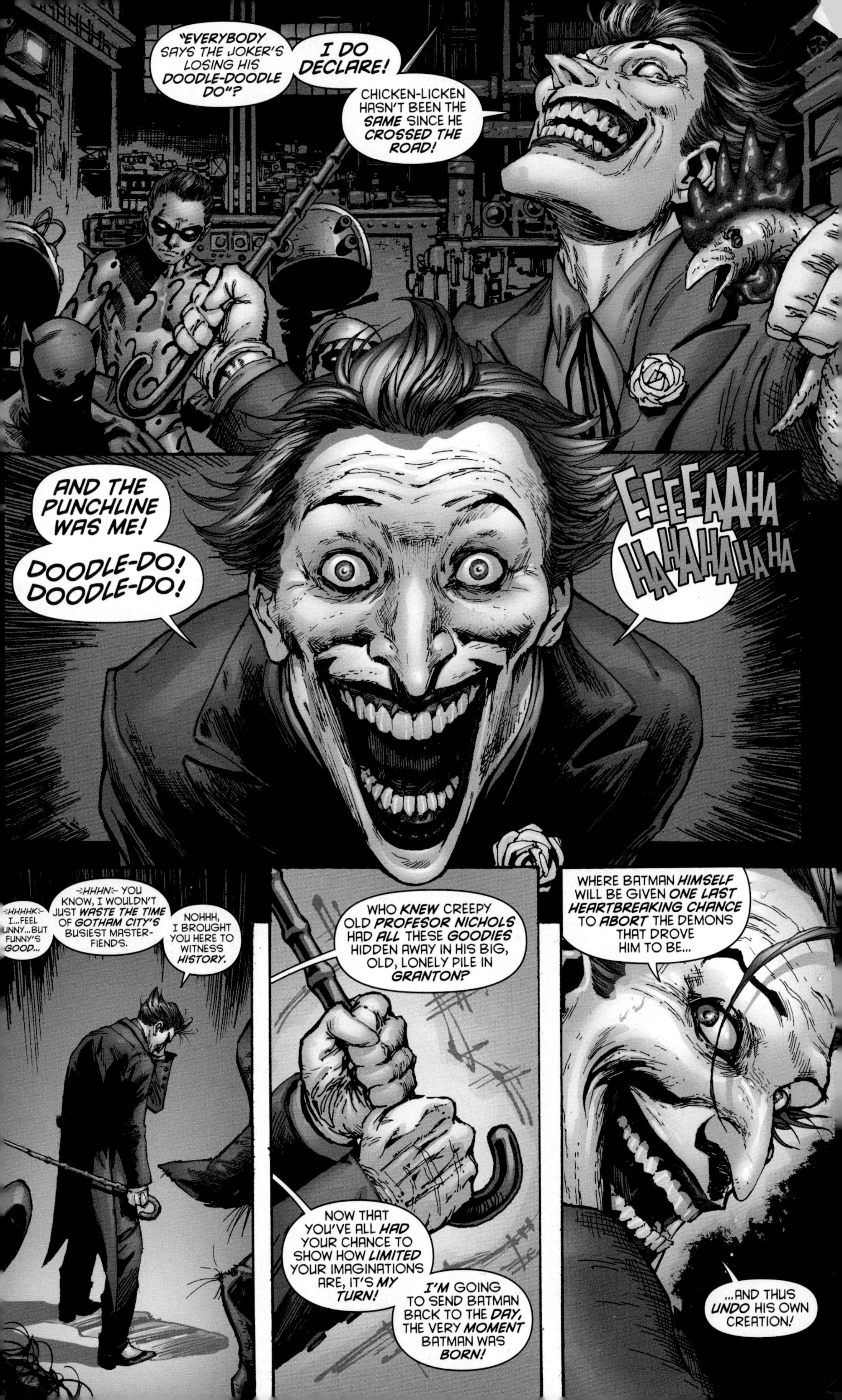

"EVERYBODY SAYS THE JOKER'S LOSING HIS DOODLE-DOODLE DO"?
I DO DECLARE!
CHICKEN-LICKEN HASN'T BEEN THE SAME SINCE HE CROSSED THE ROAD!
AND THE PUNCHLINE WAS ME!
DOODLE-DO! DOODLE-DO!
EEEEAAHA HAHAHAHAHAHA
=HHHHK= I...FEEL UNNY...BUT FUNNY'S GOOD...
=HHHN= YOU KNOW, I WOULDN'T JUST WASTE THE TIME OF GOTHAM CITY'S BUSIEST MASTER-FIENDS.
NOHHH, I BROUGHT YOU HERE TO WITNESS HISTORY.
WHO KNEW CREEPY OLD PROFESOR NICHOLS HAD ALL THESE GOODIES HIDDEN AWAY IN HIS BIG, OLD, LONELY PILE IN GRANTON?
NOW THAT YOU'VE ALL HAD YOUR CHANCE TO SHOW HOW LIMITED YOUR IMAGINATIONS ARE, IT'S MY TURN!
I'M GOING TO SEND BATMAN BACK TO THE DAY, THE VERY MOMENT BATMAN WAS BORN!
WHERE BATMAN HIMSELF WILL BE GIVEN ONE LAST HEARTBREAKING CHANCE TO ABORT THE DEMONS THAT DROVE HIM TO BE...
...AND THUS UNDO HIS OWN CREATION!

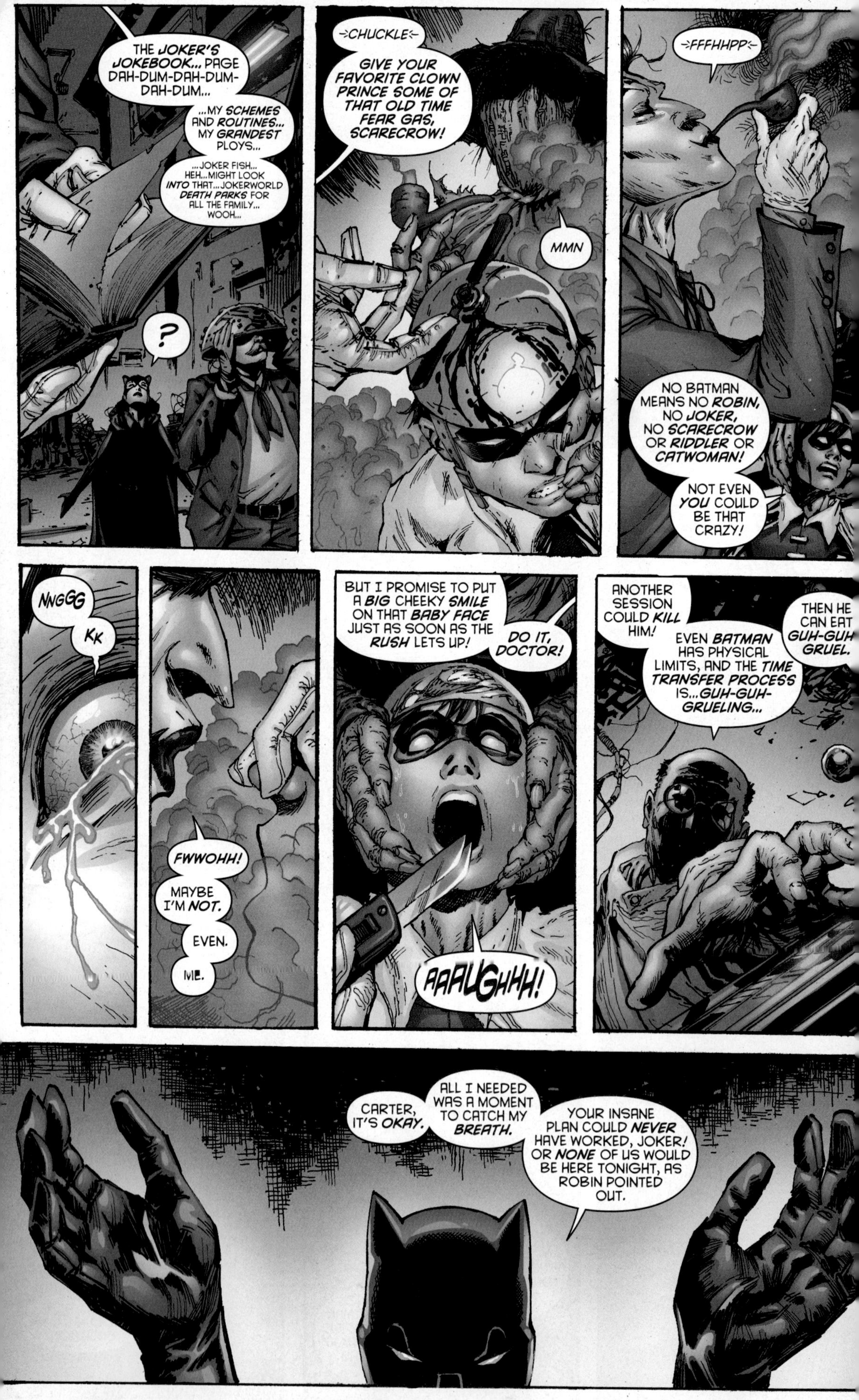
THE JOKER'S JOKEBOOK... PAGE DAH-DUM-DAH-DUM-DAH-DUM...
...MY SCHEMES AND ROUTINES... MY GRANDEST PLOYS...
...JOKER FISH... HEH... MIGHT LOOK INTO THAT... JOKERWORLD DEATH PARKS FOR ALL THE FAMILY... WOOH...
?
CHUCKLE
GIVE YOUR FAVORITE CLOWN PRINCE SOME OF THAT OLD TIME FEAR GAS, SCARECROW!
MMN
FFFHHPP
NO BATMAN MEANS NO ROBIN, NO JOKER, NO SCARECROW OR RIDDLER OR CATWOMAN!
NOT EVEN YOU COULD BE THAT CRAZY!
NNGGG
KK
FWWOHH!
MAYBE I'M NOT.
EVEN.
ME.
BUT I PROMISE TO PUT A BIG CHEEKY SMILE ON THAT BABY FACE JUST AS SOON AS THE RUSH LETS UP!
DO IT, DOCTOR!
AAAUGHHH!
ANOTHER SESSION COULD KILL HIM!
EVEN BATMAN HAS PHYSICAL LIMITS, AND THE TIME TRANSFER PROCESS IS...GUH-GUH-GRUELING...
THEN HE CAN EAT GUH-GUH GRUEL.
CARTER, IT'S OKAY.
ALL I NEEDED WAS A MOMENT TO CATCH MY BREATH.
YOUR INSANE PLAN COULD NEVER HAVE WORKED, JOKER! OR NONE OF US WOULD BE HERE TONIGHT, AS ROBIN POINTED OUT.

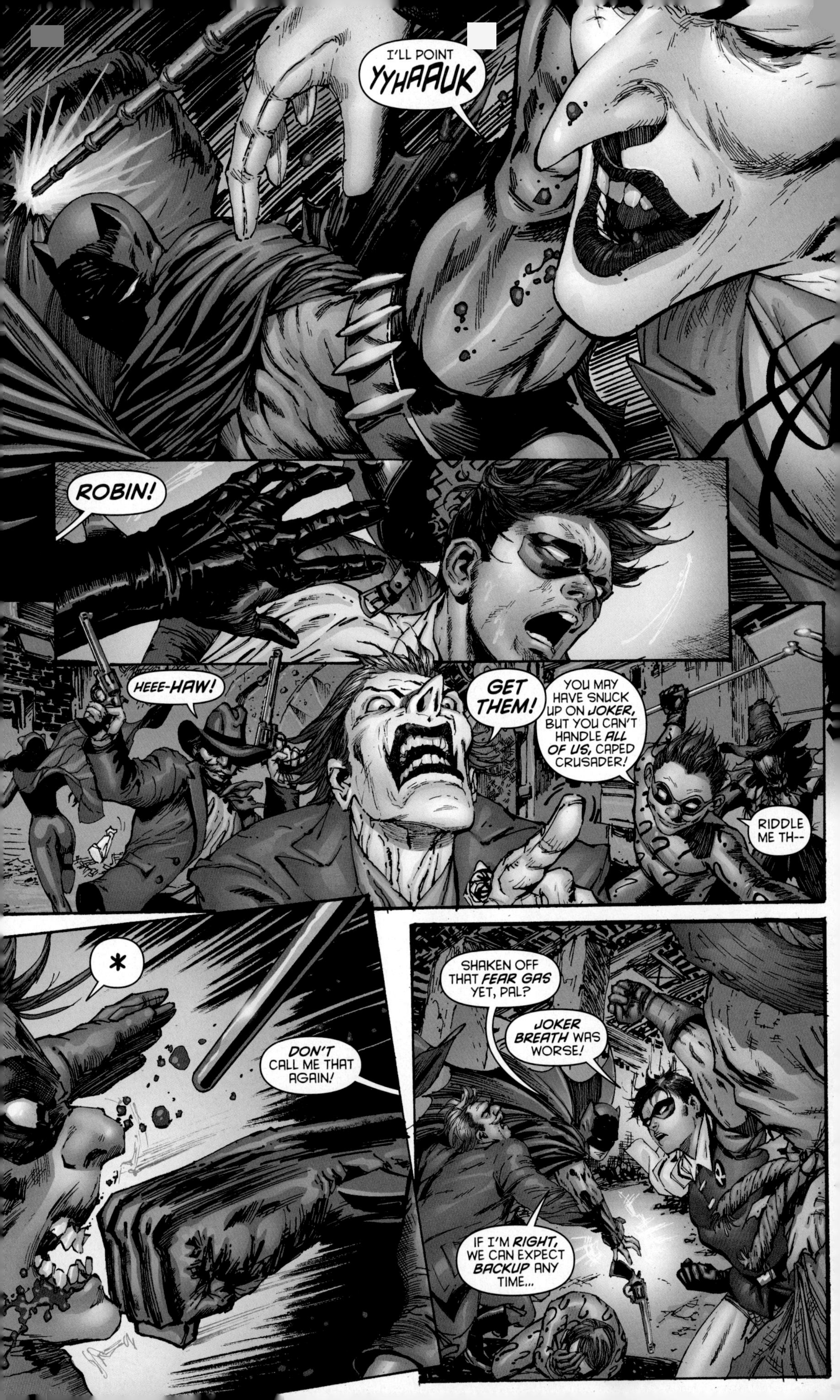
I'LL POINT
YYHAAUK
ROBIN!
HEEE-HAW!
GET THEM!
YOU MAY HAVE SNUCK UP ON JOKER, BUT YOU CAN'T HANDLE ALL OF US, CAPED CRUSADER!
RIDDLE ME TH--
*
DON'T CALL ME THAT AGAIN!
SHAKEN OFF THAT FEAR GAS YET, PAL?
JOKER BREATH WAS WORSE!
IF I'M RIGHT, WE CAN EXPECT BACKUP ANY TIME...

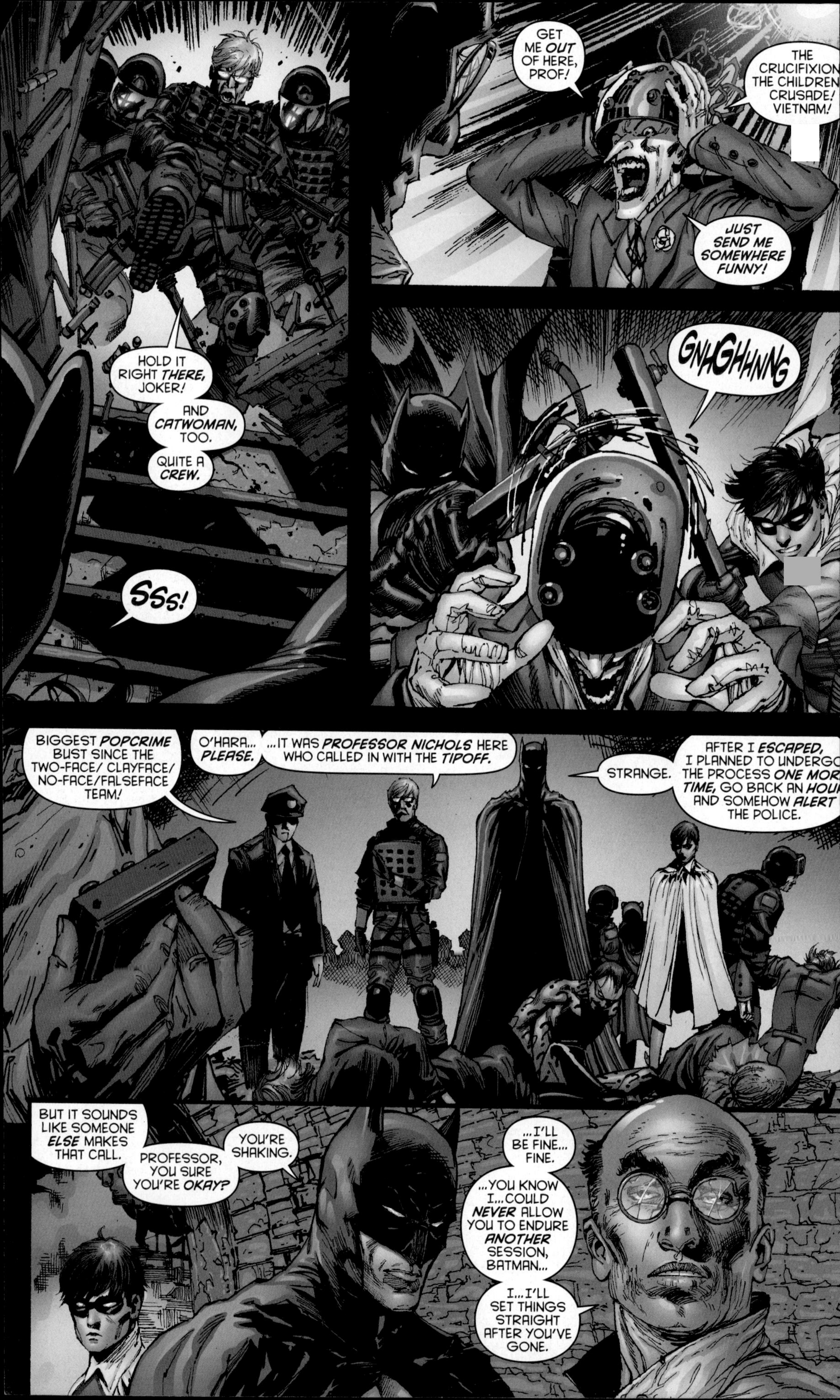
GET ME OUT OF HERE, PROF!
THE CRUCIFIXION! THE CHILDREN'S CRUSADE! VIETNAM!
JUST SEND ME SOMEWHERE FUNNY!
HOLD IT RIGHT THERE, JOKER!
AND CATWOMAN, TOO.
QUITE A CREW.
SSS!
GNHGHHNNG
BIGGEST POPCRIME BUST SINCE THE TWO-FACE/ CLAYFACE/ NO-FACE/FALSEFACE TEAM!
O'HARA... PLEASE.
...IT WAS PROFESSOR NICHOLS HERE WHO CALLED IN WITH THE TIPOFF.
STRANGE.
AFTER I ESCAPED, I PLANNED TO UNDERGO THE PROCESS ONE MORE TIME, GO BACK AN HOUR AND SOMEHOW ALERT THE POLICE.
BUT IT SOUNDS LIKE SOMEONE ELSE MAKES THAT CALL.
PROFESSOR, YOU SURE YOU'RE OKAY?
YOU'RE SHAKING.
...I'LL BE FINE... FINE.
...YOU KNOW I...COULD NEVER ALLOW YOU TO ENDURE ANOTHER SESSION, BATMAN...
I...I'LL SET THINGS STRAIGHT AFTER YOU'VE GONE.

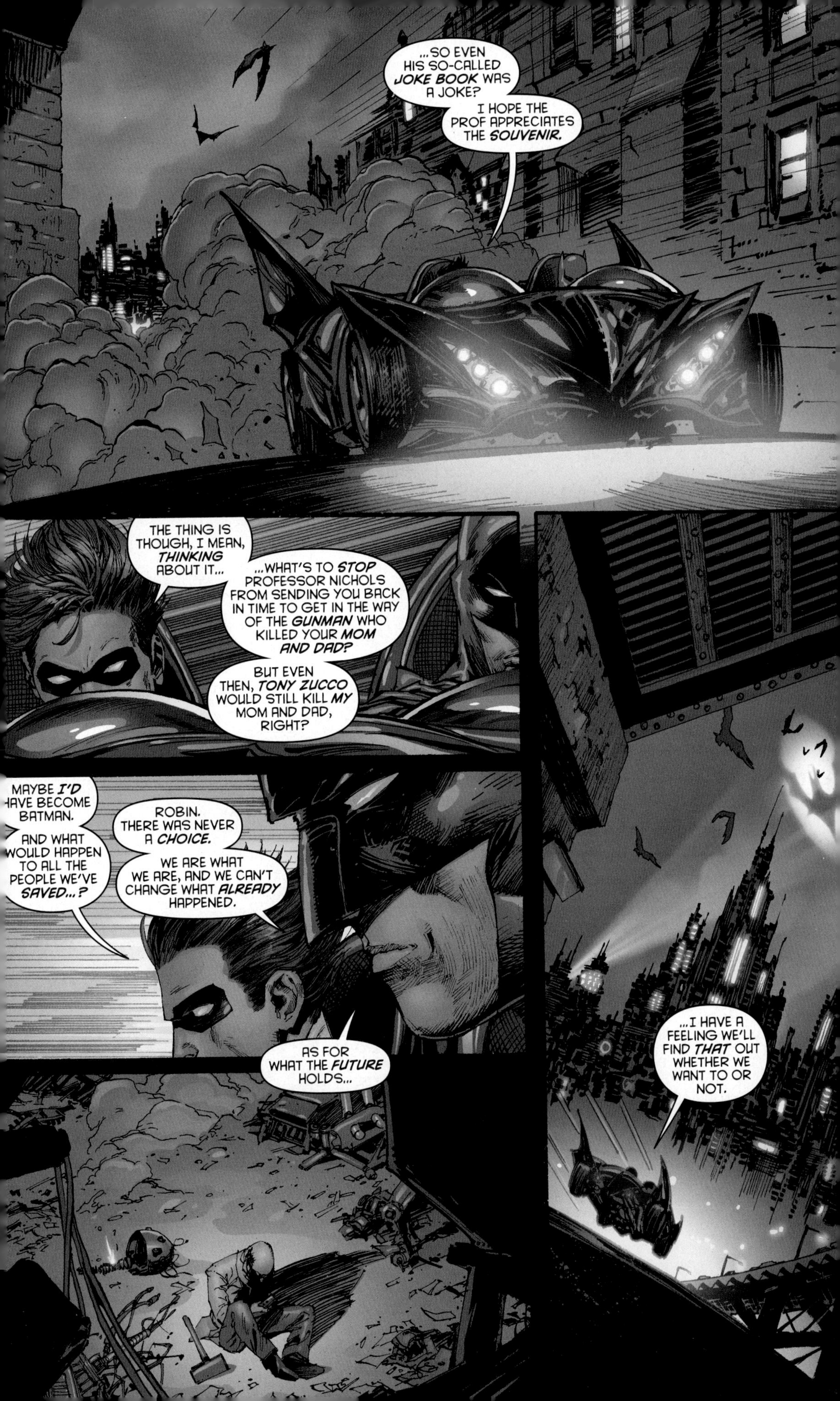
...SO EVEN HIS SO-CALLED JOKE BOOK WAS A JOKE?
I HOPE THE PROF APPRECIATES THE SOUVENIR.
THE THING IS THOUGH, I MEAN, THINKING ABOUT IT...
...WHAT'S TO STOP PROFESSOR NICHOLS FROM SENDING YOU BACK IN TIME TO GET IN THE WAY OF THE GUNMAN WHO KILLED YOUR MOM AND DAD?
BUT EVEN THEN, TONY ZUCCO WOULD STILL KILL MY MOM AND DAD, RIGHT?
MAYBE I'D HAVE BECOME BATMAN.
AND WHAT WOULD HAPPEN TO ALL THE PEOPLE WE'VE SAVED...?
ROBIN. THERE WAS NEVER A CHOICE.
WE ARE WHAT WE ARE, AND WE CAN'T CHANGE WHAT ALREADY HAPPENED.
AS FOR WHAT THE FUTURE HOLDS...
...I HAVE A FEELING WE'LL FIND THAT OUT WHETHER WE WANT TO OR NOT.

TODAY

A BASEMENT ROOM *LOCKED* FROM THE INSIDE.

THE VICTIM: *PROFESSOR CARTER NICHOLS.*

SHOT IN THE HEART, NO SIGN OF THE *WEAPON,* A *SMILE* ON HIS FACE AND *THIS* ON THE CHAIR BESIDE HIM.

SEEMED LIKE *YOUR* TERRITORY.

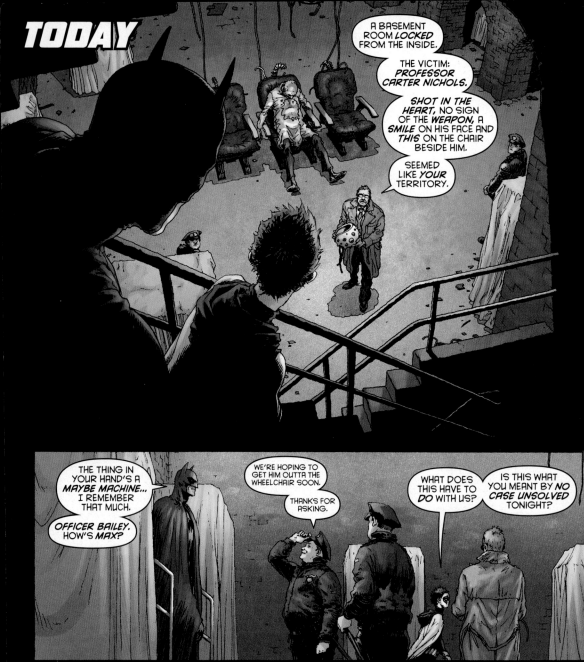

THE THING IN YOUR HAND'S A *MAYBE MACHINE*... I REMEMBER THAT MUCH.

OFFICER BAILEY. HOW'S *MAX*?

WE'RE HOPING TO GET HIM OUTTA THE WHEELCHAIR SOON.

THANKS FOR ASKING.

WHAT DOES THIS HAVE TO DO WITH US?

IS THIS WHAT YOU MEANT BY *NO CASE UNSOLVED* TONIGHT?

...THE WOUND'S CLEAN. *CAUTERIZED.* MEDICATION'S... *EXELON.* FOR *DEMENTIA,* I THINK.

THING IS, CARTER NICHOLS WOULD BE IN HIS *SIXTIES.*

THIS MAN IS *EIGHTY,* AT LEAST.

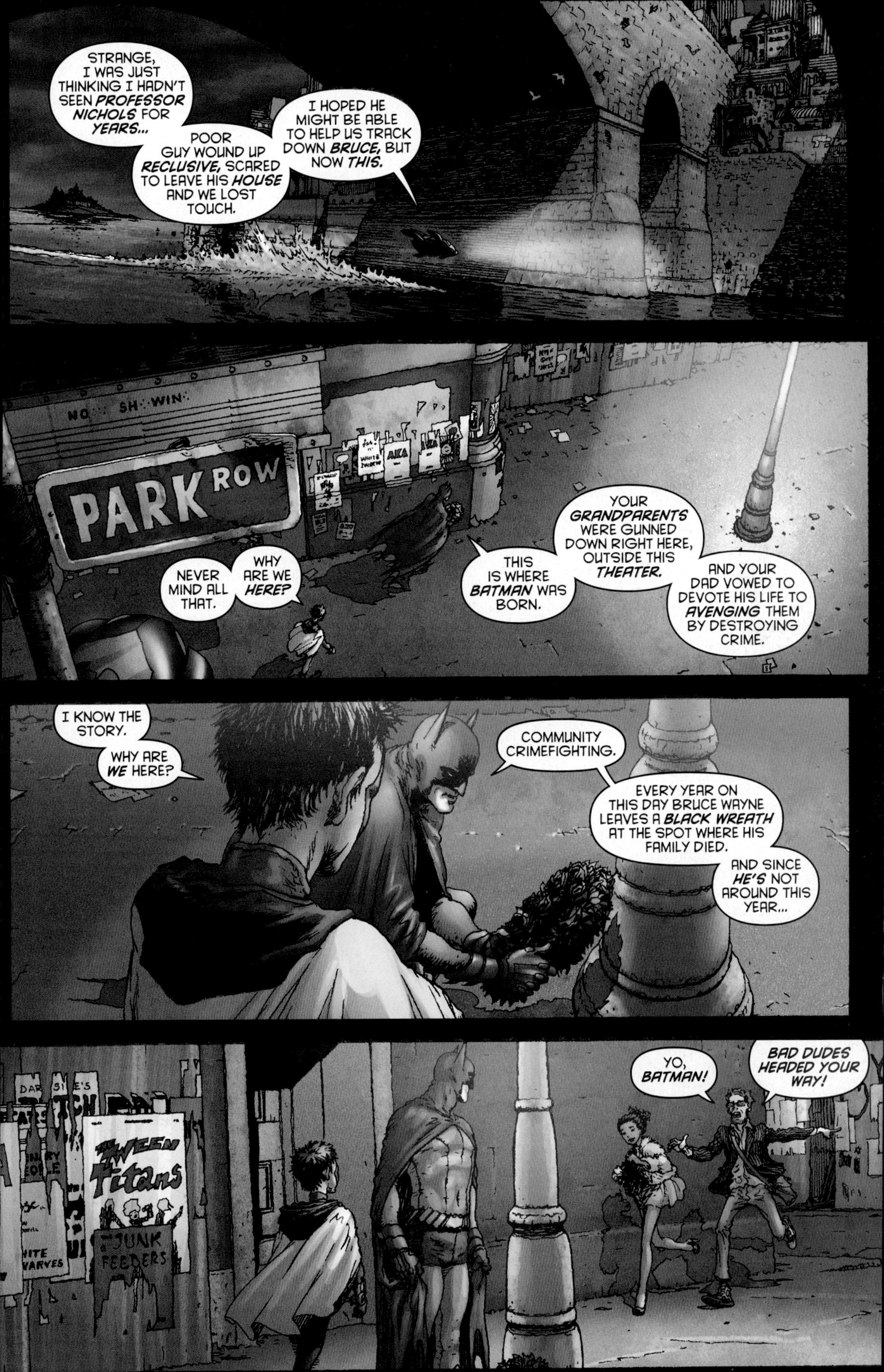

STRANGE, I WAS JUST THINKING I HADN'T SEEN PROFESSOR NICHOLS FOR YEARS...
POOR GUY WOUND UP RECLUSIVE, SCARED TO LEAVE HIS HOUSE AND WE LOST TOUCH.
I HOPED HE MIGHT BE ABLE TO HELP US TRACK DOWN BRUCE, BUT NOW THIS.
PARK ROW
NEVER MIND ALL THAT.
WHY ARE WE HERE?
THIS IS WHERE BATMAN WAS BORN.
YOUR GRANDPARENTS WERE GUNNED DOWN RIGHT HERE, OUTSIDE THIS THEATER.
AND YOUR DAD VOWED TO DEVOTE HIS LIFE TO AVENGING THEM BY DESTROYING CRIME.
I KNOW THE STORY.
WHY ARE WE HERE?
COMMUNITY CRIMEFIGHTING.
EVERY YEAR ON THIS DAY BRUCE WAYNE LEAVES A BLACK WREATH AT THE SPOT WHERE HIS FAMILY DIED.
AND SINCE HE'S NOT AROUND THIS YEAR...
YO, BATMAN!
BAD DUDES HEADED YOUR WAY!

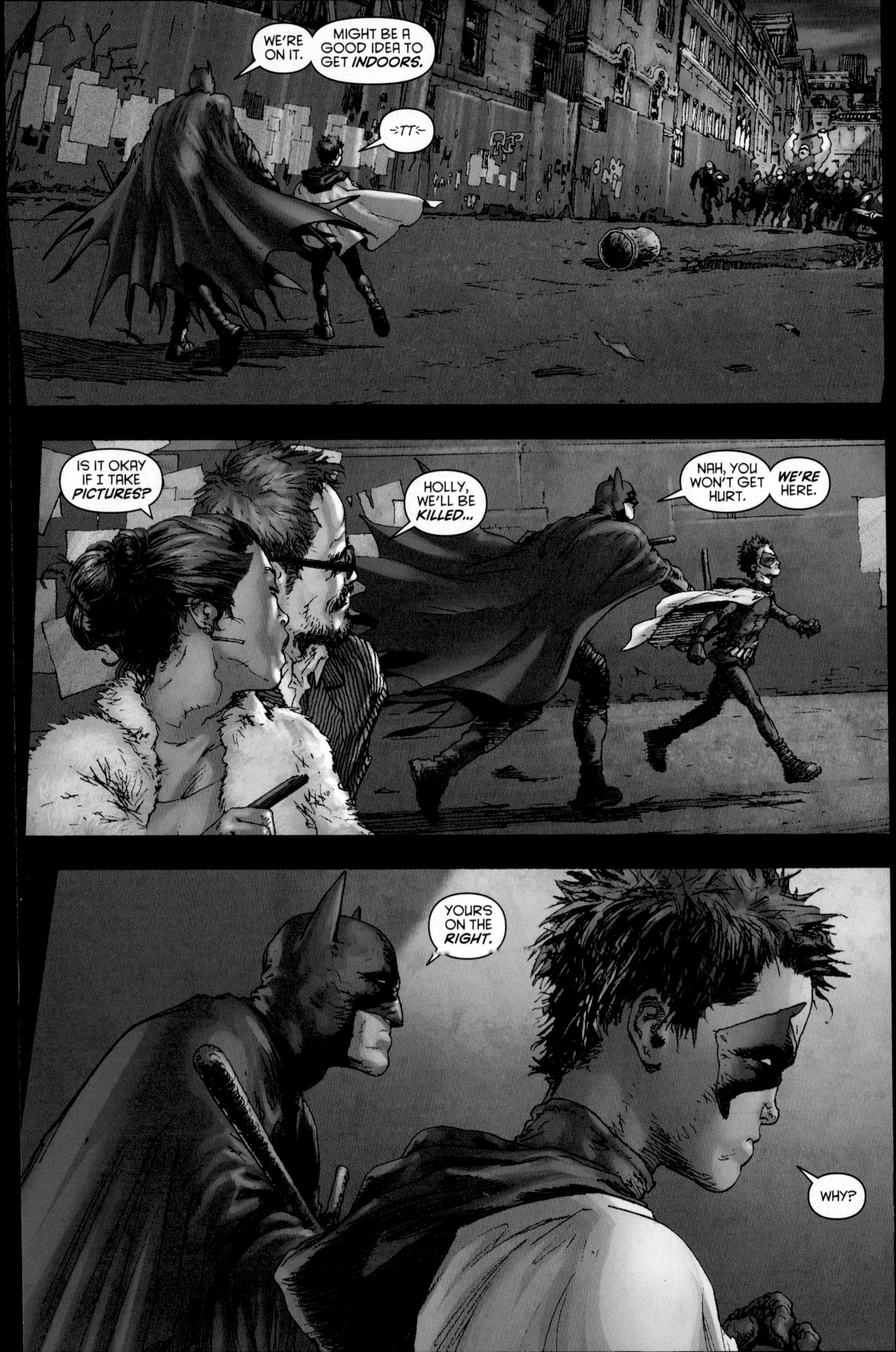

WE'RE ON IT.
MIGHT BE A GOOD IDEA TO GET INDOORS.
TT
IS IT OKAY IF I TAKE PICTURES?
HOLLY, WE'LL BE KILLED...
NAH, YOU WON'T GET HURT.
WE'RE HERE.
YOURS ON THE RIGHT.
WHY?

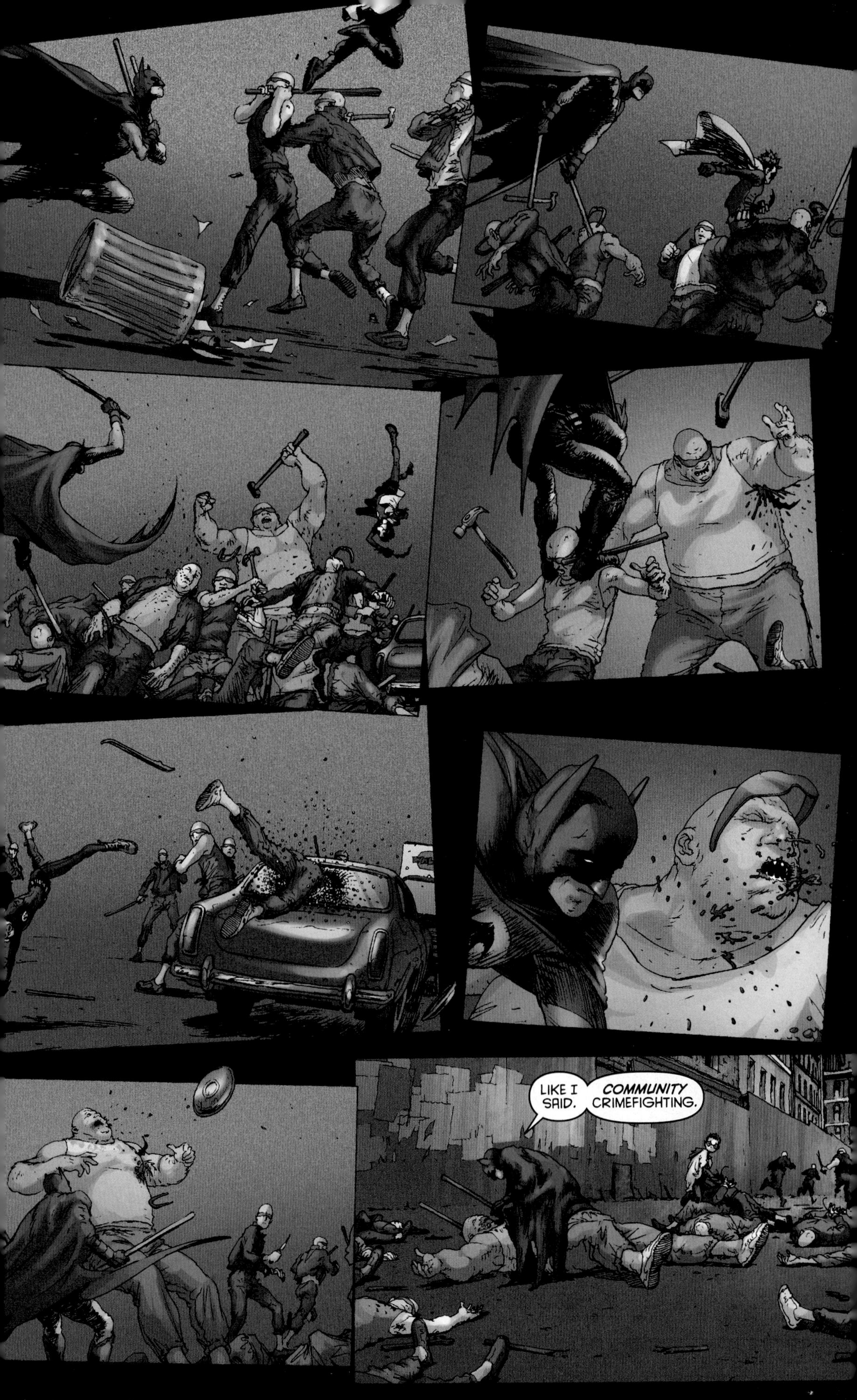
LIKE I SAID.
COMMUNITY CRIMEFIGHTING.

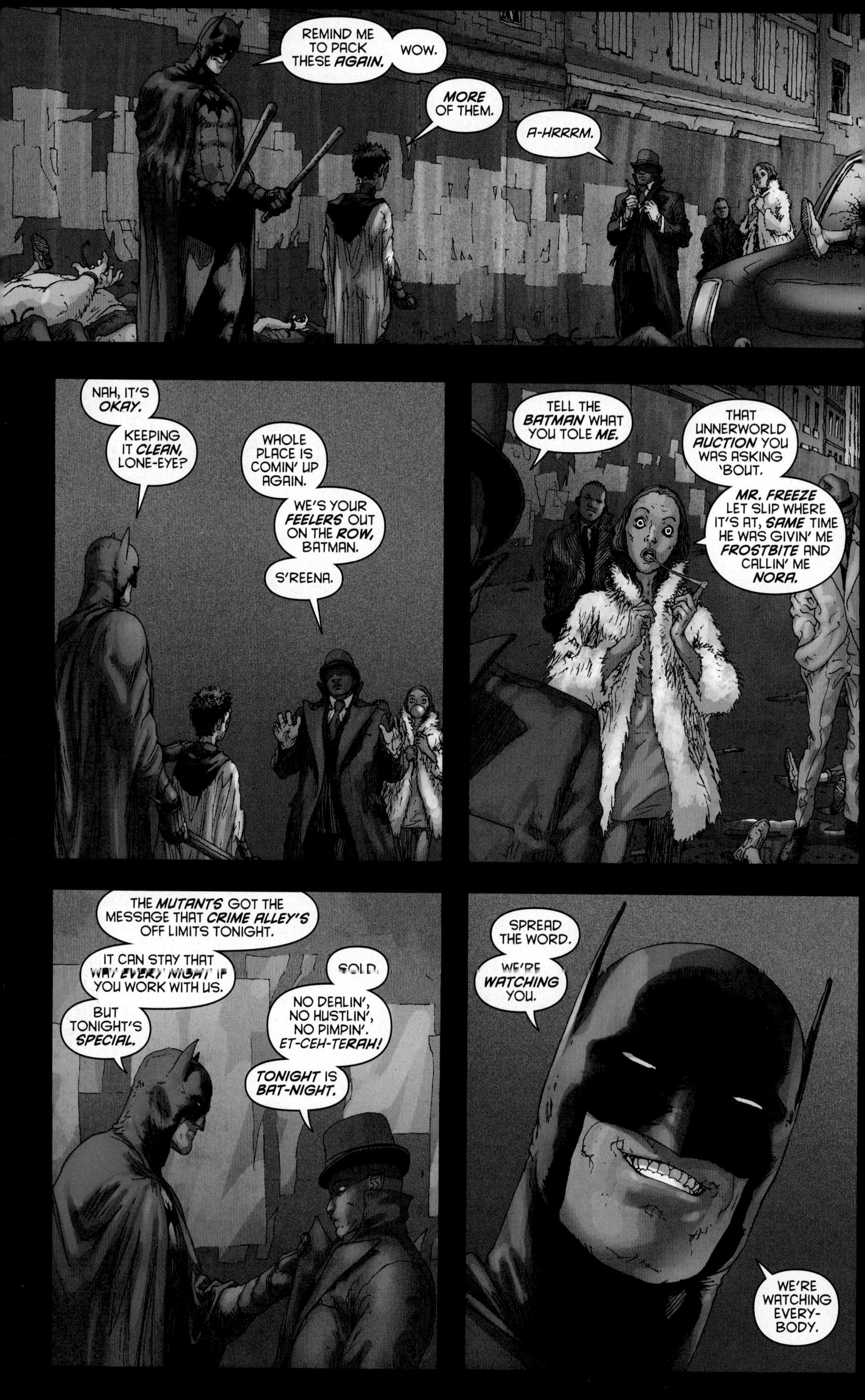
REMIND ME TO PACK THESE AGAIN.
WOW.
MORE OF THEM.
A-HRRRM.
NAH, IT'S OKAY.
KEEPING IT CLEAN, LONE-EYE?
WHOLE PLACE IS COMIN' UP AGAIN.
WE'S YOUR FEELERS OUT ON THE ROW, BATMAN.
S'REENA.
TELL THE BATMAN WHAT YOU TOLE ME.
THAT UNNERWORLD AUCTION YOU WAS ASKING 'BOUT.
MR. FREEZE LET SLIP WHERE IT'S AT, SAME TIME HE WAS GIVIN' ME FROSTBITE AND CALLIN' ME NORA.
THE MUTANTS GOT THE MESSAGE THAT CRIME ALLEY'S OFF LIMITS TONIGHT.
IT CAN STAY THAT WAY EVERY NIGHT IF YOU WORK WITH US.
BUT TONIGHT'S SPECIAL.
SOLD.
NO DEALIN', NO HUSTLIN', NO PIMPIN'. ET-CEH-TERAH!
TONIGHT IS BAT-NIGHT.
SPREAD THE WORD.
WE'RE WATCHING YOU.
WE'RE WATCHING EVERY-BODY.

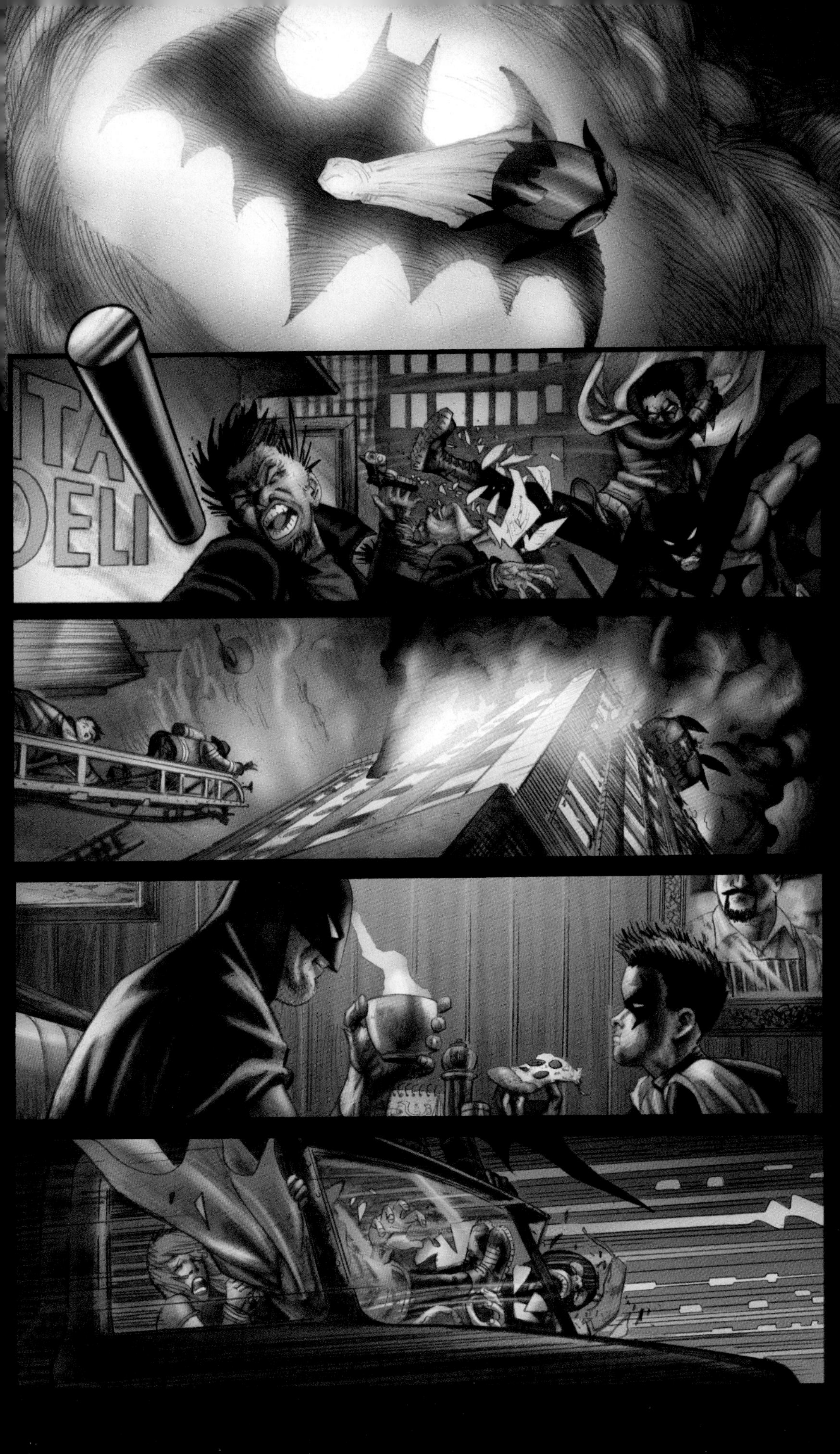
ITA
DELI

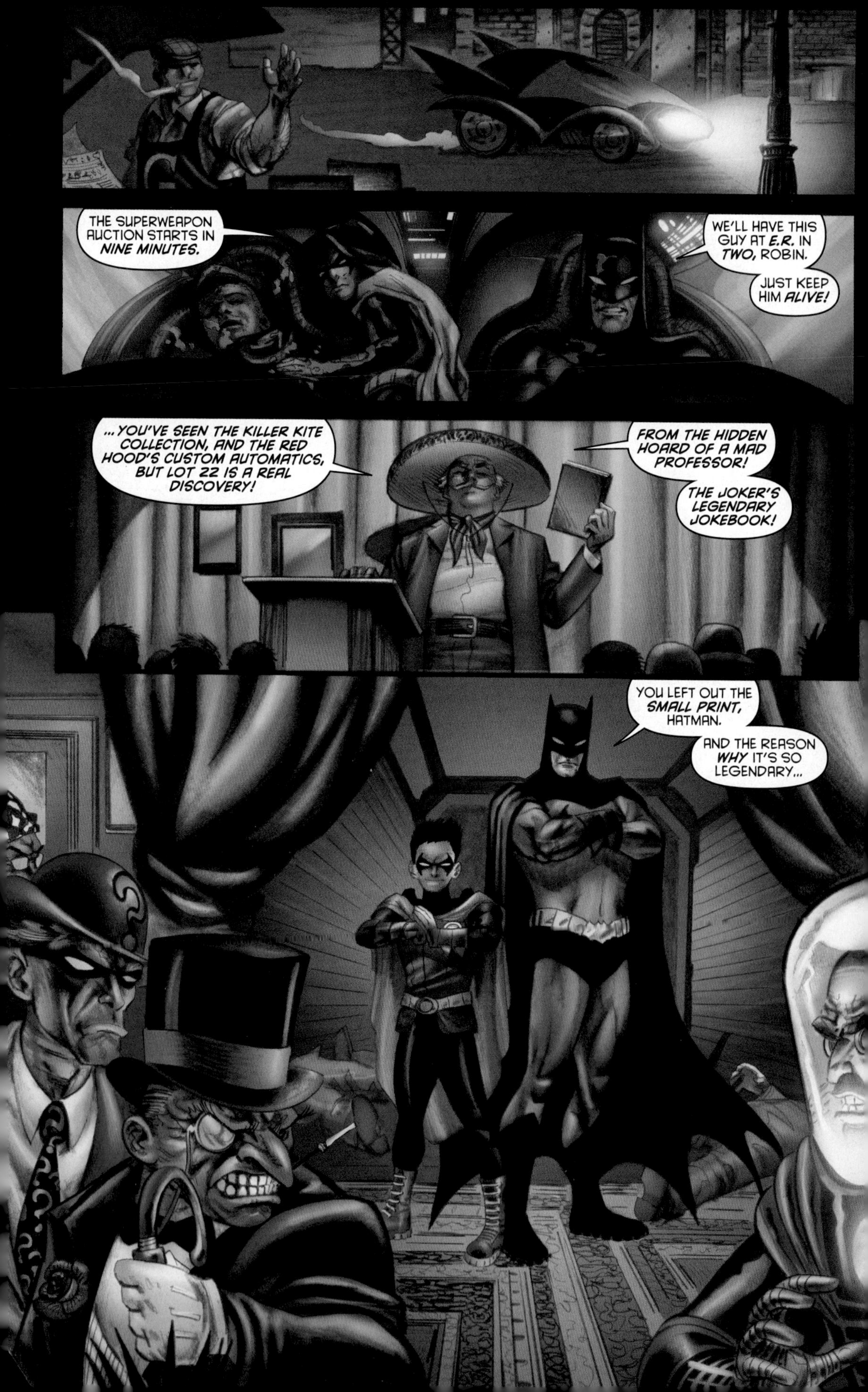
THE SUPERWEAPON AUCTION STARTS IN NINE MINUTES.
WE'LL HAVE THIS GUY AT E.R. IN TWO, ROBIN.
JUST KEEP HIM ALIVE!
...YOU'VE SEEN THE KILLER KITE COLLECTION, AND THE RED HOOD'S CUSTOM AUTOMATICS, BUT LOT 22 IS A REAL DISCOVERY!
FROM THE HIDDEN HOARD OF A MAD PROFESSOR!
THE JOKER'S LEGENDARY JOKEBOOK!
YOU LEFT OUT THE SMALL PRINT, HATMAN.
AND THE REASON WHY IT'S SO LEGENDARY...

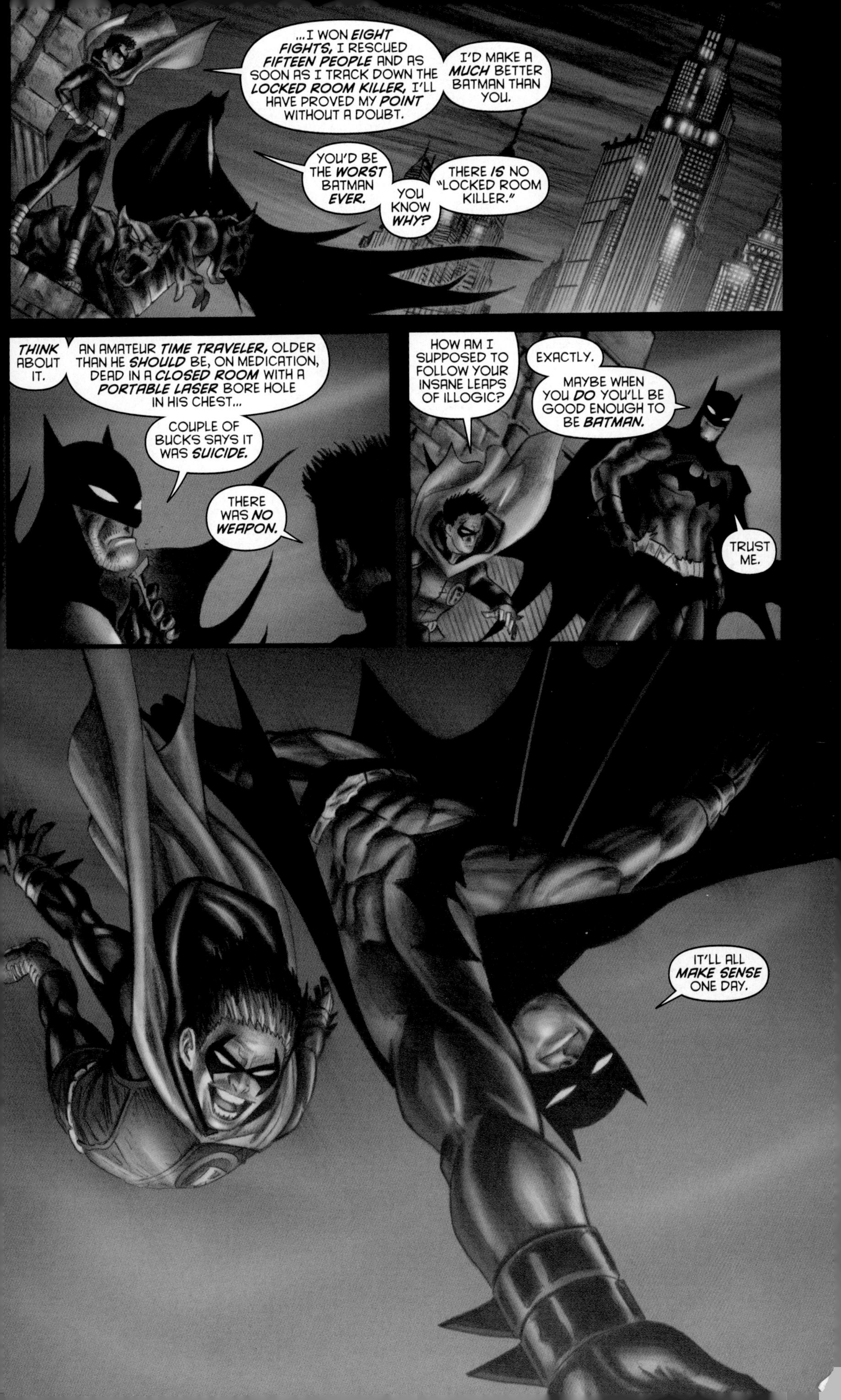
...I WON EIGHT FIGHTS, I RESCUED FIFTEEN PEOPLE AND AS SOON AS I TRACK DOWN THE LOCKED ROOM KILLER, I'LL HAVE PROVED MY POINT WITHOUT A DOUBT.
I'D MAKE A MUCH BETTER BATMAN THAN YOU.
YOU'D BE THE WORST BATMAN EVER.
YOU KNOW WHY?
THERE IS NO "LOCKED ROOM KILLER."
THINK ABOUT IT.
AN AMATEUR TIME TRAVELER, OLDER THAN HE SHOULD BE, ON MEDICATION, DEAD IN A CLOSED ROOM WITH A PORTABLE LASER BORE HOLE IN HIS CHEST...
COUPLE OF BUCKS SAYS IT WAS SUICIDE.
THERE WAS NO WEAPON.
HOW AM I SUPPOSED TO FOLLOW YOUR INSANE LEAPS OF ILLOGIC?
EXACTLY.
MAYBE WHEN YOU DO YOU'LL BE GOOD ENOUGH TO BE BATMAN.
TRUST ME.
IT'LL ALL MAKE SENSE ONE DAY.

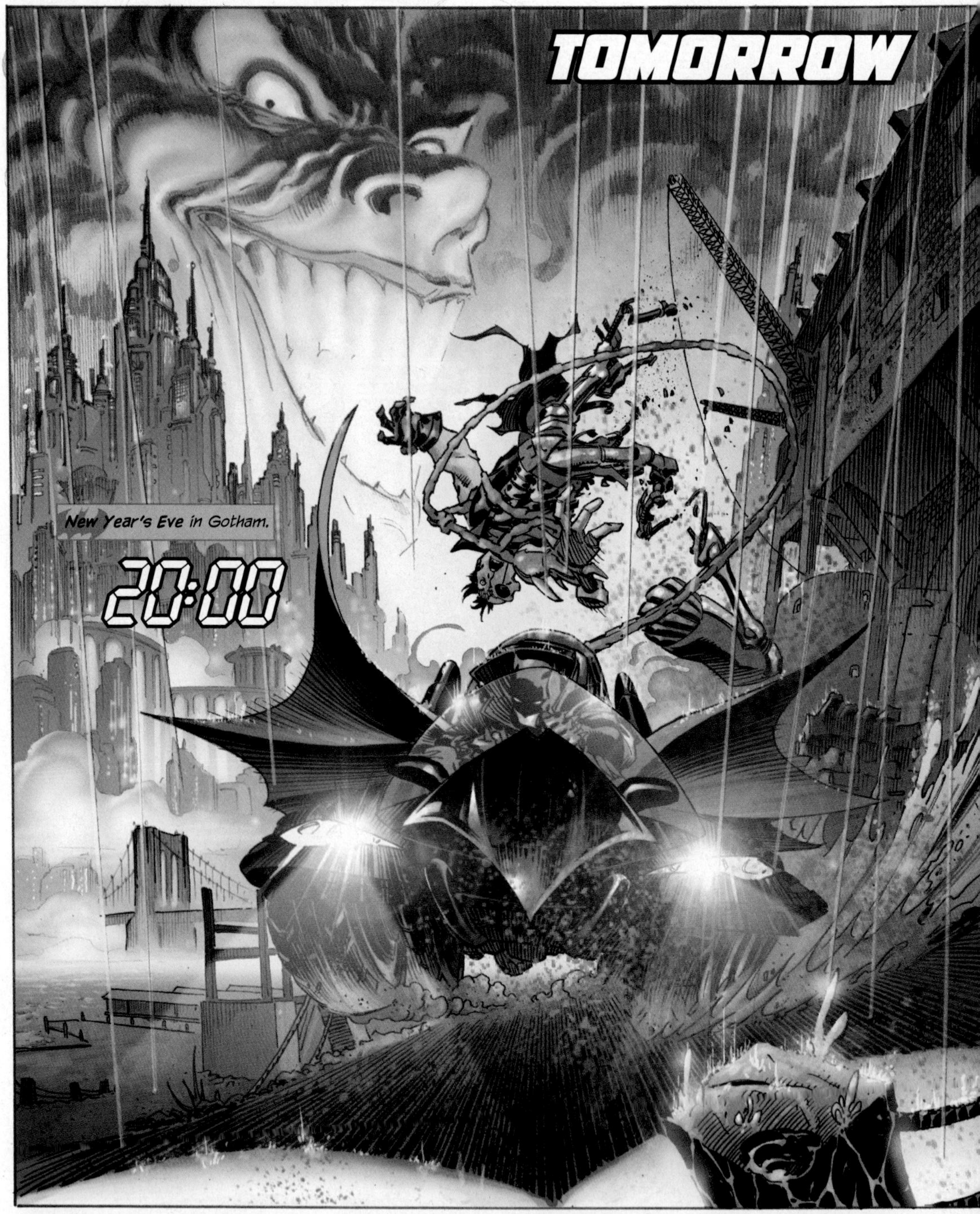
TOMORROW
New Year's Eve in Gotham.
20:00

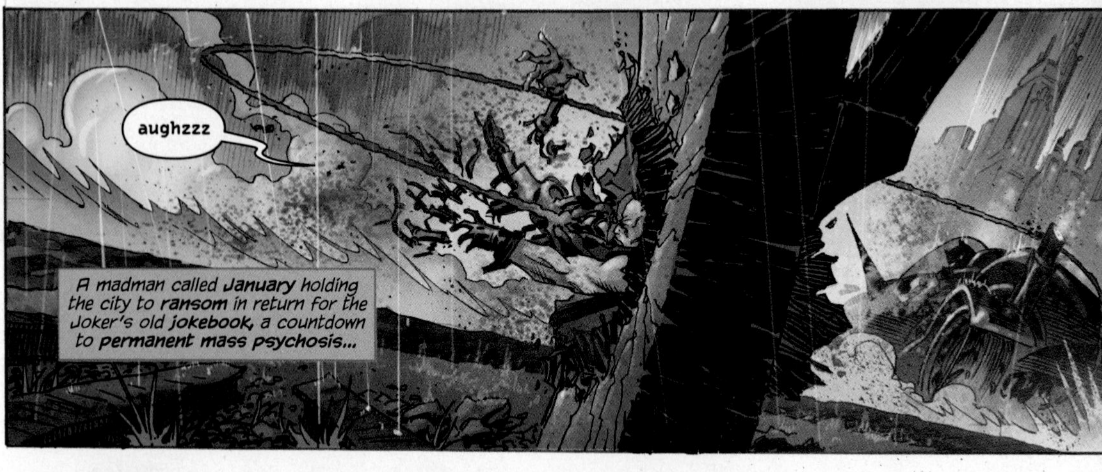
augzzz
A madman called January holding the city to ransom in return for the Joker's old jokebook, a countdown to permanent mass psychosis...

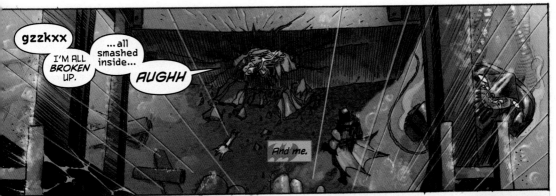

gzzkxx

I'M ALL BROKEN UP.

...all smashed inside...

AUGHH

And me.

YOU REPROGRAMMED CLIMATE CONTROL TO MAKE JOKERZOMBIES, BUT YOU PAID FOR IMMUNIZATION WITH YOUR EYE, RIGHT?

JANUARY, MAX.

...UNGGH... CAN'T MOVE... YOU'LL HAVE TO LEAN IN CLOSER...

it was.

TELL ME WHERE YOUR BOSS TOOK THE BABY AND THE OLD MAN AND I'LL BREAK YOUR NECK CLEAN.

-PTTFF-

YOUR CALL, ROBOTO.

THEY SAY THE RATS DOWN HERE ARE CANNIBAL FLESH EATERS.

BUT YOU'RE ONLY ABOUT 40% RAT, RIGHT?

NO! NO! NO!

it's some place in granton!

YOU CAN'T LEAVE ME HERE!

BATMAN, YOU BASTARD!

Weaponized Joker Venom in the form of neurotoxic rain.

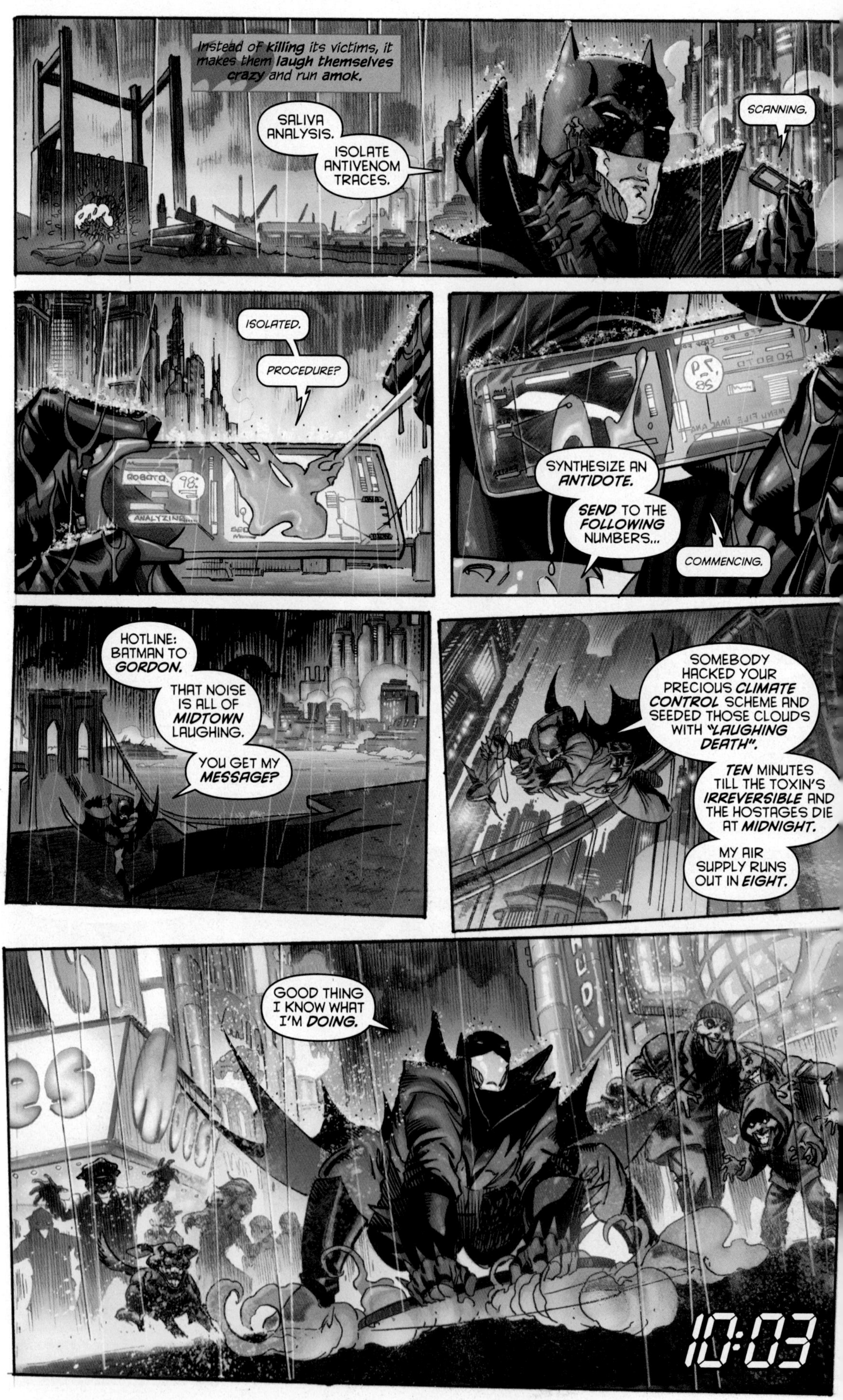

Instead of killing its victims, it makes them laugh themselves crazy and run amok.
SALIVA ANALYSIS.
ISOLATE ANTIVENOM TRACES.
SCANNING.
ISOLATED.
PROCEDURE?
SYNTHESIZE AN ANTIDOTE.
SEND TO THE FOLLOWING NUMBERS...
COMMENCING.
HOTLINE: BATMAN TO GORDON.
THAT NOISE IS ALL OF MIDTOWN LAUGHING.
YOU GET MY MESSAGE?
SOMEBODY HACKED YOUR PRECIOUS CLIMATE CONTROL SCHEME AND SEEDED THOSE CLOUDS WITH "LAUGHING DEATH".
TEN MINUTES TILL THE TOXIN'S IRREVERSIBLE AND THE HOSTAGES DIE AT MIDNIGHT.
MY AIR SUPPLY RUNS OUT IN EIGHT.
GOOD THING I KNOW WHAT I'M DOING.
10:03

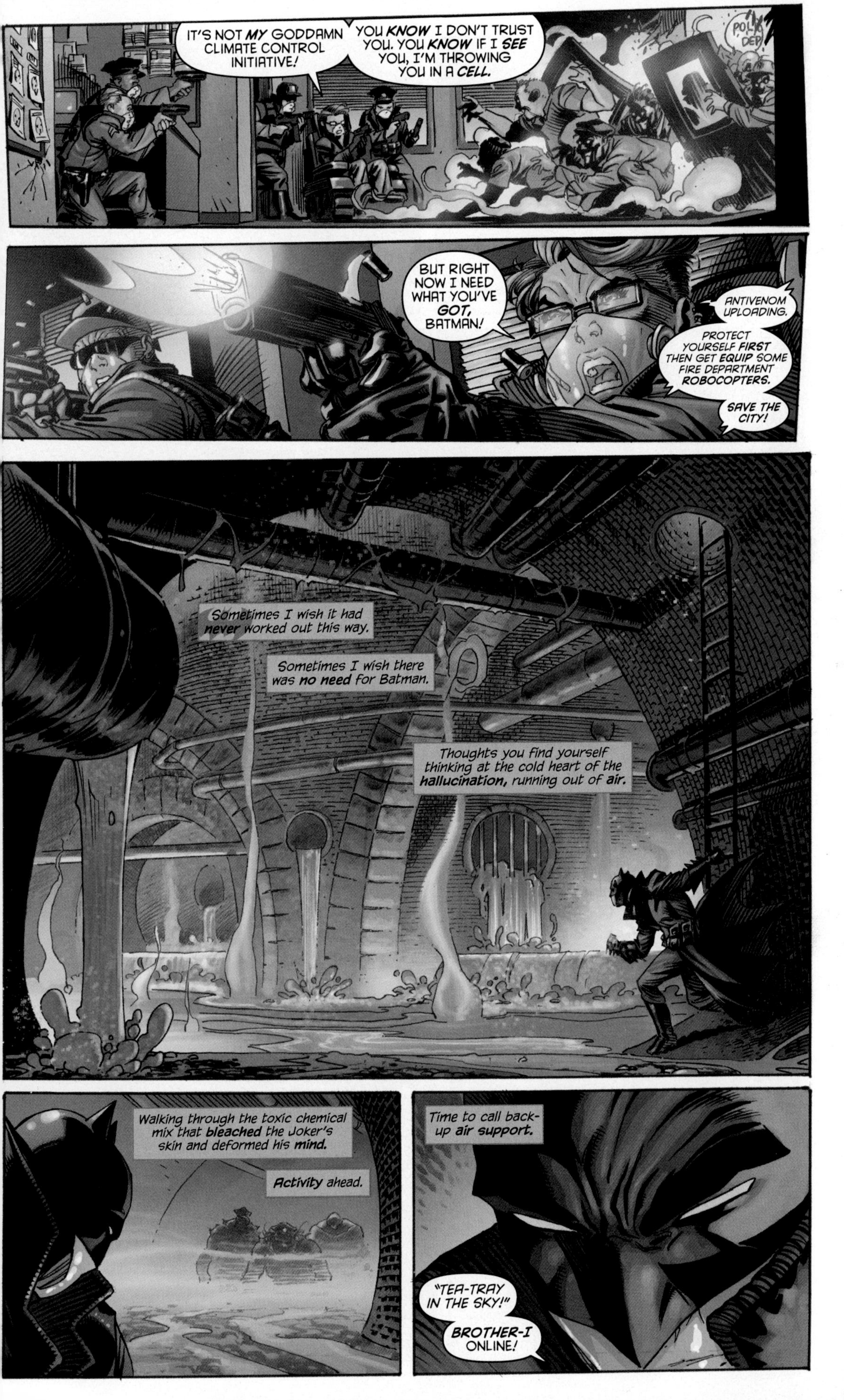

IT'S NOT MY GODDAMN CLIMATE CONTROL INITIATIVE!
YOU KNOW I DON'T TRUST YOU. YOU KNOW IF I SEE YOU, I'M THROWING YOU IN A CELL.
BUT RIGHT NOW I NEED WHAT YOU'VE GOT, BATMAN!
ANTIVENOM UPLOADING.
PROTECT YOURSELF FIRST THEN GET EQUIP SOME FIRE DEPARTMENT ROBOCOPTERS.
SAVE THE CITY!
Sometimes I wish it had never worked out this way.
Sometimes I wish there was no need for Batman.
Thoughts you find yourself thinking at the cold heart of the hallucination, running out of air.
Walking through the toxic chemical mix that bleached the Joker's skin and deformed his mind.
Activity ahead.
Time to call back-up air support.
"TEA-TRAY IN THE SKY!"
BROTHER-I ONLINE!

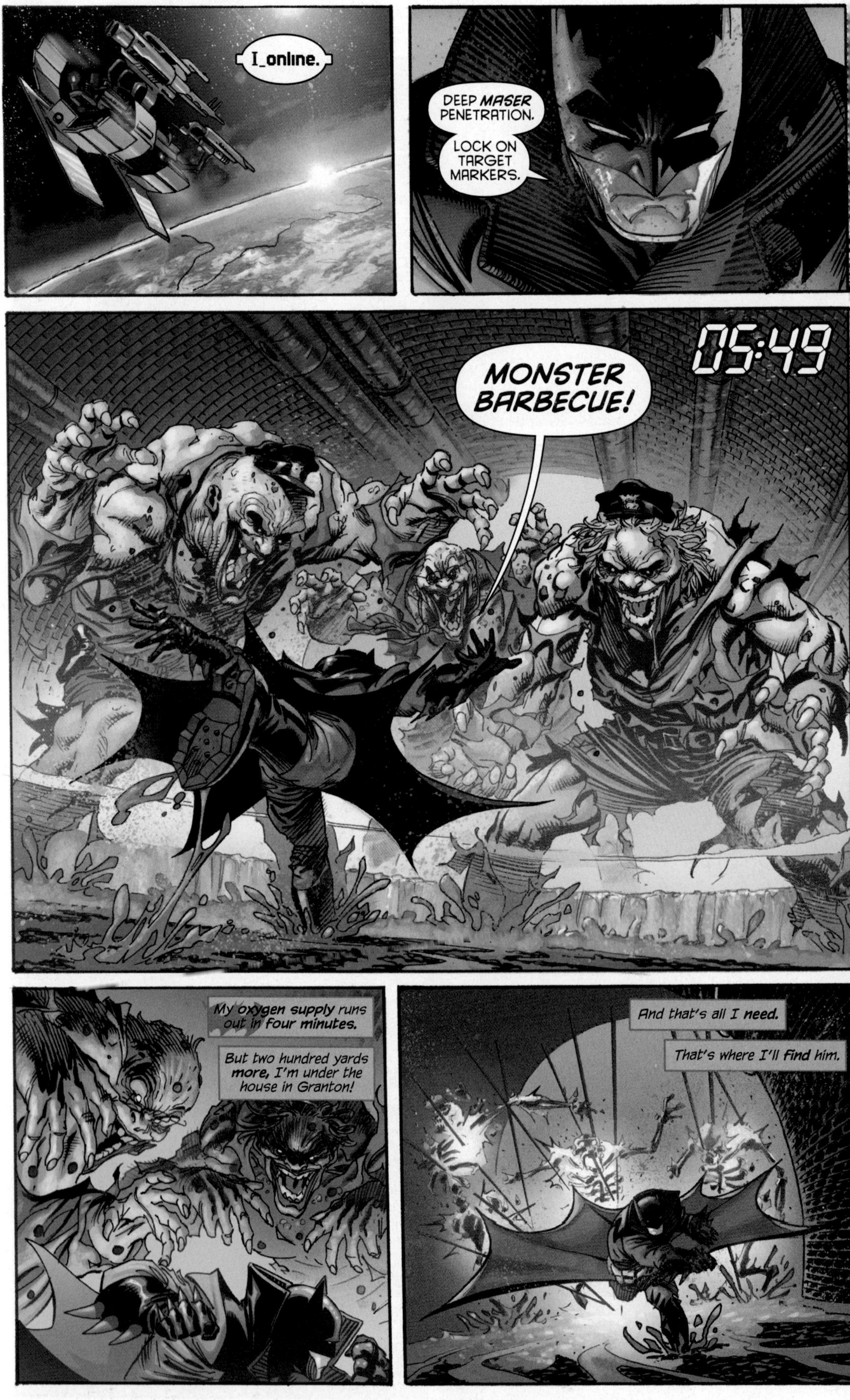

I_online.
DEEP MASER PENETRATION.
LOCK ON TARGET MARKERS.
05:49
MONSTER BARBECUE!
My oxygen supply runs out in four minutes.
But two hundred yards more, I'm under the house in Granton!
And that's all I need.
That's where I'll find him.

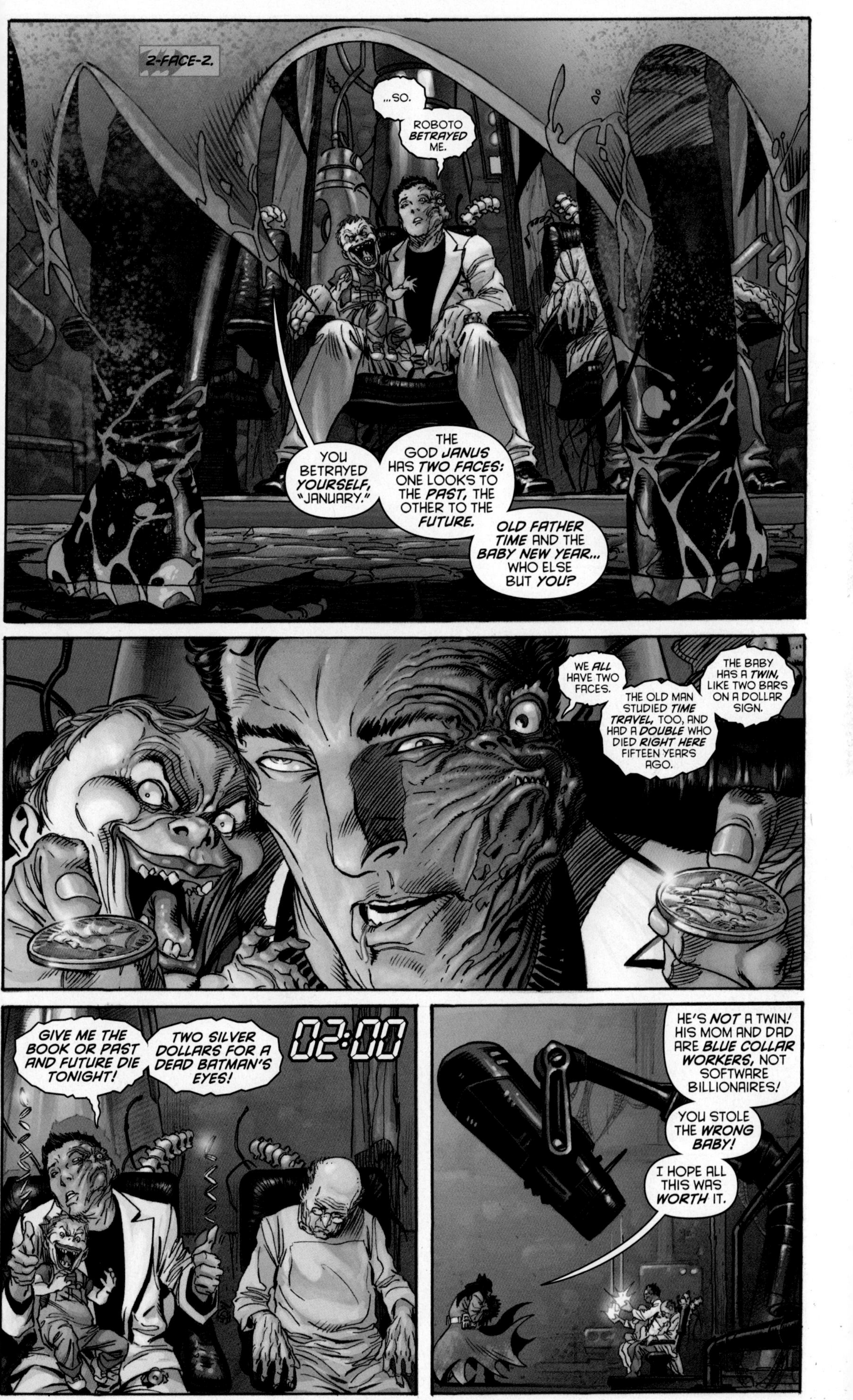
2-FACE-2.
...SO.
ROBOTO BETRAYED ME.
YOU BETRAYED YOURSELF, "JANUARY."
THE GOD JANUS HAS TWO FACES: ONE LOOKS TO THE PAST, THE OTHER TO THE FUTURE.
OLD FATHER TIME AND THE BABY NEW YEAR... WHO ELSE BUT YOU?
WE ALL HAVE TWO FACES.
THE OLD MAN STUDIED TIME TRAVEL, TOO, AND HAD A DOUBLE WHO DIED RIGHT HERE FIFTEEN YEARS AGO.
THE BABY HAS A TWIN, LIKE TWO BARS ON A DOLLAR SIGN.
GIVE ME THE BOOK OR PAST AND FUTURE DIE TONIGHT!
TWO SILVER DOLLARS FOR A DEAD BATMAN'S EYES!
02:00
HE'S NOT A TWIN! HIS MOM AND DAD ARE BLUE COLLAR WORKERS, NOT SOFTWARE BILLIONAIRES!
YOU STOLE THE WRONG BABY!
I HOPE ALL THIS WAS WORTH IT.

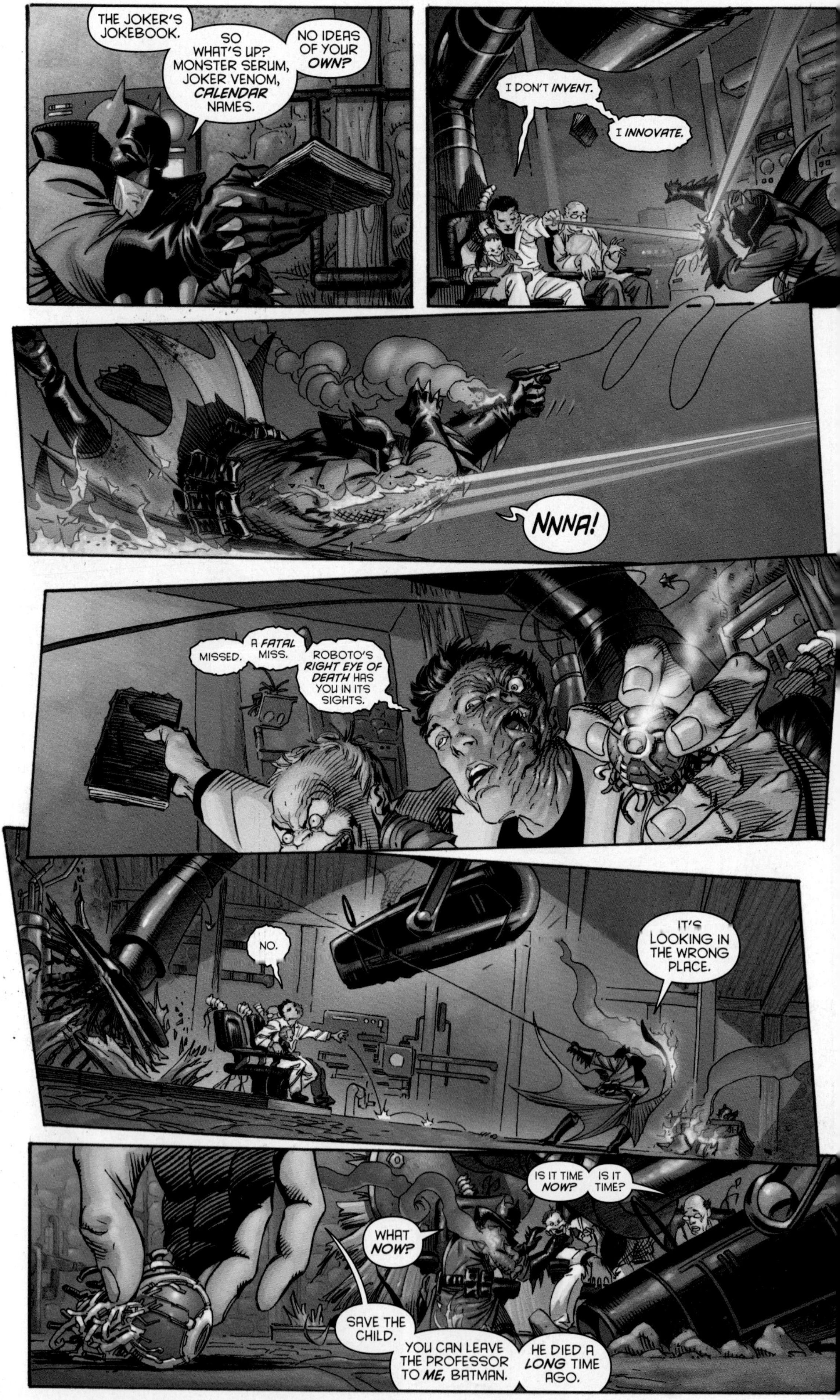
THE JOKER'S JOKEBOOK.
SO WHAT'S UP? MONSTER SERUM, JOKER VENOM, CALENDAR NAMES.
NO IDEAS OF YOUR OWN?
I DON'T INVENT.
I INNOVATE.
NNNA!
MISSED.
A FATAL MISS.
ROBOTO'S RIGHT EYE OF DEATH HAS YOU IN ITS SIGHTS.
NO.
IT'S LOOKING IN THE WRONG PLACE.
IS IT TIME NOW?
IS IT TIME?
WHAT NOW?
SAVE THE CHILD.
YOU CAN LEAVE THE PROFESSOR TO ME, BATMAN.
HE DIED A LONG TIME AGO.

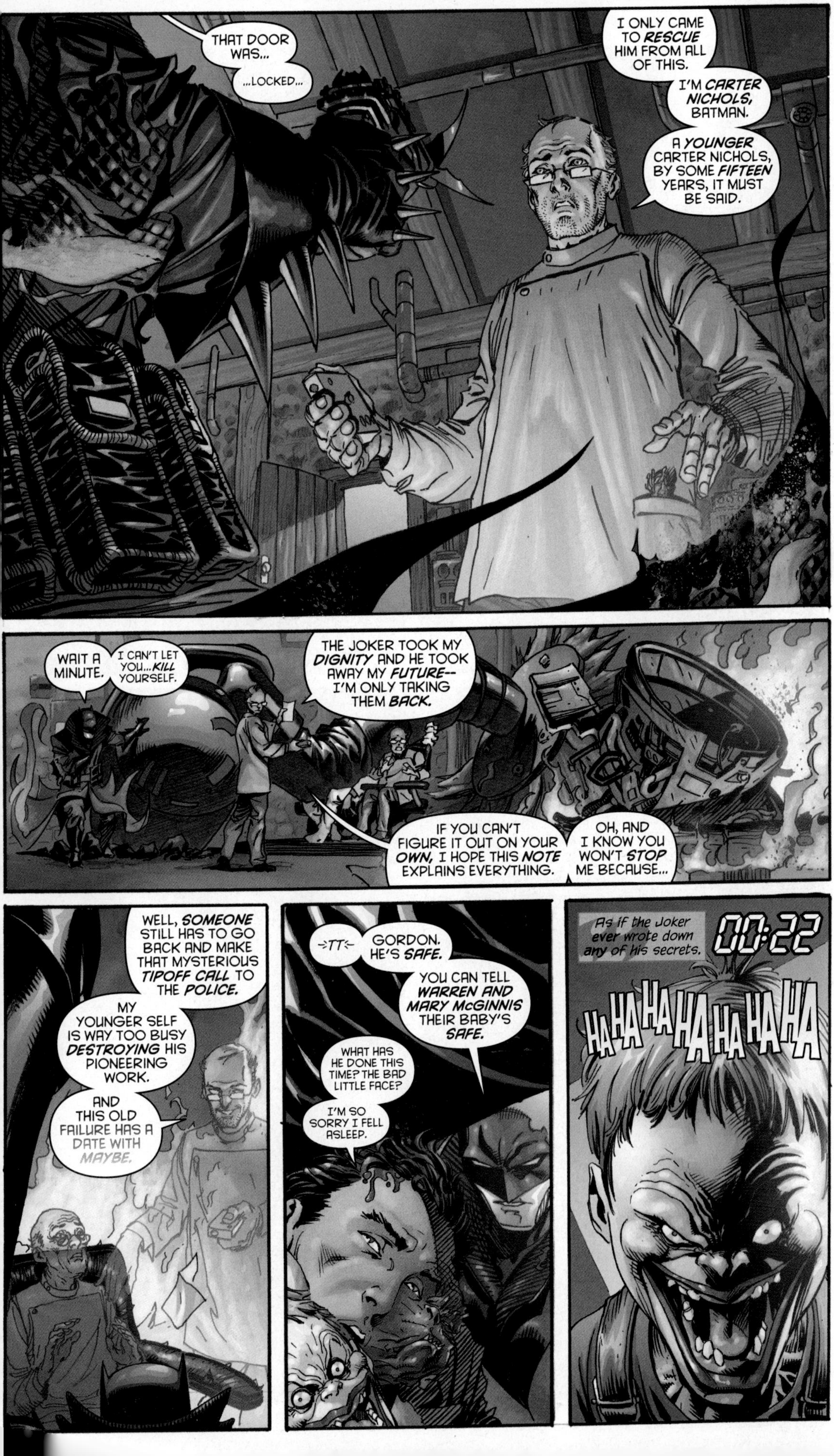
THAT DOOR WAS...
...LOCKED...
I ONLY CAME TO RESCUE HIM FROM ALL OF THIS.
I'M CARTER NICHOLS, BATMAN.
A YOUNGER CARTER NICHOLS, BY SOME FIFTEEN YEARS, IT MUST BE SAID.
WAIT A MINUTE.
I CAN'T LET YOU...KILL YOURSELF.
THE JOKER TOOK MY DIGNITY AND HE TOOK AWAY MY FUTURE-- I'M ONLY TAKING THEM BACK.
IF YOU CAN'T FIGURE IT OUT ON YOUR OWN, I HOPE THIS NOTE EXPLAINS EVERYTHING.
OH, AND I KNOW YOU WON'T STOP ME BECAUSE...
WELL, SOMEONE STILL HAS TO GO BACK AND MAKE THAT MYSTERIOUS TIPOFF CALL TO THE POLICE.
MY YOUNGER SELF IS WAY TOO BUSY DESTROYING HIS PIONEERING WORK.
AND THIS OLD FAILURE HAS A DATE WITH MAYBE.
TT
GORDON. HE'S SAFE.
YOU CAN TELL WARREN AND MARY McGINNIS THEIR BABY'S SAFE.
WHAT HAS HE DONE THIS TIME? THE BAD LITTLE FACE?
I'M SO SORRY I FELL ASLEEP.
As if the Joker ever wrote down any of his secrets.
00:22
HAHAHAHAHAHAHAHA

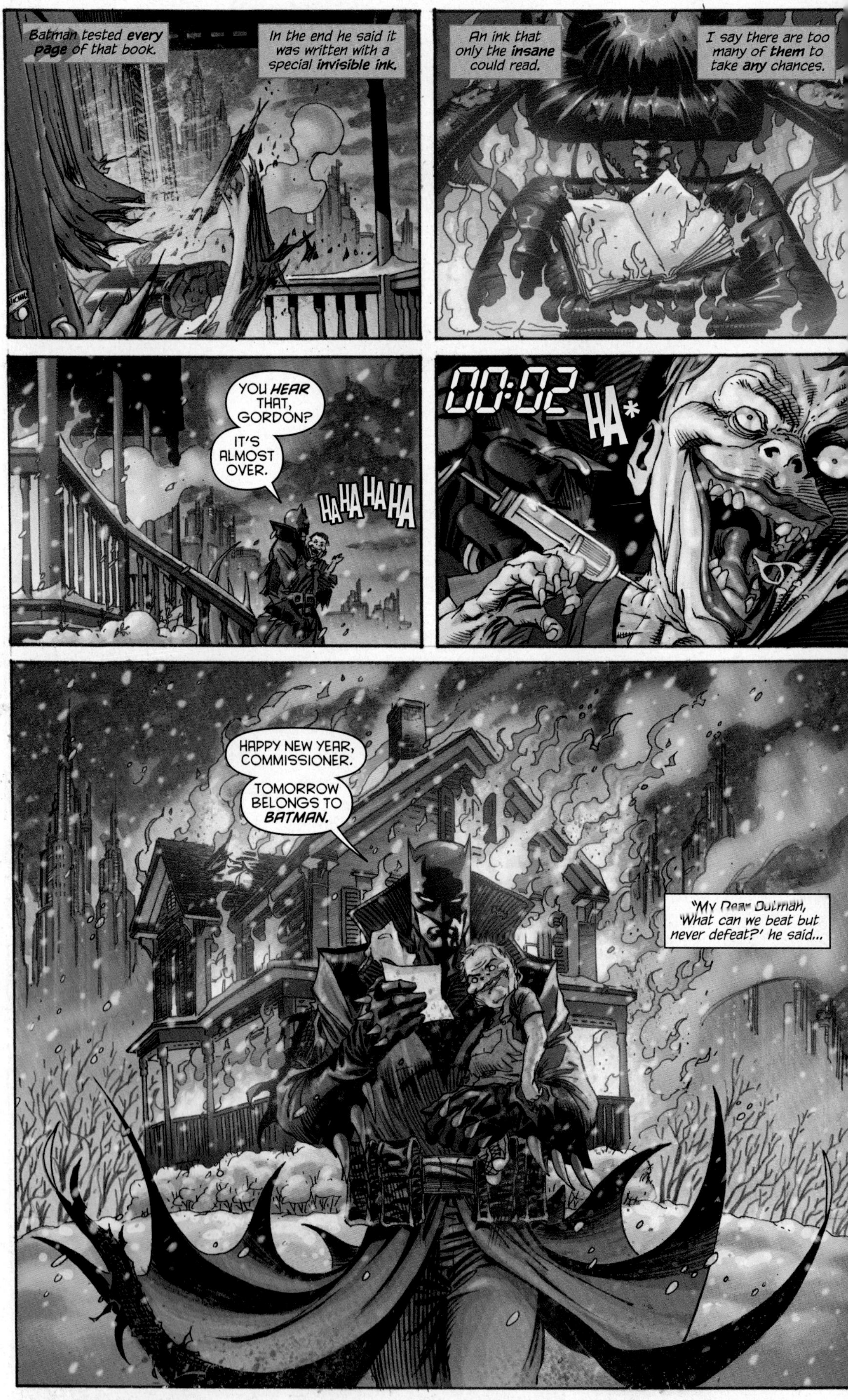
Batman tested **every** **page** of that book.
In the end he said it was written with a special **invisible ink.**
An ink that only the **insane** could read.
I say there are too many of **them** to take **any** chances.
YOU **HEAR** THAT, GORDON?
IT'S ALMOST OVER.
HAHAHAHA
00:02
HA*
HAPPY NEW YEAR, COMMISSIONER.
TOMORROW BELONGS TO **BATMAN.**
"My Dear Batman,
'What can we beat but never defeat?' he said...

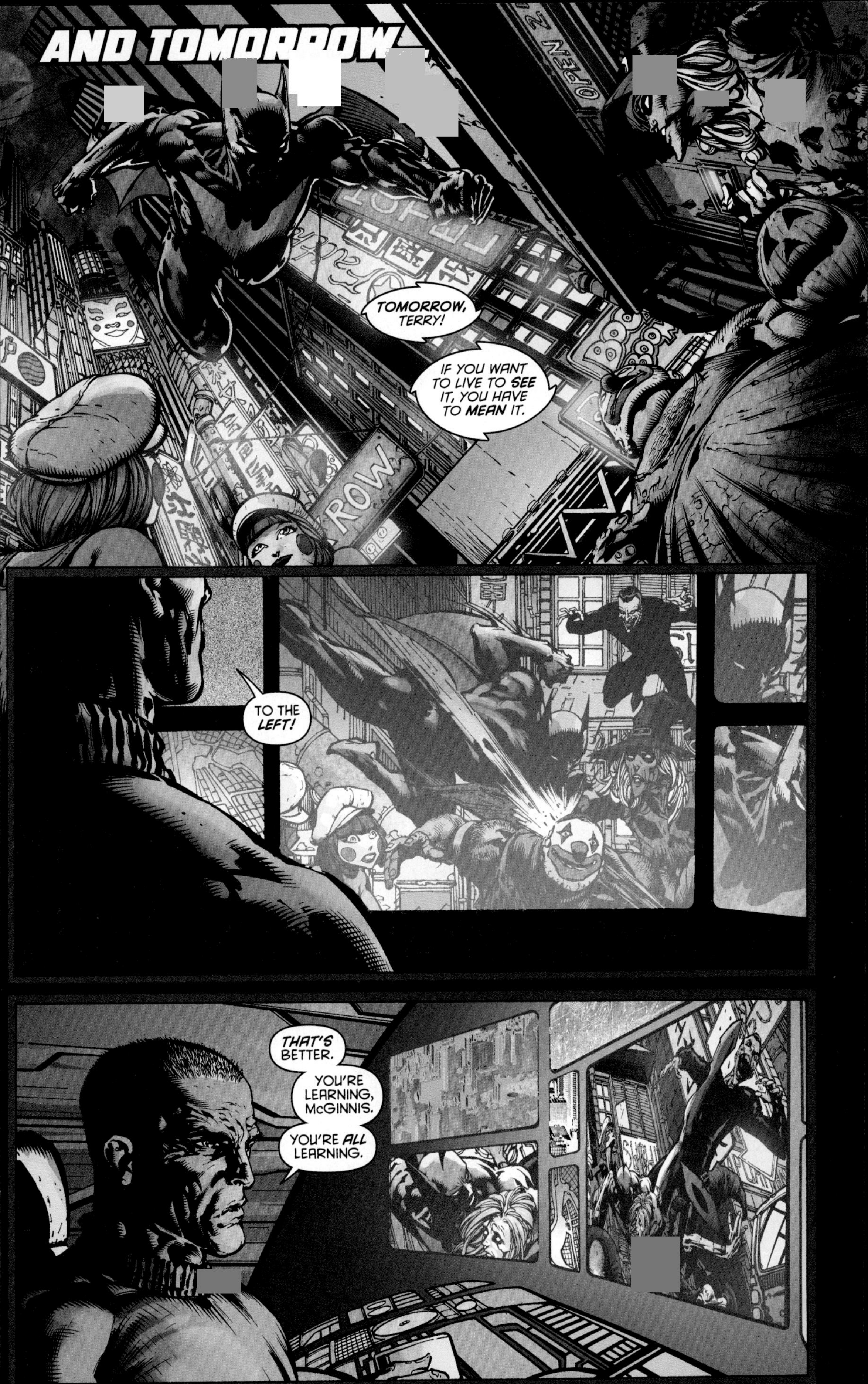
AND TOMORROW...
TOMORROW, TERRY!
IF YOU WANT TO LIVE TO SEE IT, YOU HAVE TO MEAN IT.
ROW
TO THE LEFT!
THAT'S BETTER.
YOU'RE LEARNING, McGINNIS.
YOU'RE ALL LEARNING.

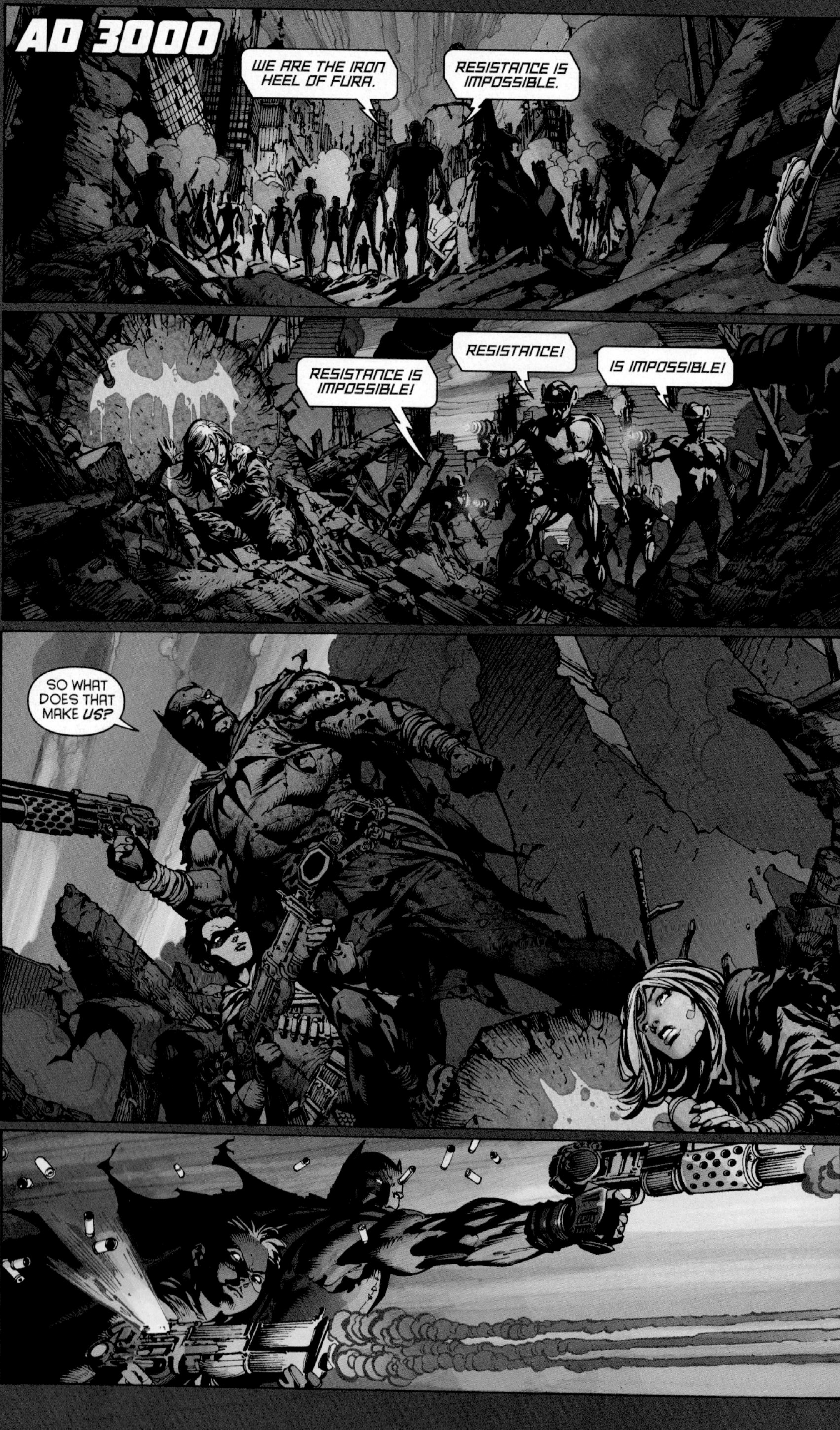
AD 3000
WE ARE THE IRON HEEL OF FURA.
RESISTANCE IS IMPOSSIBLE.
RESISTANCE IS IMPOSSIBLE!
RESISTANCE!
IS IMPOSSIBLE!
SO WHAT DOES THAT MAKE US?

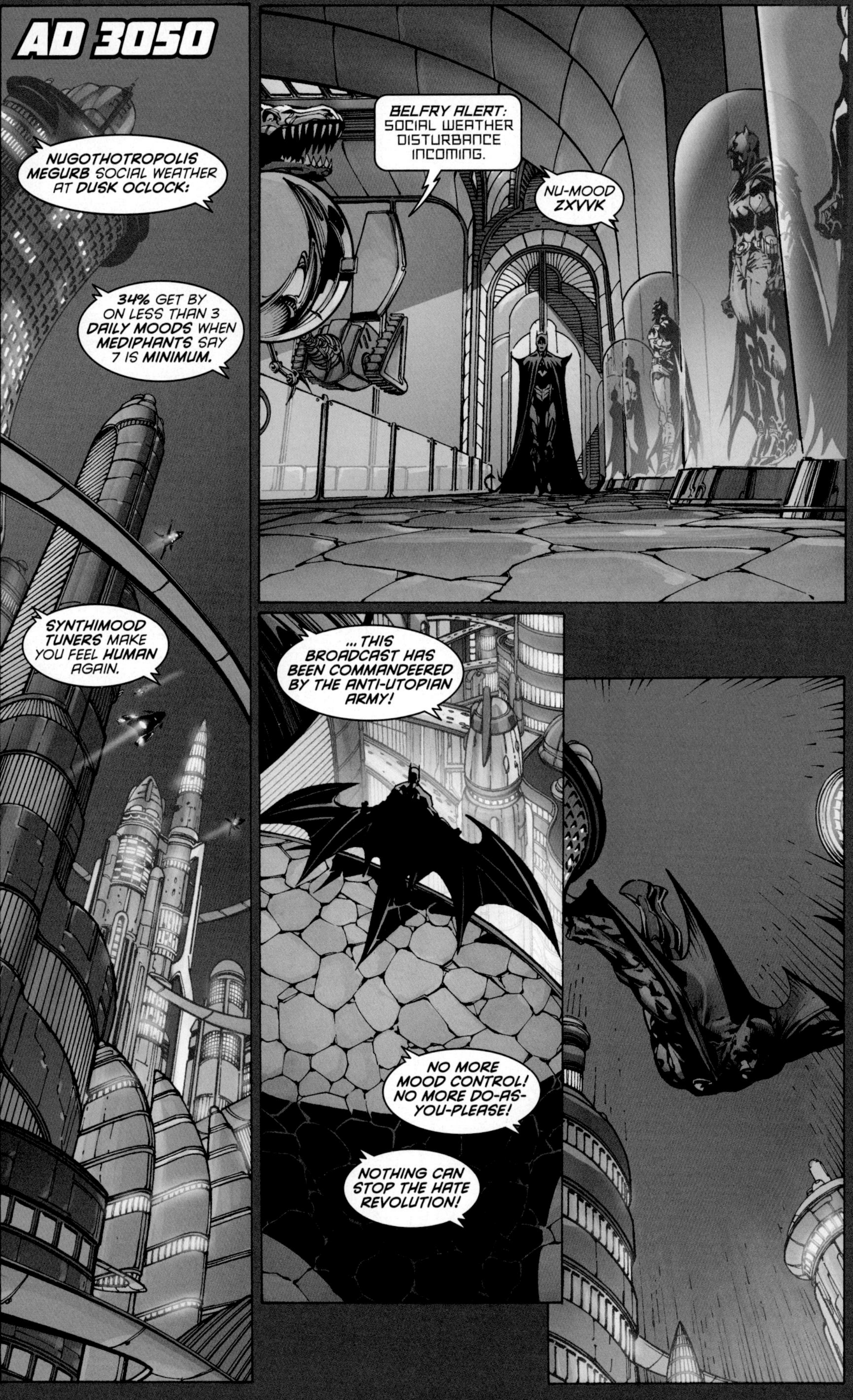
AD 3050
NUGOTHOTROPOLIS MEGURB SOCIAL WEATHER AT DUSK OCLOCK:
34% GET BY ON LESS THAN 3 DAILY MOODS WHEN MEDIPHANTS SAY 7 IS MINIMUM.
SYNTHIMOOD TUNERS MAKE YOU FEEL HUMAN AGAIN.
BELFRY ALERT: SOCIAL WEATHER DISTURBANCE INCOMING.
NU-MOOD ZXVVK
...THIS BROADCAST HAS BEEN COMMANDEERED BY THE ANTI-UTOPIAN ARMY!
NO MORE MOOD CONTROL! NO MORE DO-AS-YOU-PLEASE!
NOTHING CAN STOP THE HATE REVOLUTION!

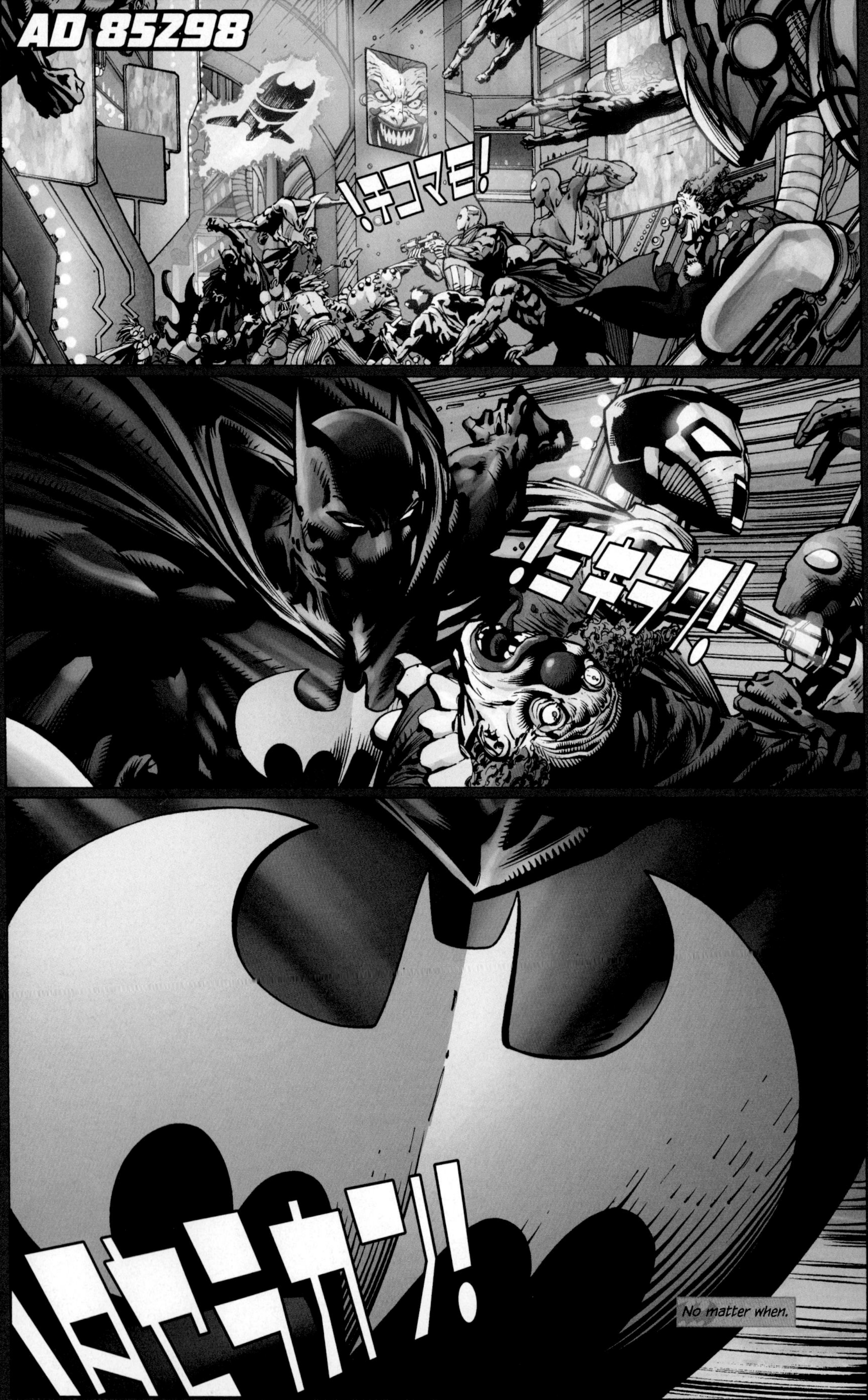
AD 85298
No matter when.

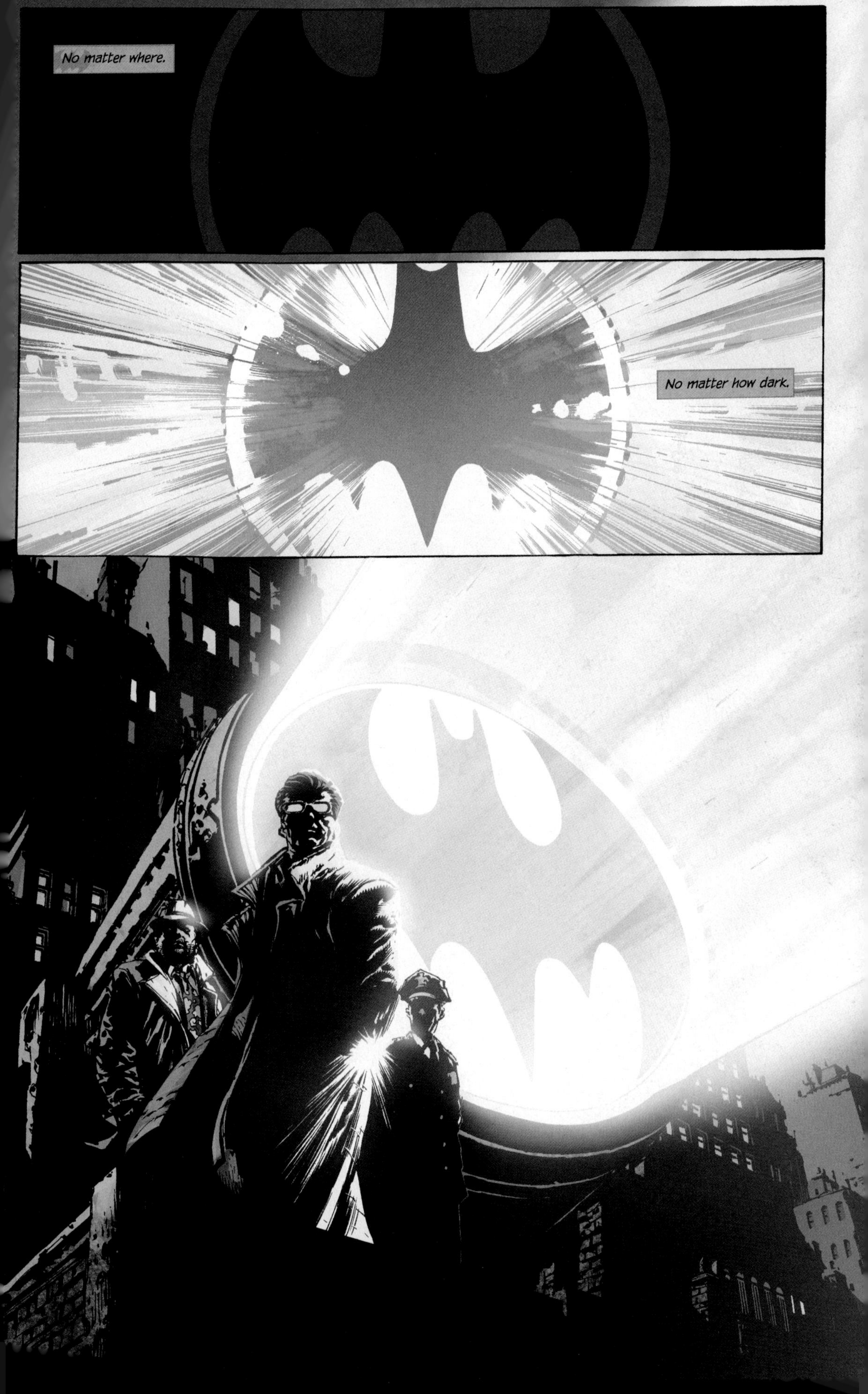
No matter where.
No matter how dark.

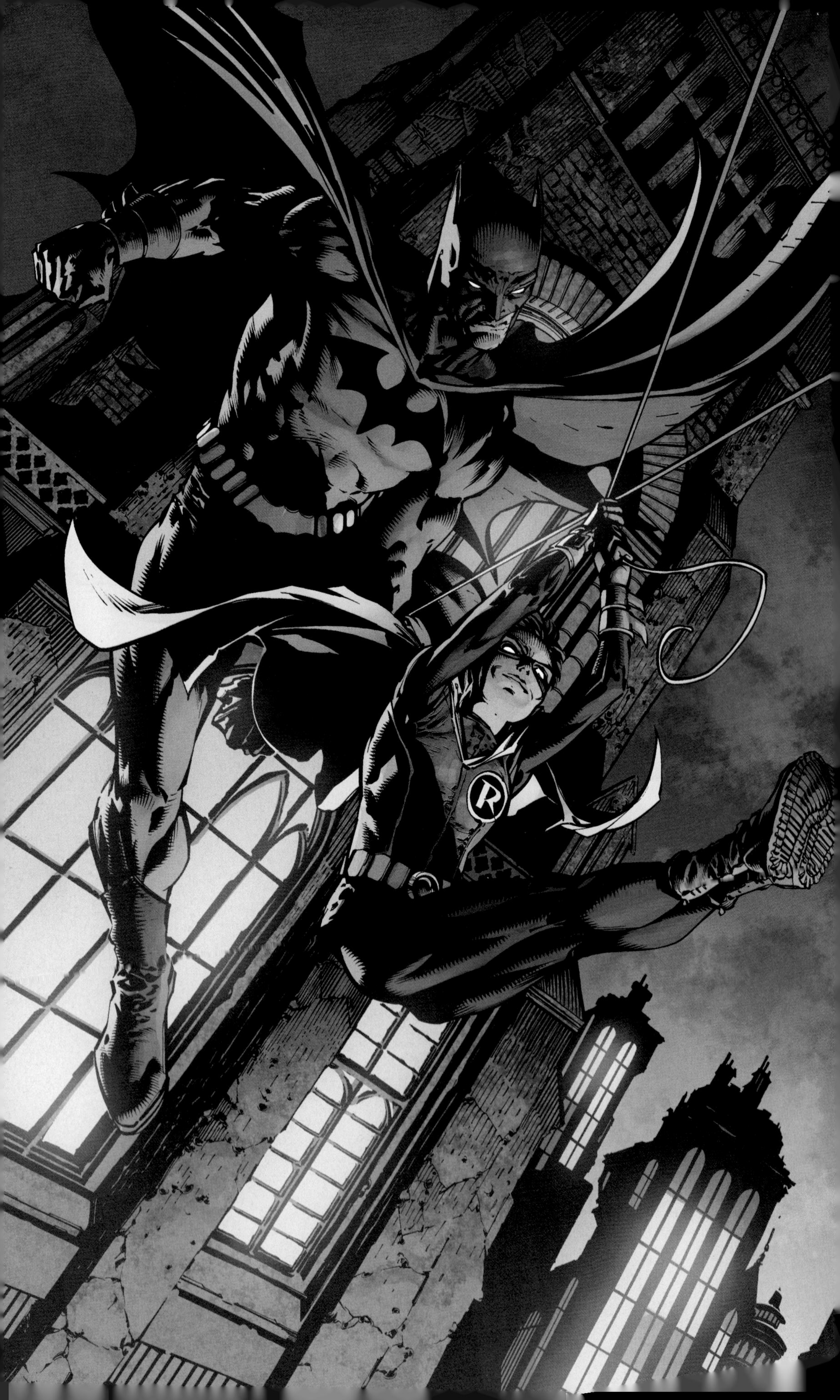

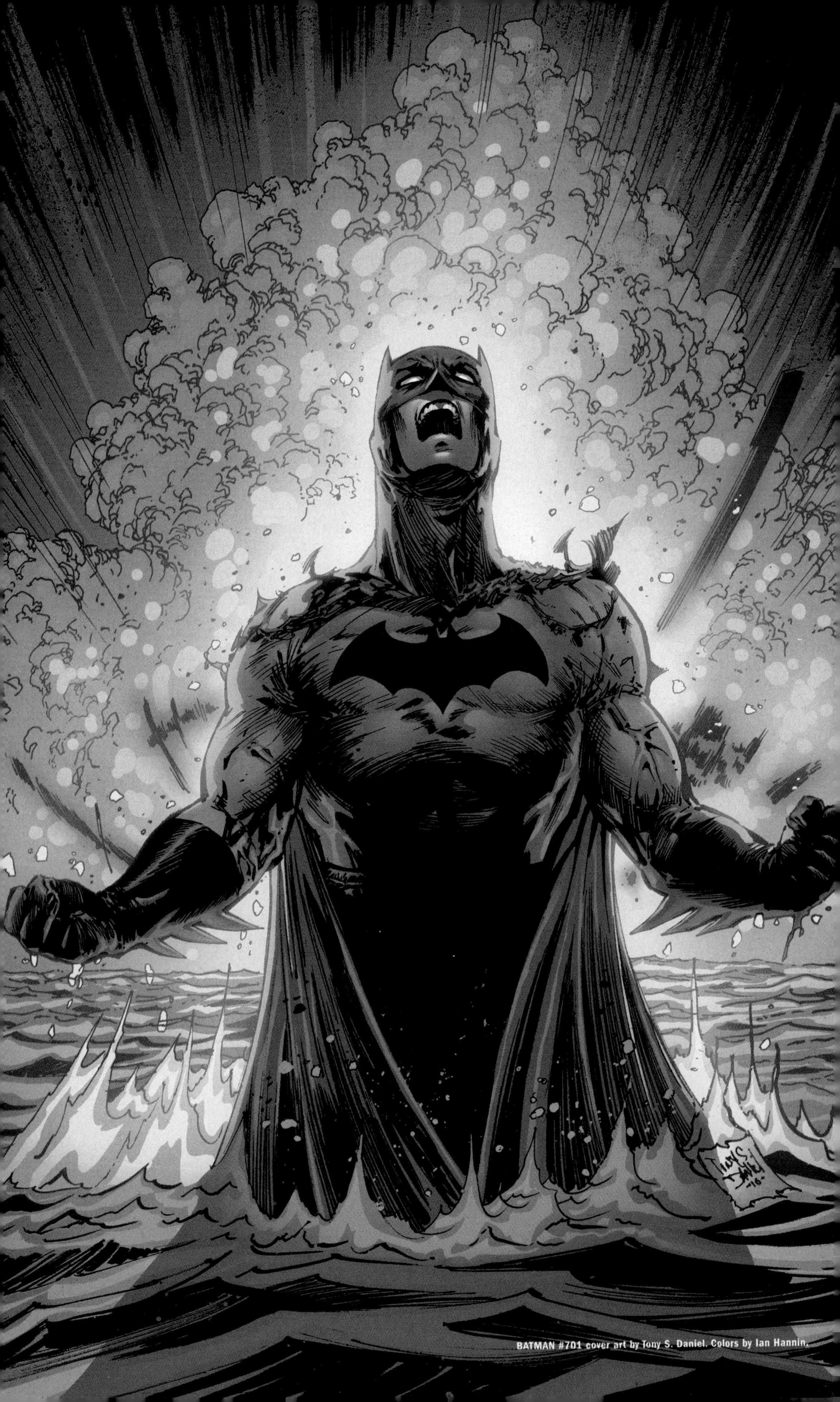

BATMAN #701 cover art by Tony S. Daniel. Colors by Ian Hannin.

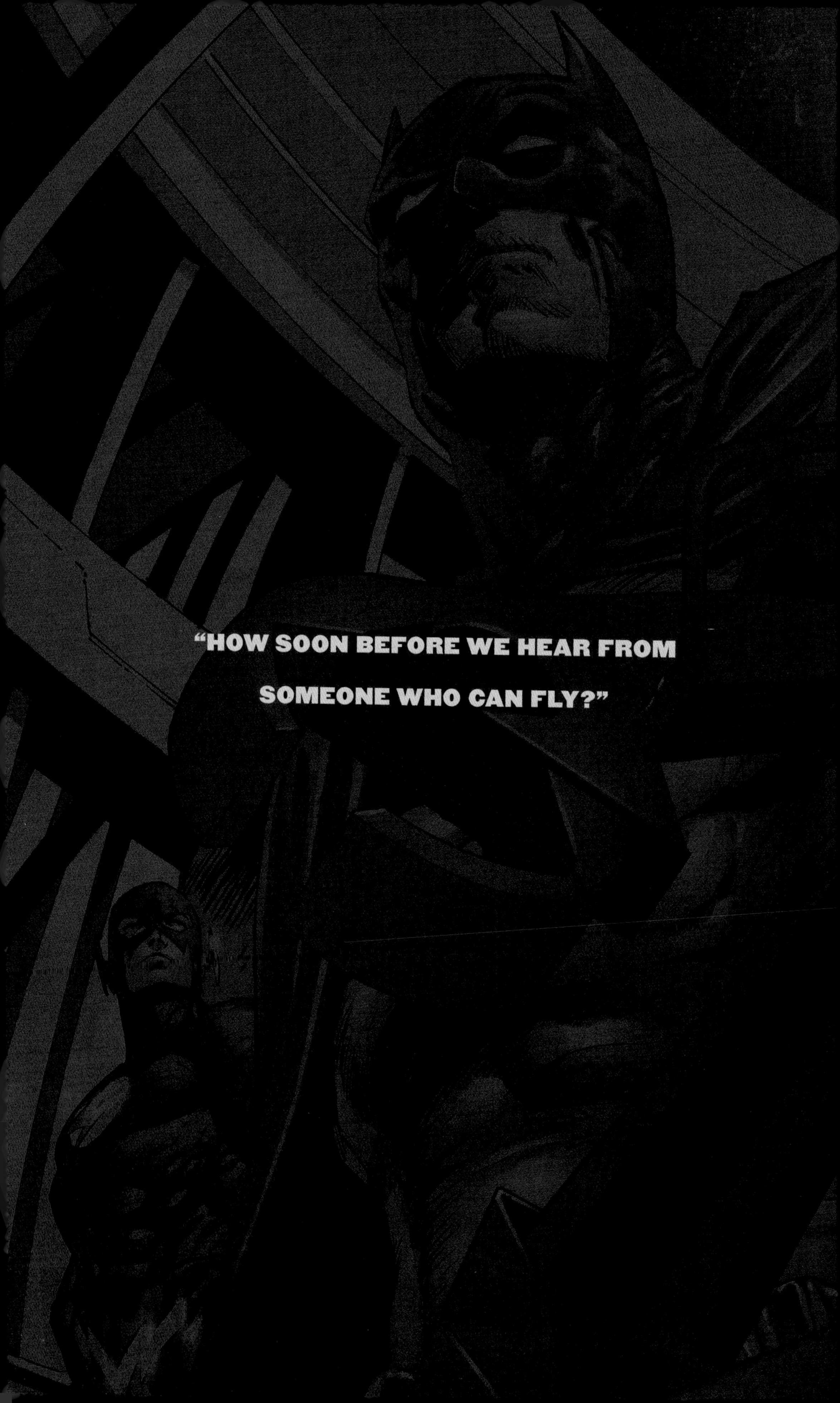
"HOW SOON BEFORE WE HEAR FROM
SOMEONE WHO CAN FLY?"

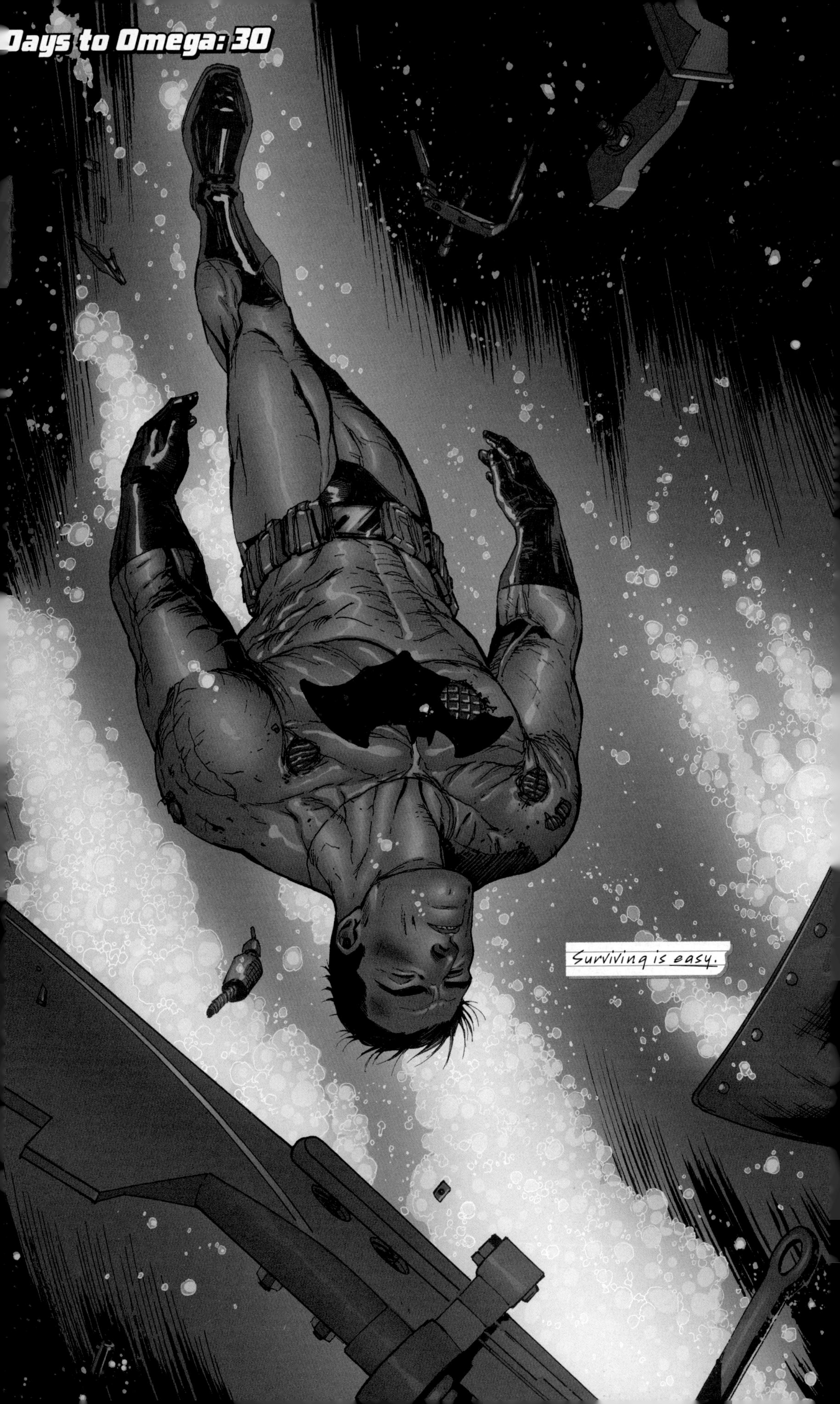
Days to Omega: 30
Surviving is easy.

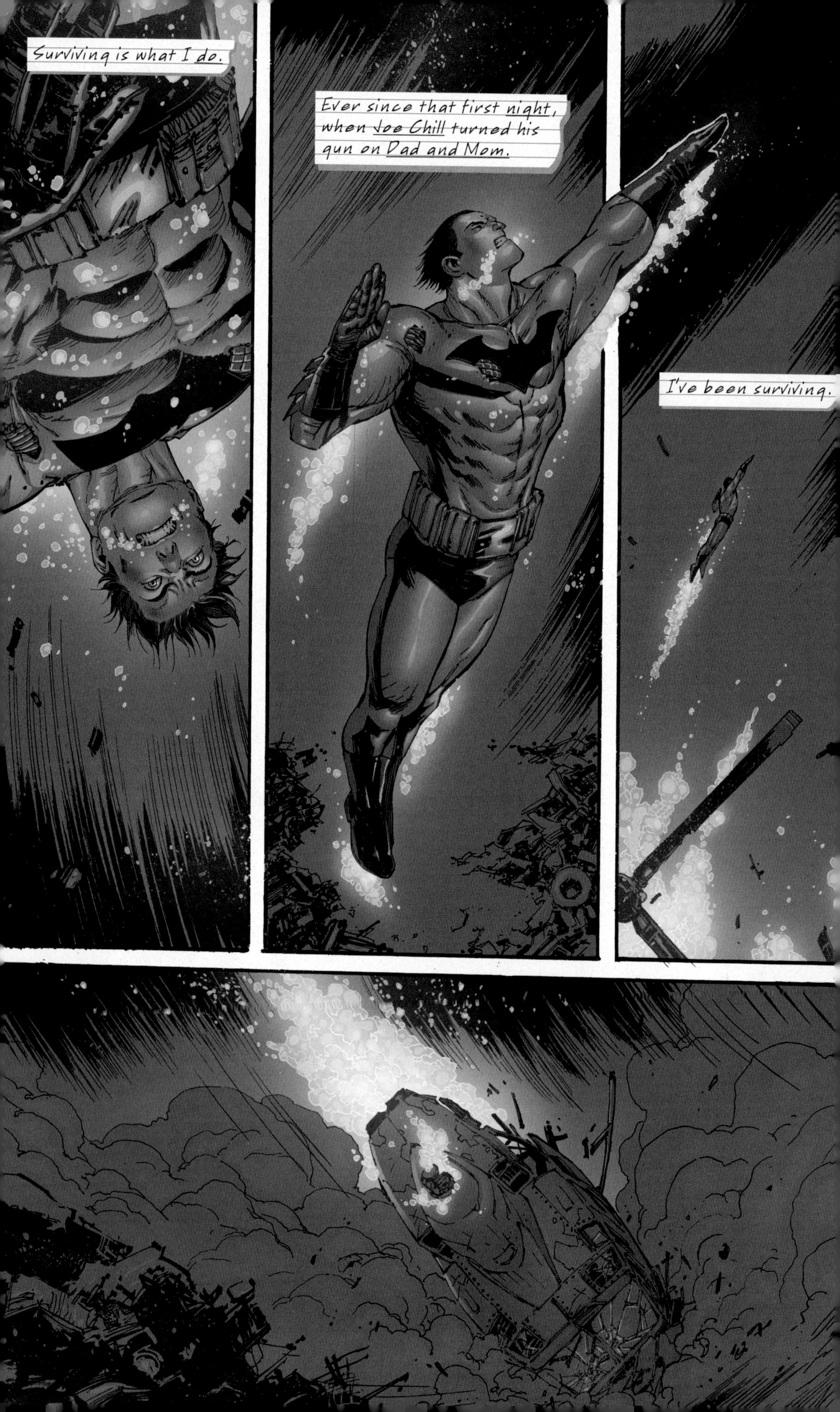
Surviving is what I do.
Ever since that first night, when Joe Chill turned his gun on Dad and Mom.
I've been surviving.

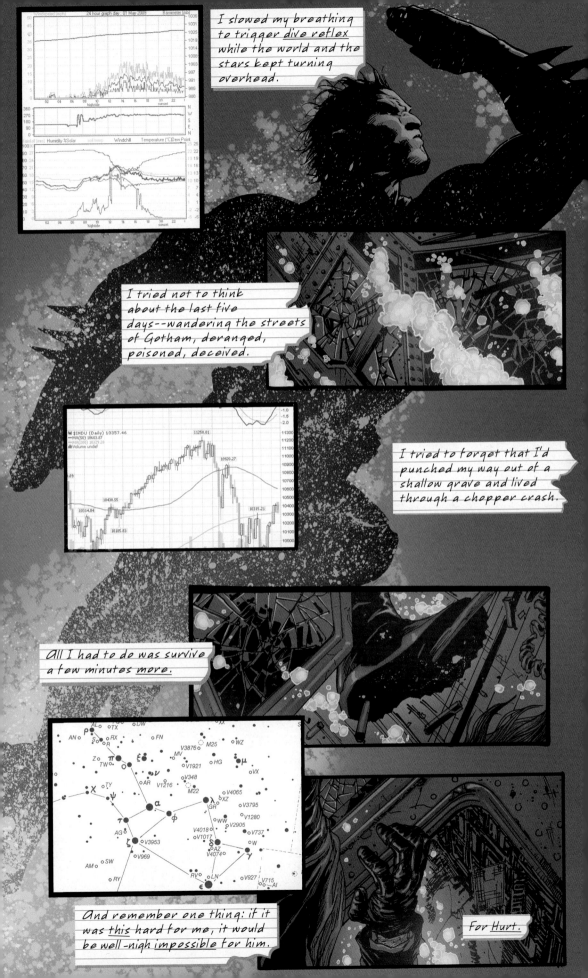

I slowed my breathing to trigger dive reflex while the world and the stars kept turning overhead.

I tried not to think about the last five days--wandering the streets of Gotham, deranged, poisoned, deceived.

I tried to forget that I'd punched my way out of a shallow grave and lived through a chopper crash.

All I had to do was survive a few minutes more.

And remember one thing: if it was this hard for me, it would be well-nigh impossible for him.

For Hurt.

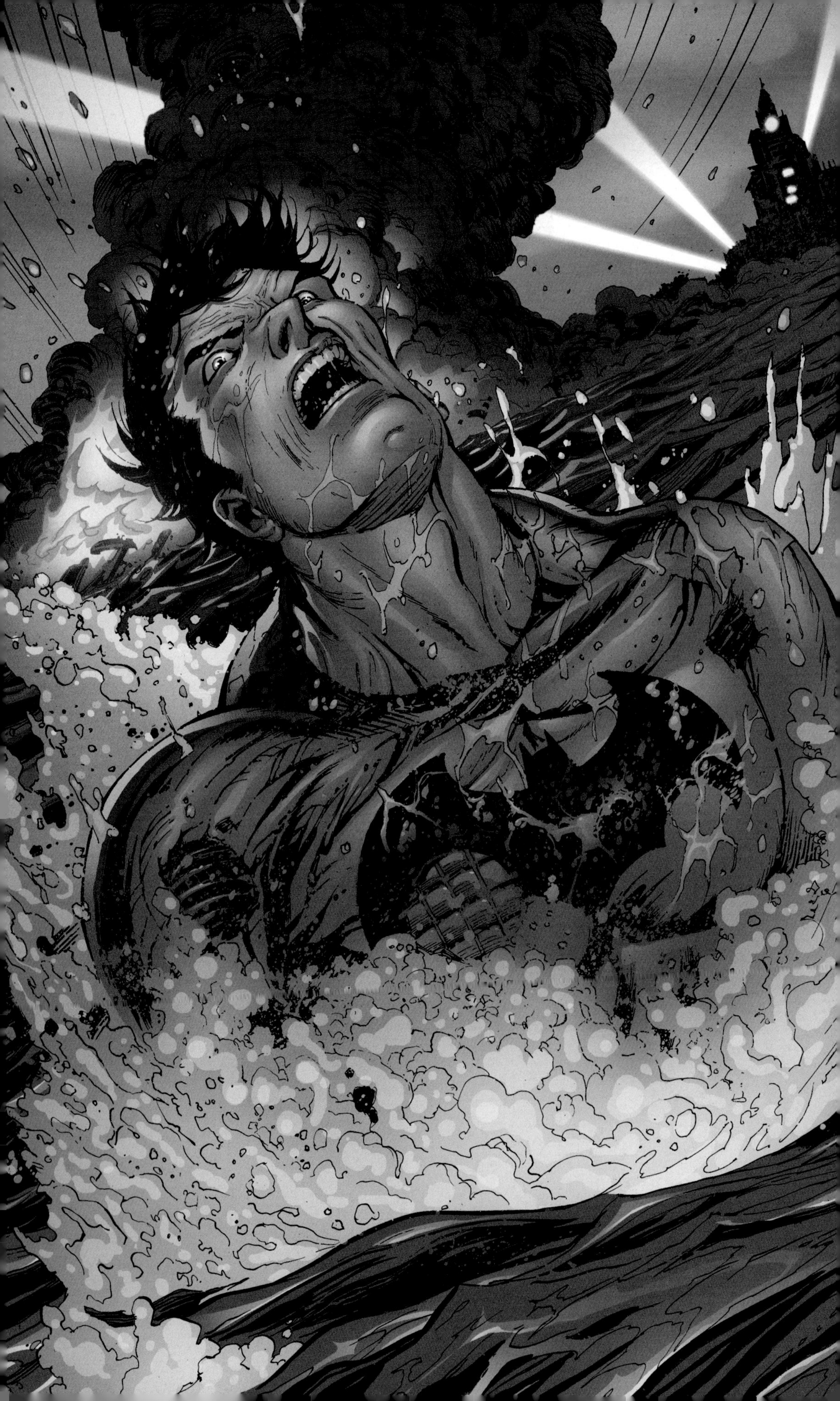

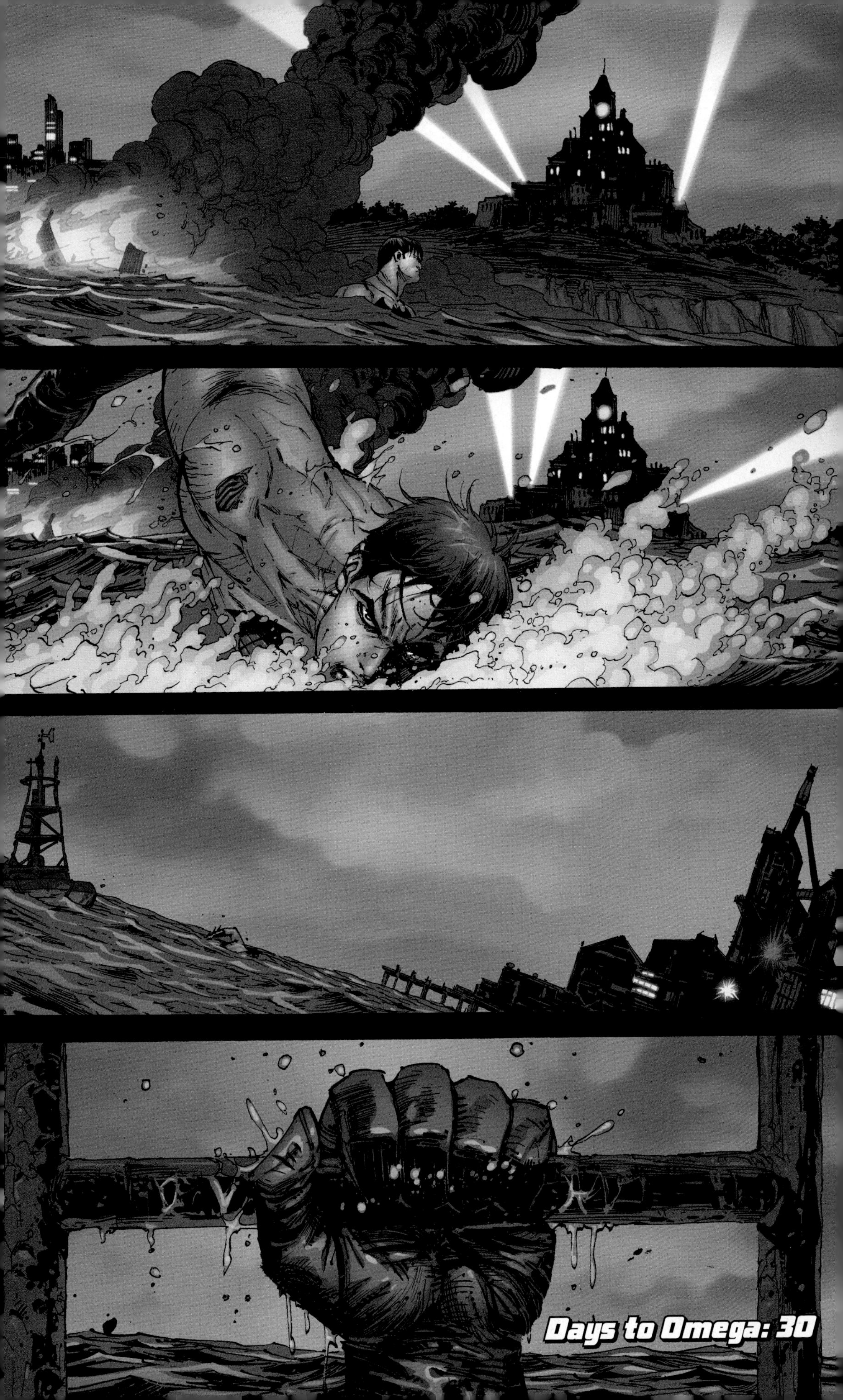
Days to Omega: 30

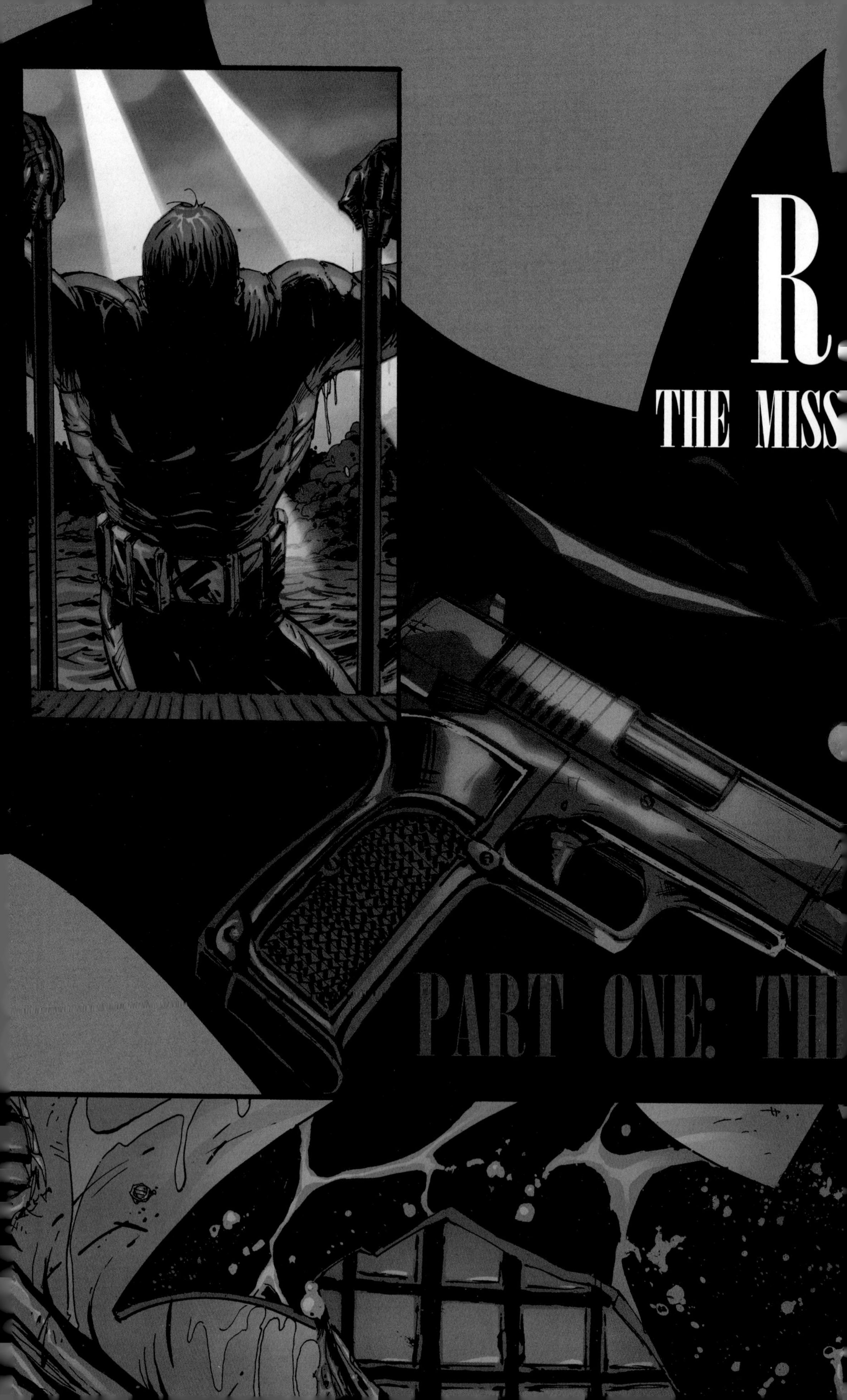
R
THE MISS
PART ONE: TH

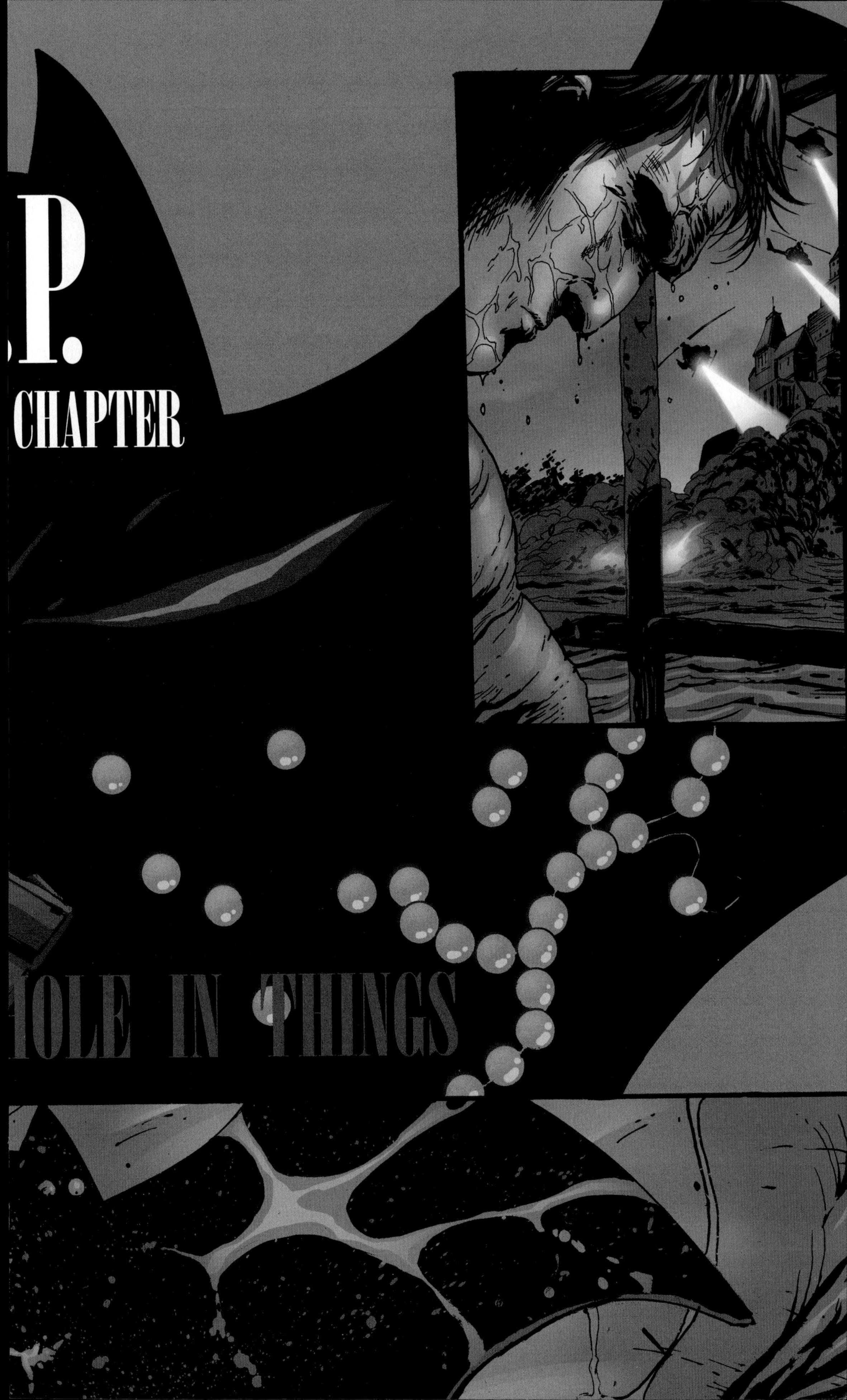
CHAPTER
IN THINGS

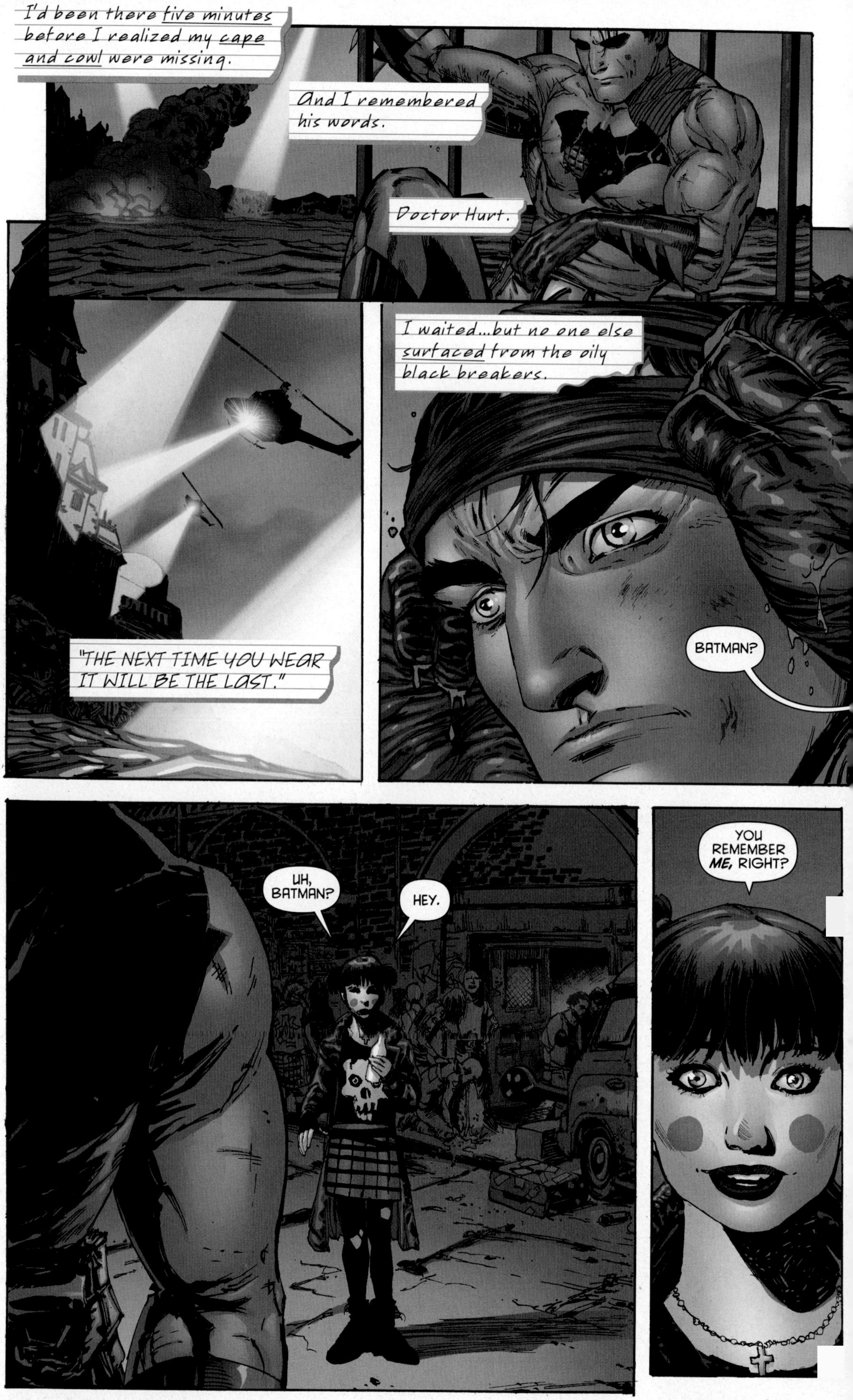
I'd been there five minutes before I realized my cape and cowl were missing.
And I remembered his words.
Doctor Hurt.
"THE NEXT TIME YOU WEAR IT WILL BE THE LAST."
I waited...but no one else surfaced from the oily black breakers.
BATMAN?
UH, BATMAN?
HEY.
YOU REMEMBER ME, RIGHT?

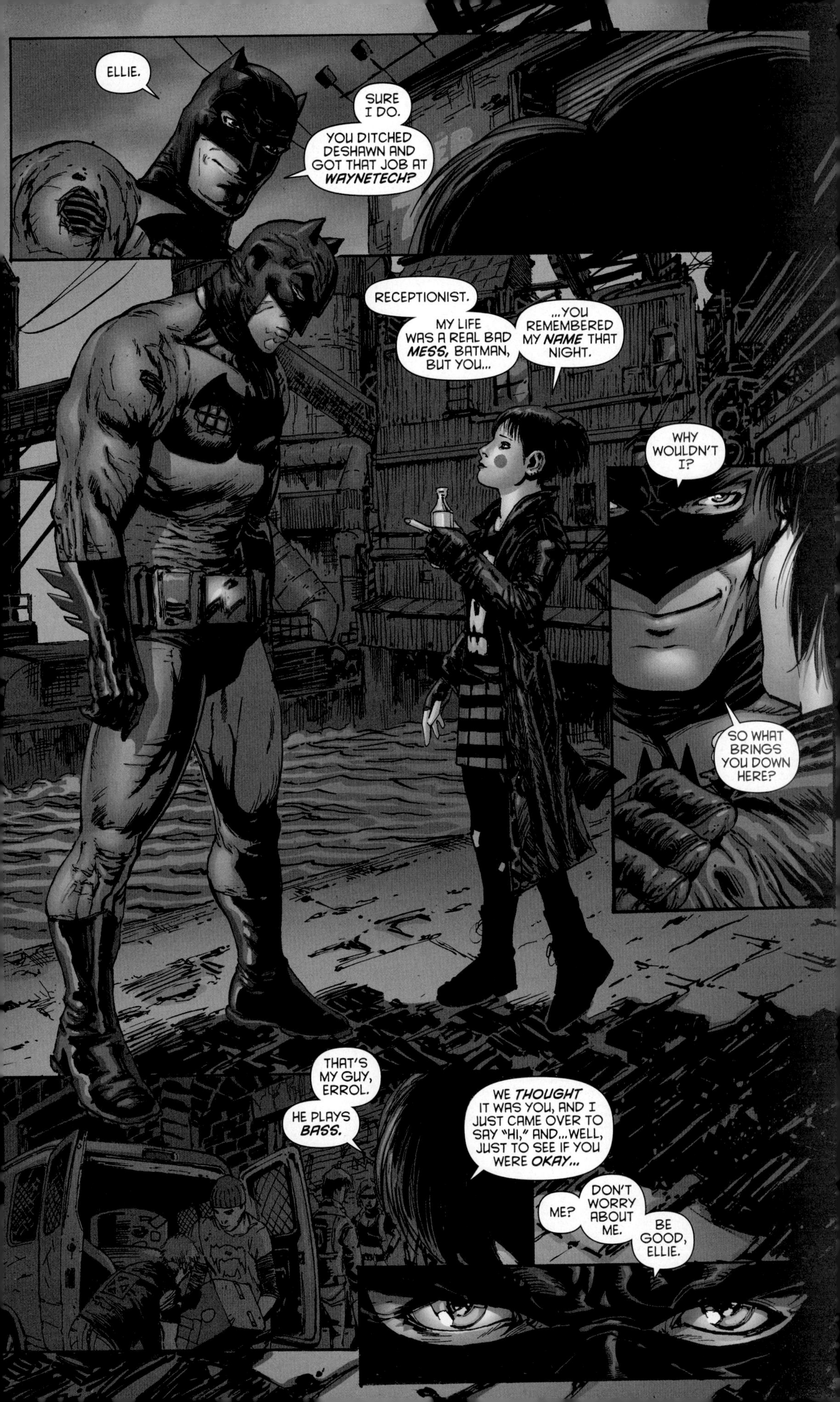

ELLIE.
SURE I DO.
YOU DITCHED DESHAWN AND GOT THAT JOB AT *WAYNETECH?*
RECEPTIONIST.
MY LIFE WAS A REAL BAD *MESS,* BATMAN, BUT YOU...
...YOU REMEMBERED MY *NAME* THAT NIGHT.
WHY WOULDN'T I?
SO WHAT BRINGS YOU DOWN HERE?
THAT'S MY GUY, ERROL.
HE PLAYS *BASS.*
WE *THOUGHT* IT WAS YOU, AND I JUST CAME OVER TO SAY "HI," AND...WELL, JUST TO SEE IF YOU WERE *OKAY...*
ME?
DON'T WORRY ABOUT ME.
BE GOOD, ELLIE.

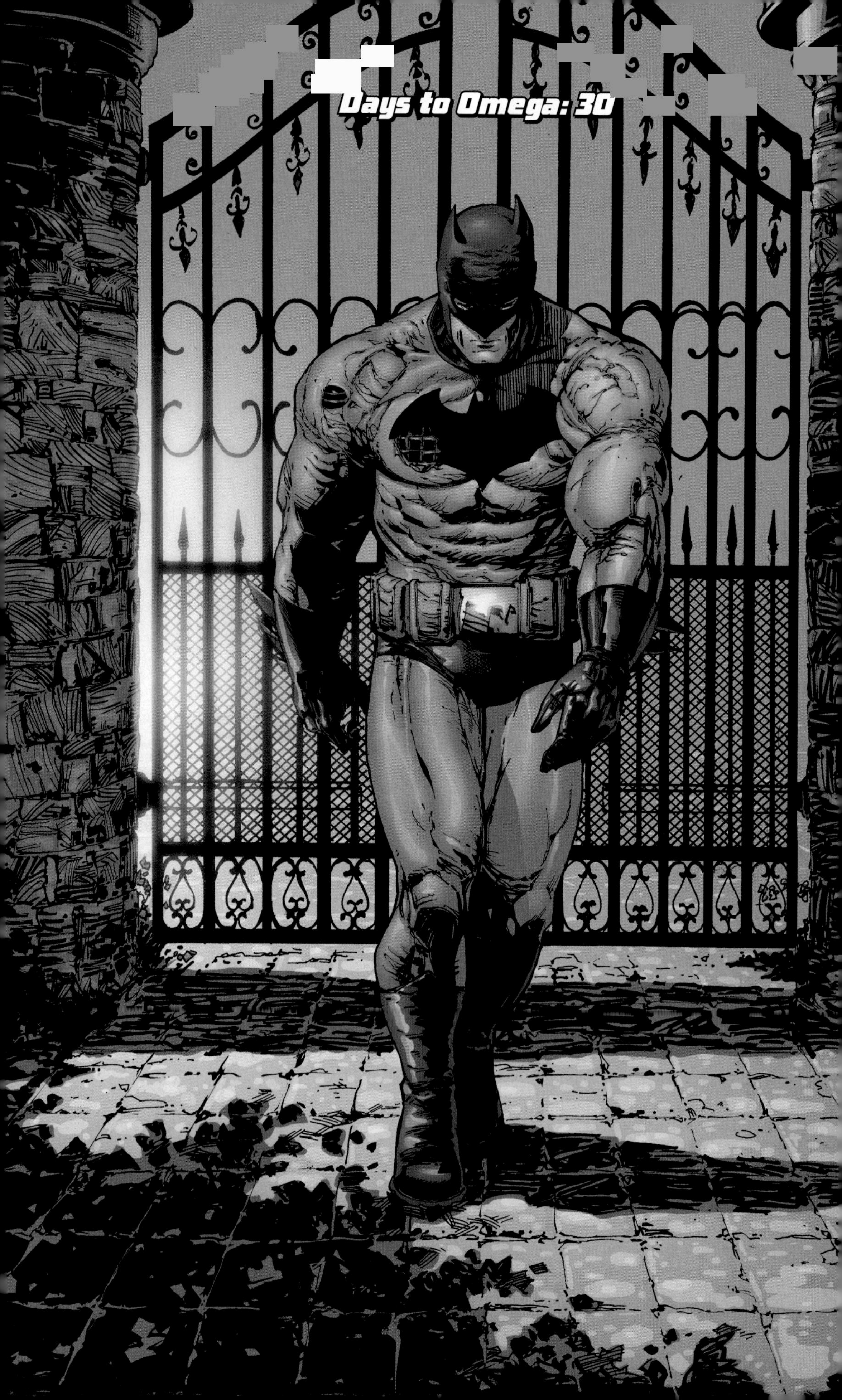
Days to Omega: 30

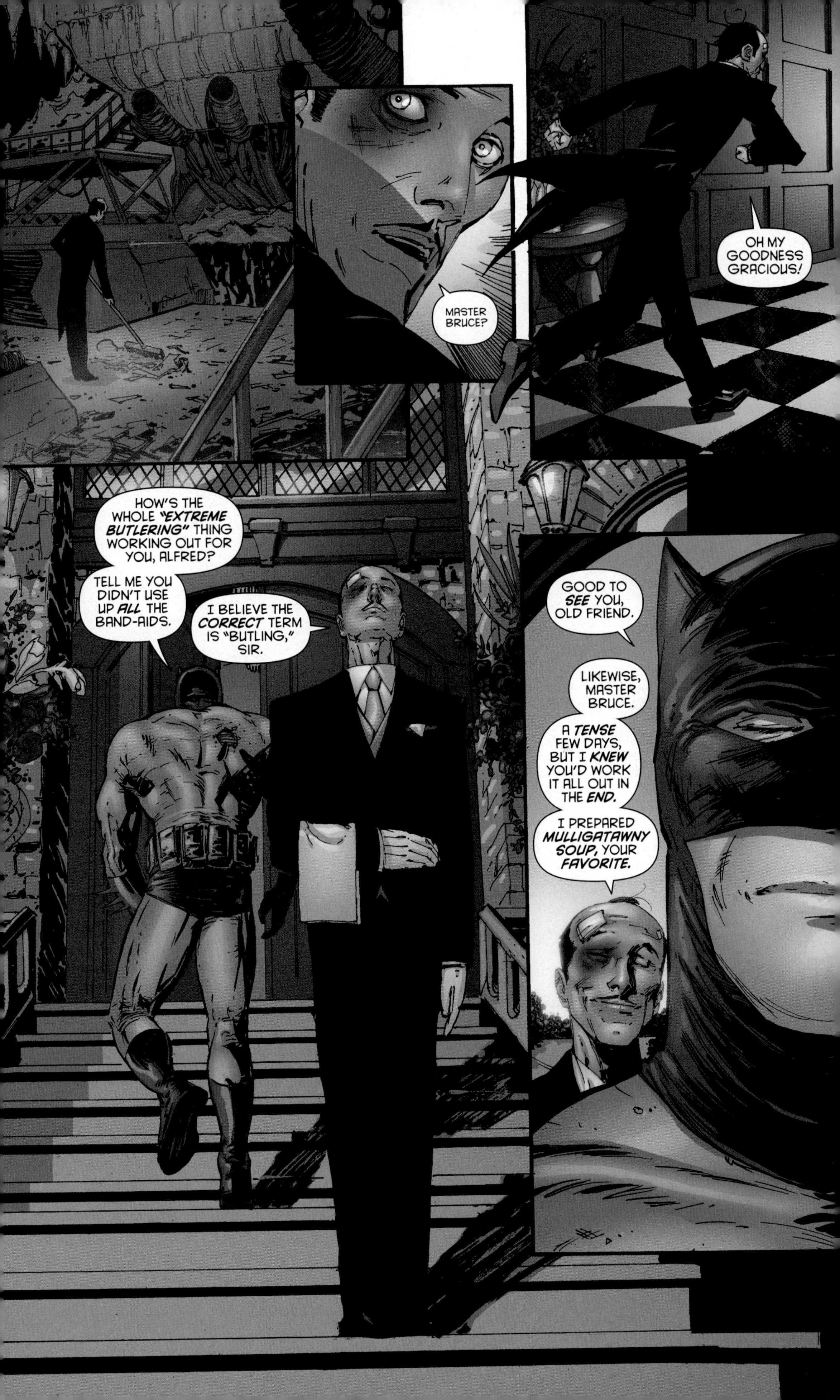
MASTER BRUCE?
OH MY GOODNESS GRACIOUS!
HOW'S THE WHOLE "EXTREME BUTLERING" THING WORKING OUT FOR YOU, ALFRED?
TELL ME YOU DIDN'T USE UP ALL THE BAND-AIDS.
I BELIEVE THE CORRECT TERM IS "BUTLING," SIR.
GOOD TO SEE YOU, OLD FRIEND.
LIKEWISE, MASTER BRUCE.
A TENSE FEW DAYS, BUT I KNEW YOU'D WORK IT ALL OUT IN THE END.
I PREPARED MULLIGATAWNY SOUP, YOUR FAVORITE.

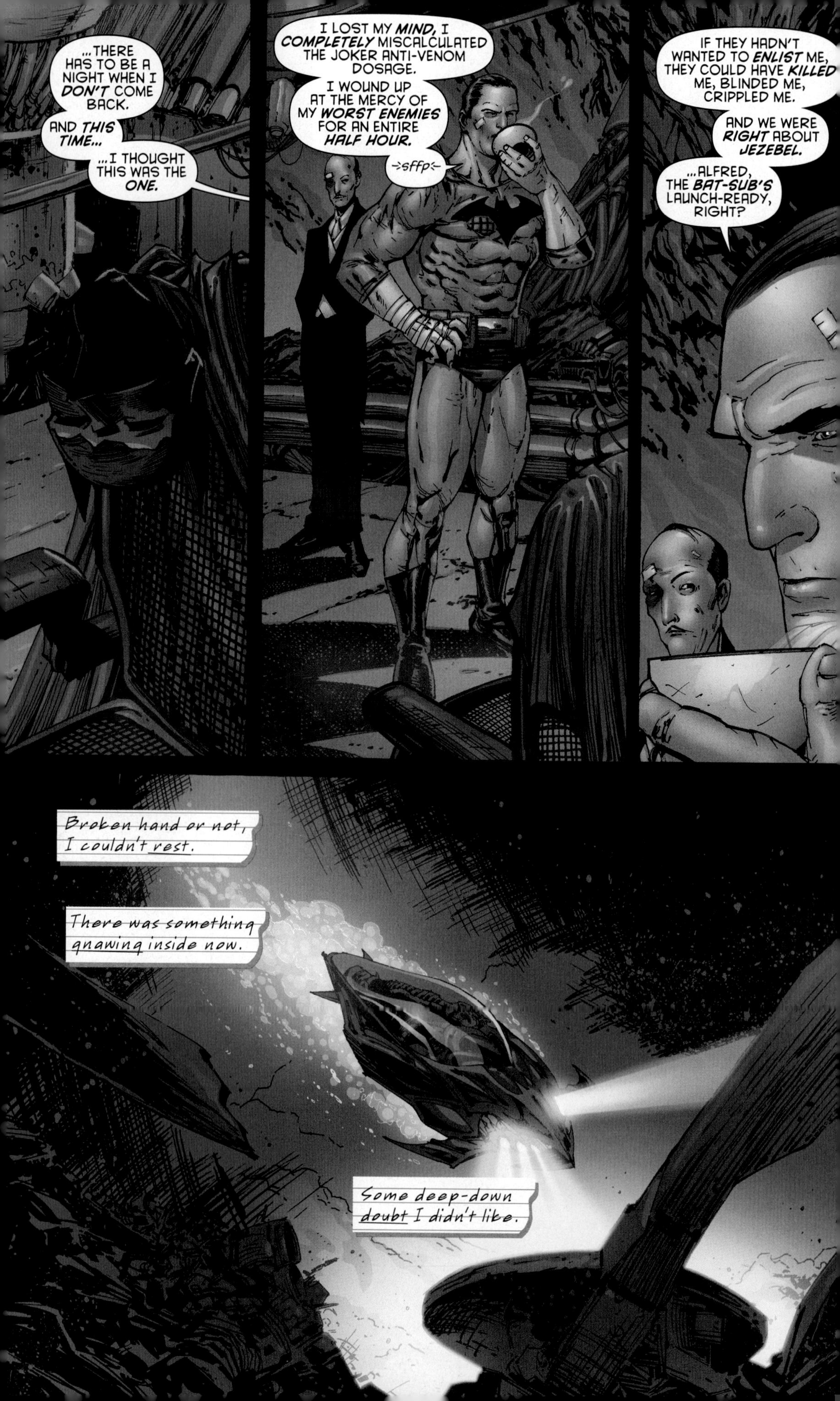

...THERE HAS TO BE A NIGHT WHEN I DON'T COME BACK.
AND THIS TIME...
...I THOUGHT THIS WAS THE ONE.
I LOST MY MIND, I COMPLETELY MISCALCULATED THE JOKER ANTI-VENOM DOSAGE.
I WOUND UP AT THE MERCY OF MY WORST ENEMIES FOR AN ENTIRE HALF HOUR.
sffp
IF THEY HADN'T WANTED TO ENLIST ME, THEY COULD HAVE KILLED ME, BLINDED ME, CRIPPLED ME.
AND WE WERE RIGHT ABOUT JEZEBEL.
...ALFRED, THE BAT-SUB'S LAUNCH-READY, RIGHT?
Broken hand or not, I couldn't rest.
There was something gnawing inside now.
Some deep-down doubt I didn't like.

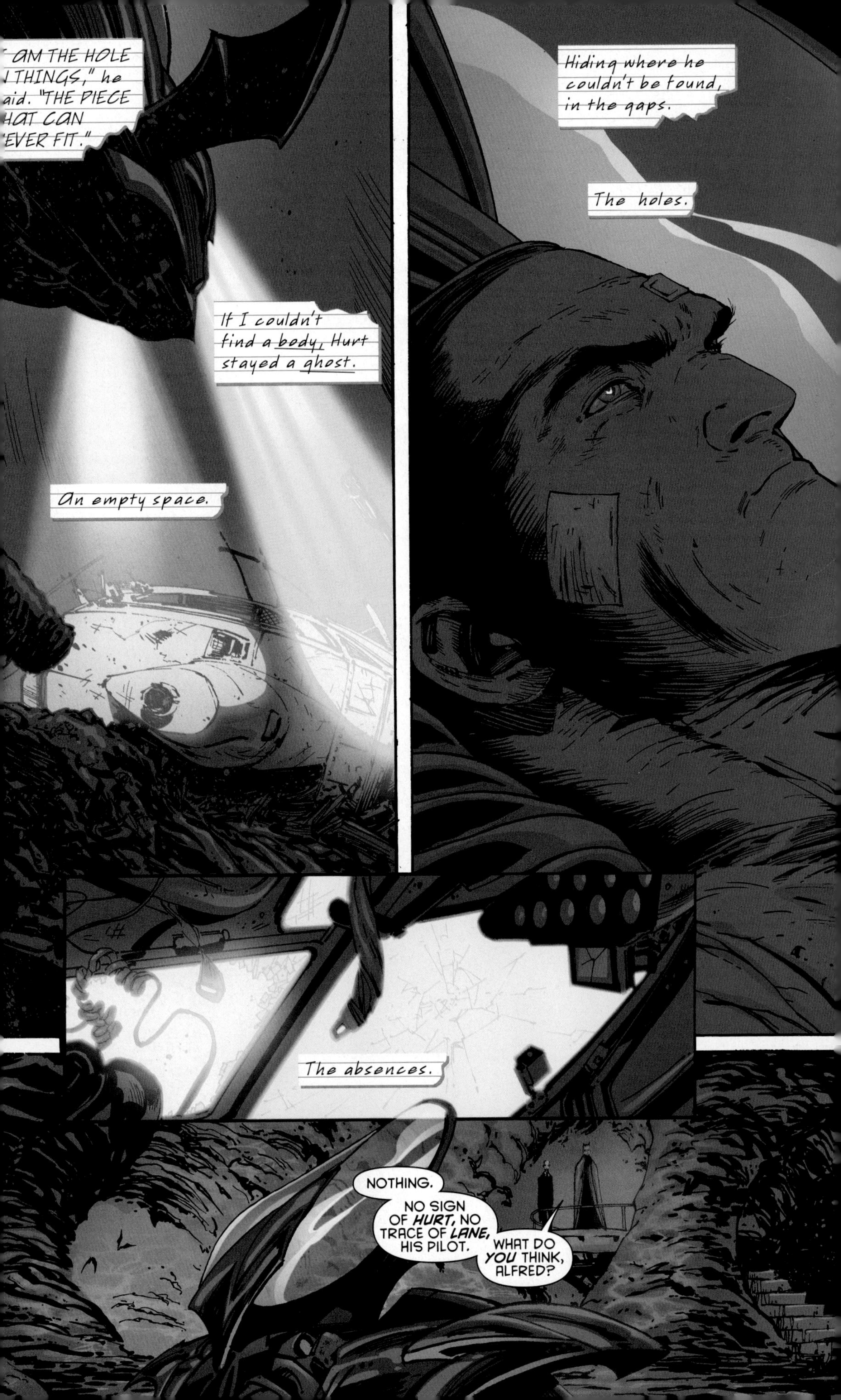
AM THE HOLE
THINGS," he
aid. "THE PIECE
HAT CAN
EVER FIT."
If I couldn't find a body, Hurt stayed a ghost.
An empty space.
Hiding where he couldn't be found, in the gaps.
The holes.
The absences.
NOTHING.
NO SIGN OF HURT, NO TRACE OF LANE, HIS PILOT.
WHAT DO YOU THINK, ALFRED?

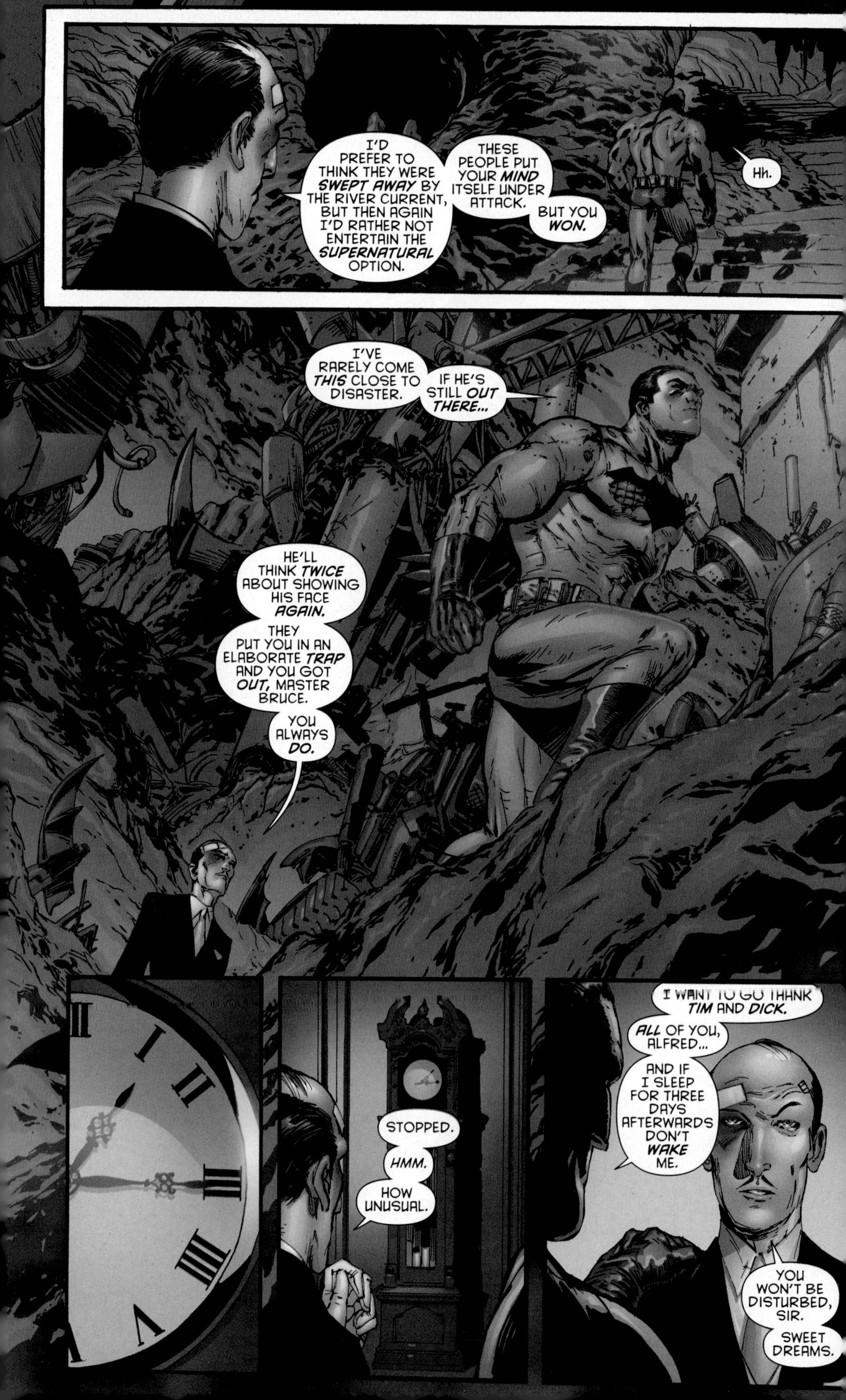

I'D PREFER TO THINK THEY WERE SWEPT AWAY BY THE RIVER CURRENT, BUT THEN AGAIN I'D RATHER NOT ENTERTAIN THE SUPERNATURAL OPTION.
THESE PEOPLE PUT YOUR MIND ITSELF UNDER ATTACK.
BUT YOU WON.
Hh.
I'VE RARELY COME THIS CLOSE TO DISASTER.
IF HE'S STILL OUT THERE...
HE'LL THINK TWICE ABOUT SHOWING HIS FACE AGAIN.
THEY PUT YOU IN AN ELABORATE TRAP AND YOU GOT OUT, MASTER BRUCE.
YOU ALWAYS DO.
STOPPED.
HMM.
HOW UNUSUAL.
I WANT TO GO THANK TIM AND DICK.
ALL OF YOU, ALFRED...
AND IF I SLEEP FOR THREE DAYS AFTERWARDS DON'T WAKE ME.
YOU WON'T BE DISTURBED, SIR.
SWEET DREAMS.

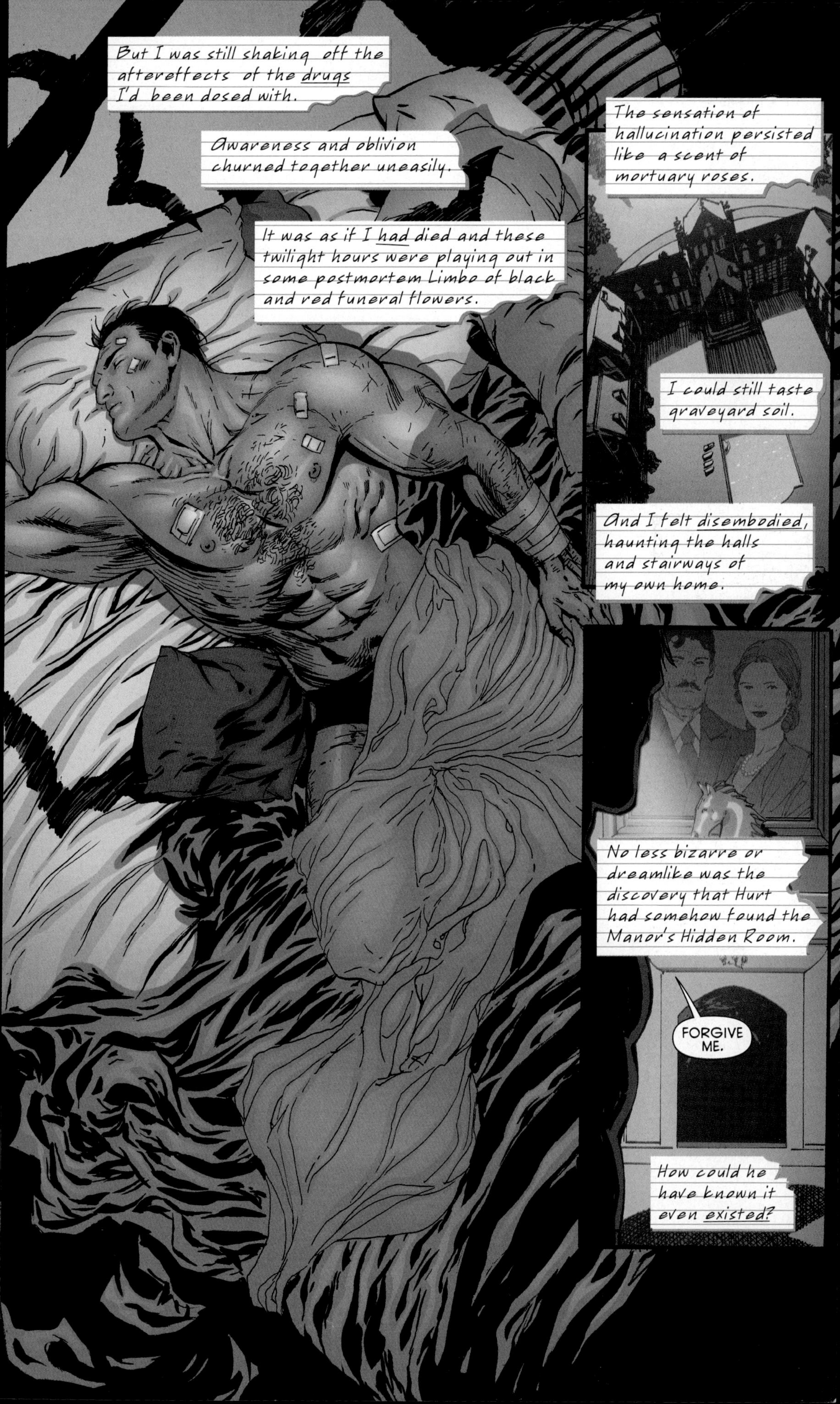
But I was still shaking off the aftereffects of the drugs I'd been dosed with.
Awareness and oblivion churned together uneasily.
It was as if I had died and these twilight hours were playing out in some postmortem Limbo of black and red funeral flowers.
The sensation of hallucination persisted like a scent of mortuary roses.
I could still taste graveyard soil.
And I felt disembodied, haunting the halls and stairways of my own home.
No less bizarre or dreamlike was the discovery that Hurt had somehow found the Manor's Hidden Room.
FORGIVE ME.
How could he have known it even existed?

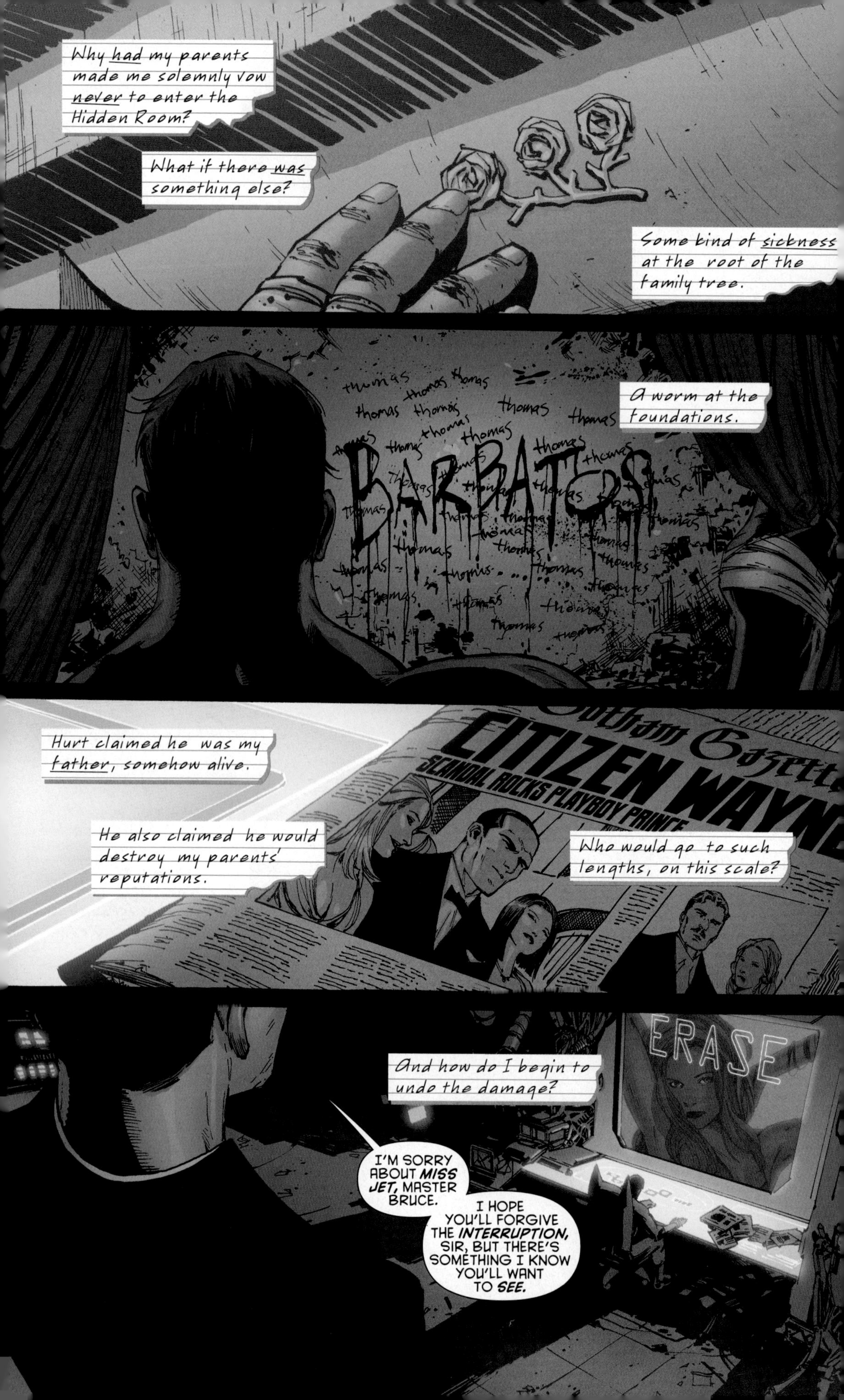

Why had my parents made me solemnly vow never to enter the Hidden Room?
What if there was something else?
Some kind of sickness at the root of the family tree.
A worm at the foundations.
BARBATOS
Hurt claimed he was my father, somehow alive.
He also claimed he would destroy my parents' reputations.
CITIZEN WAYNE
SCANDAL ROCKS PLAYBOY PRINCE
Who would go to such lengths, on this scale?
And how do I begin to undo the damage?
ERASE
I'M SORRY ABOUT MISS JET, MASTER BRUCE.
I HOPE YOU'LL FORGIVE THE INTERRUPTION, SIR, BUT THERE'S SOMETHING I KNOW YOU'LL WANT TO SEE.

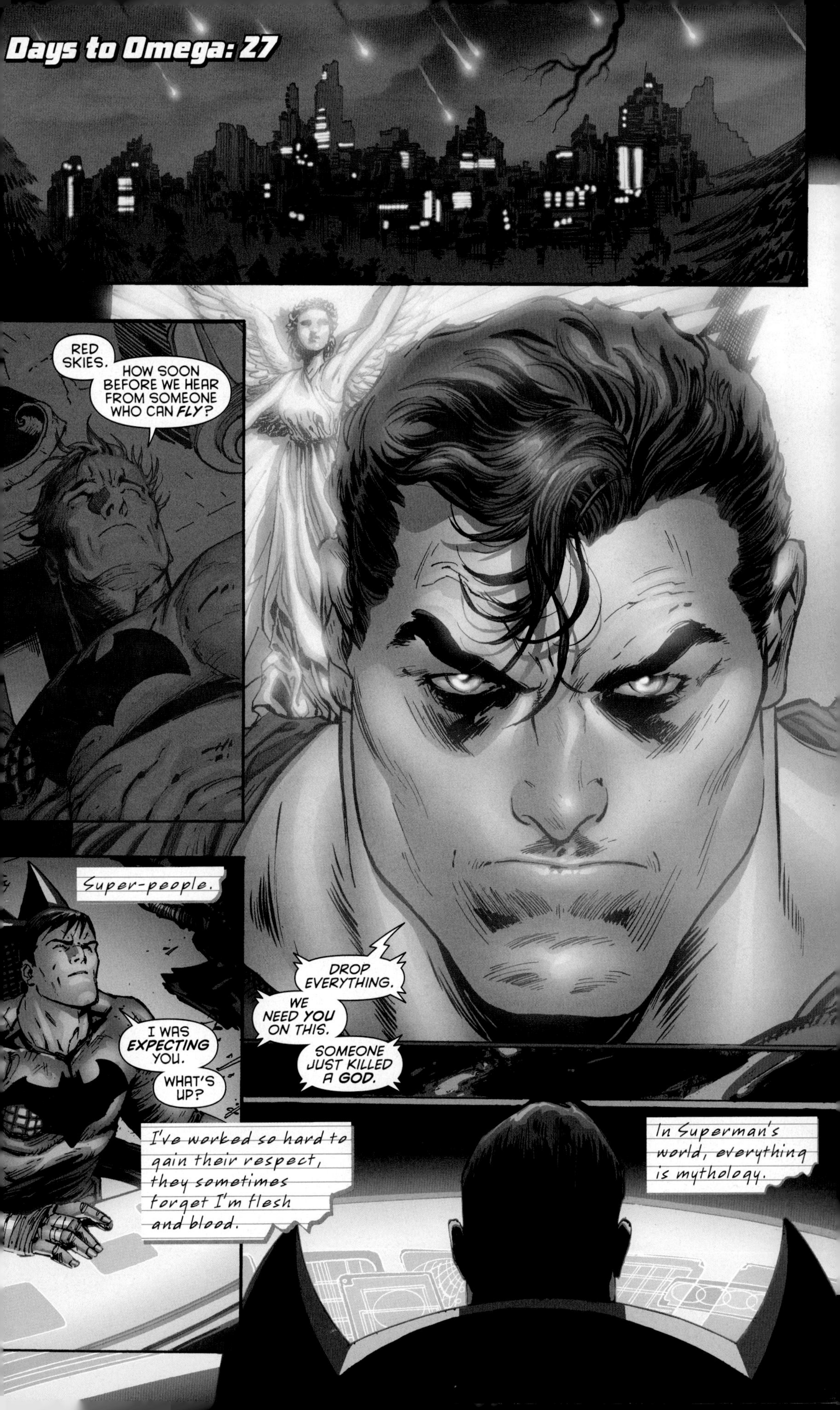
Days to Omega: 27
RED SKIES.
HOW SOON BEFORE WE HEAR FROM SOMEONE WHO CAN FLY?
Super-people.
I WAS EXPECTING YOU.
WHAT'S UP?
DROP EVERYTHING.
WE NEED YOU ON THIS.
SOMEONE JUST KILLED A GOD.
I've worked so hard to gain their respect, they sometimes forget I'm flesh and blood.
In Superman's world, everything is mythology.

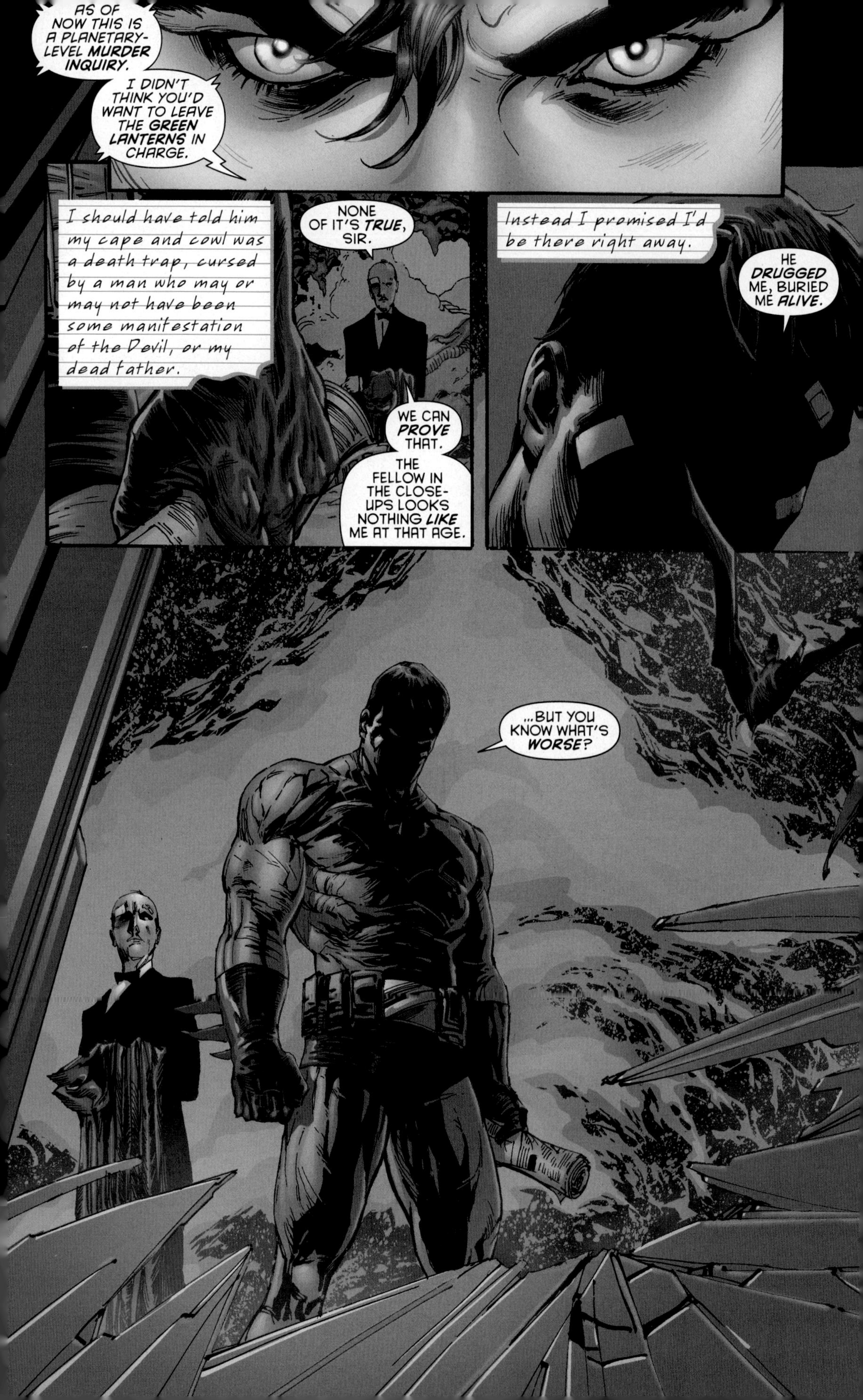
AS OF NOW THIS IS A PLANETARY-LEVEL MURDER INQUIRY.
I DIDN'T THINK YOU'D WANT TO LEAVE THE GREEN LANTERNS IN CHARGE.
I should have told him my cape and cowl was a death trap, cursed by a man who may or may not have been some manifestation of the Devil, or my dead father.
NONE OF IT'S TRUE, SIR.
WE CAN PROVE THAT.
THE FELLOW IN THE CLOSE-UPS LOOKS NOTHING LIKE ME AT THAT AGE.
Instead I promised I'd be there right away.
HE DRUGGED ME, BURIED ME ALIVE.
...BUT YOU KNOW WHAT'S WORSE?

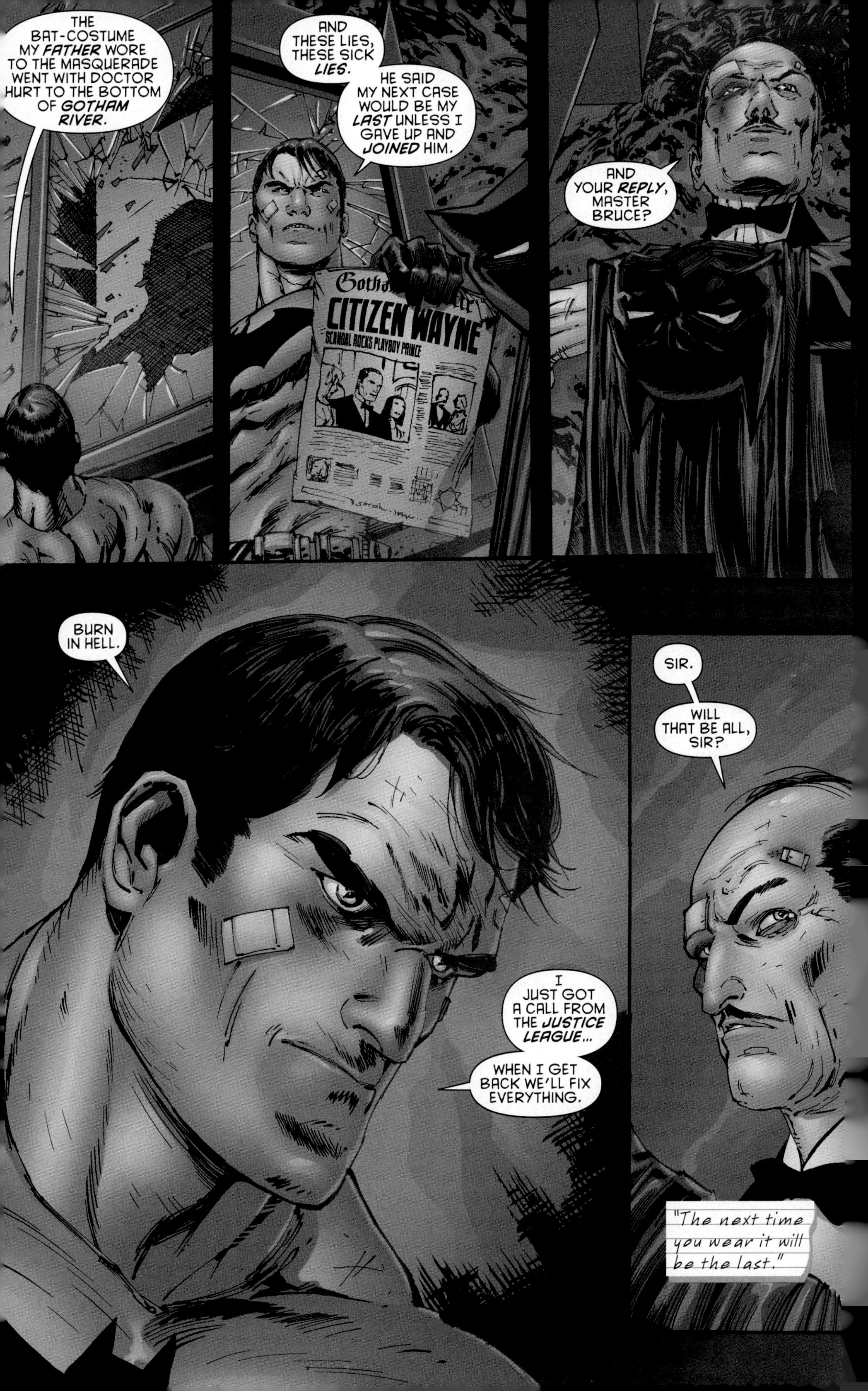
THE BAT-COSTUME MY FATHER WORE TO THE MASQUERADE WENT WITH DOCTOR HURT TO THE BOTTOM OF GOTHAM RIVER.
AND THESE LIES, THESE SICK LIES.
HE SAID MY NEXT CASE WOULD BE MY LAST UNLESS I GAVE UP AND JOINED HIM.
CITIZEN WAYNE
SCANDAL ROCKS PLAYBOY PRINCE
AND YOUR REPLY, MASTER BRUCE?
BURN IN HELL.
SIR.
WILL THAT BE ALL, SIR?
I JUST GOT A CALL FROM THE JUSTICE LEAGUE...
WHEN I GET BACK WE'LL FIX EVERYTHING.
"The next time you wear it will be the last."

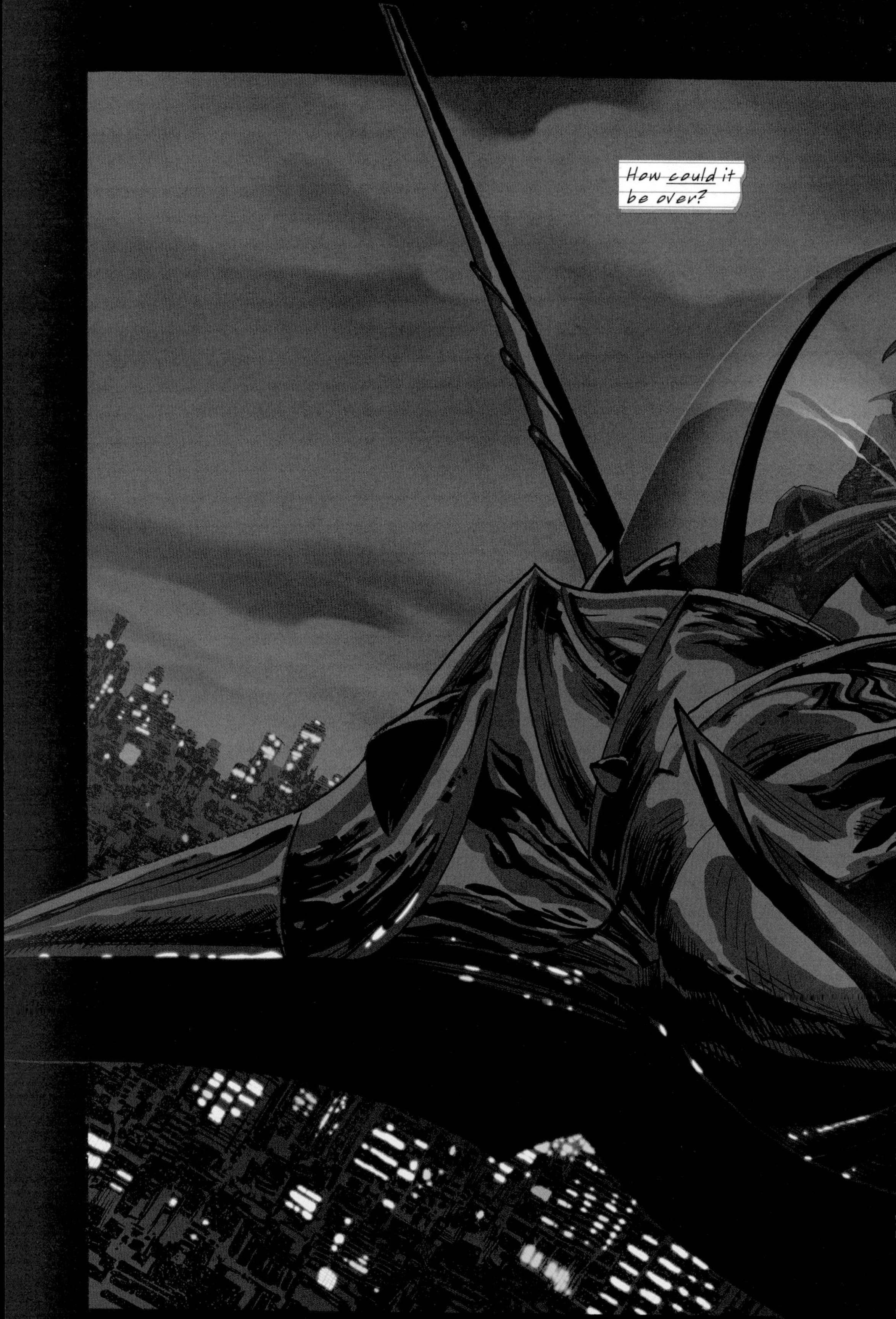
How could it be over?

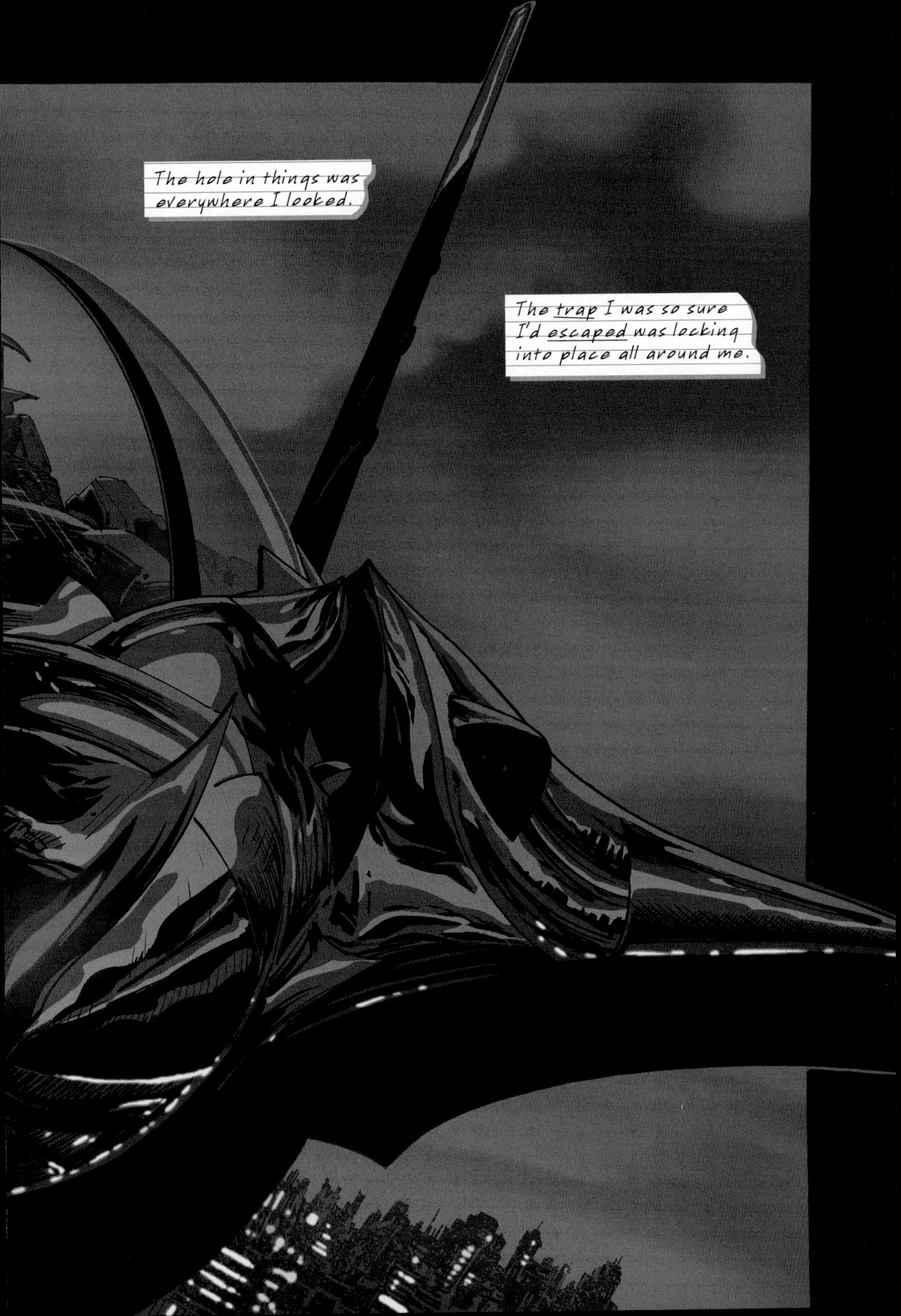
The hole in things was everywhere I looked.
The trap I was so sure I'd escaped was locking into place all around me.

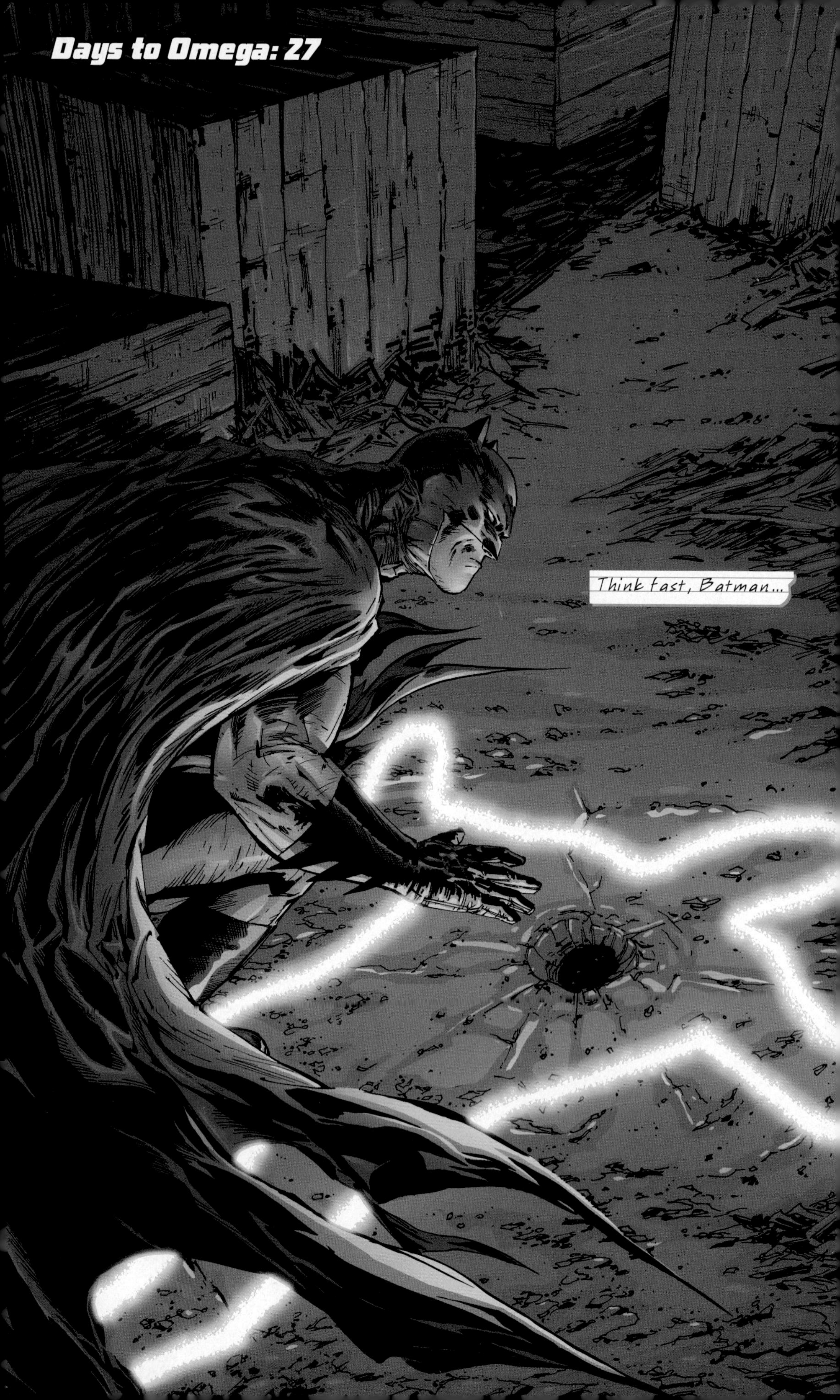
Days to Omega: 27
Think fast, Batman...

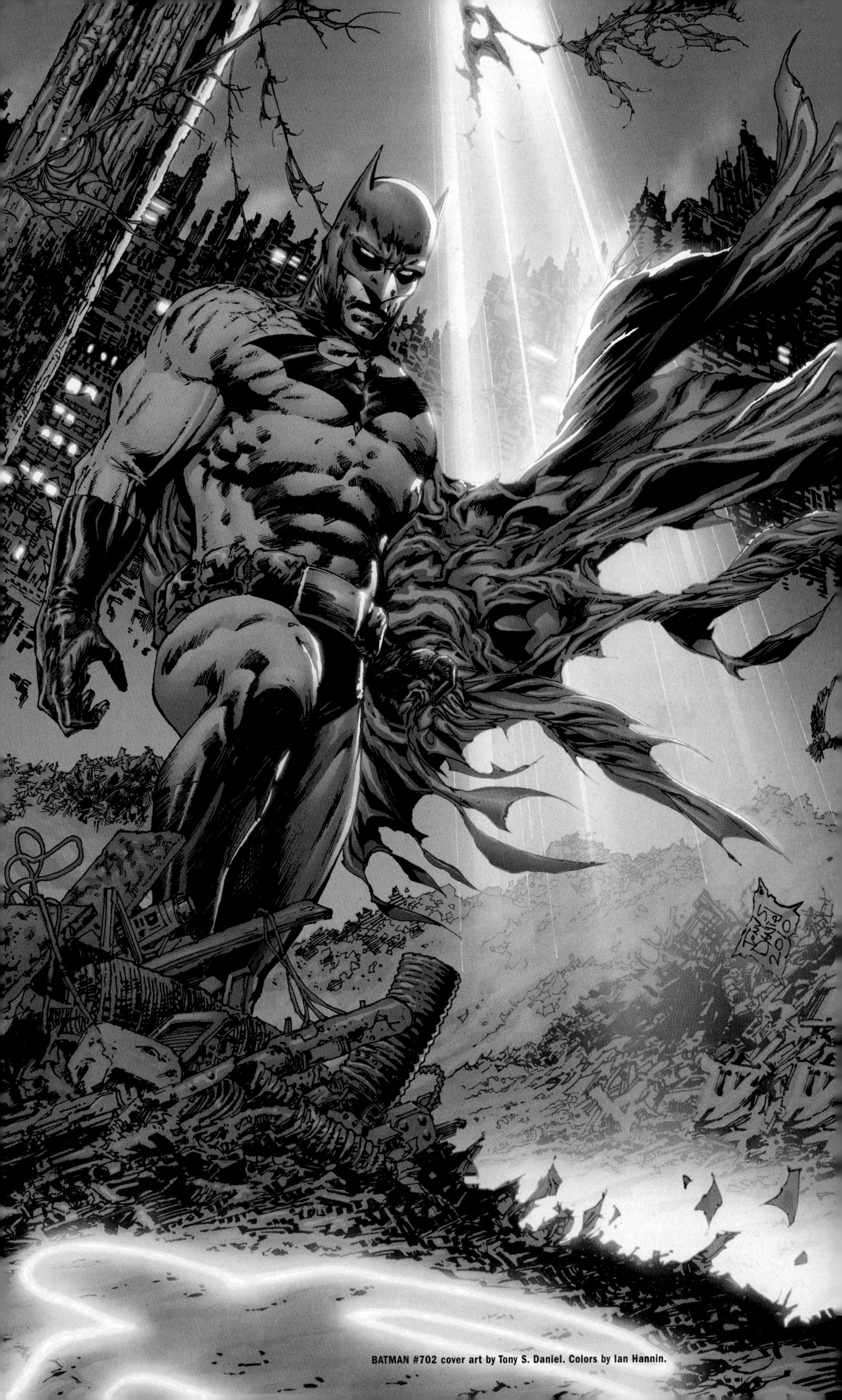

BATMAN #702 cover art by Tony S. Daniel. Colors by Ian Hannin.

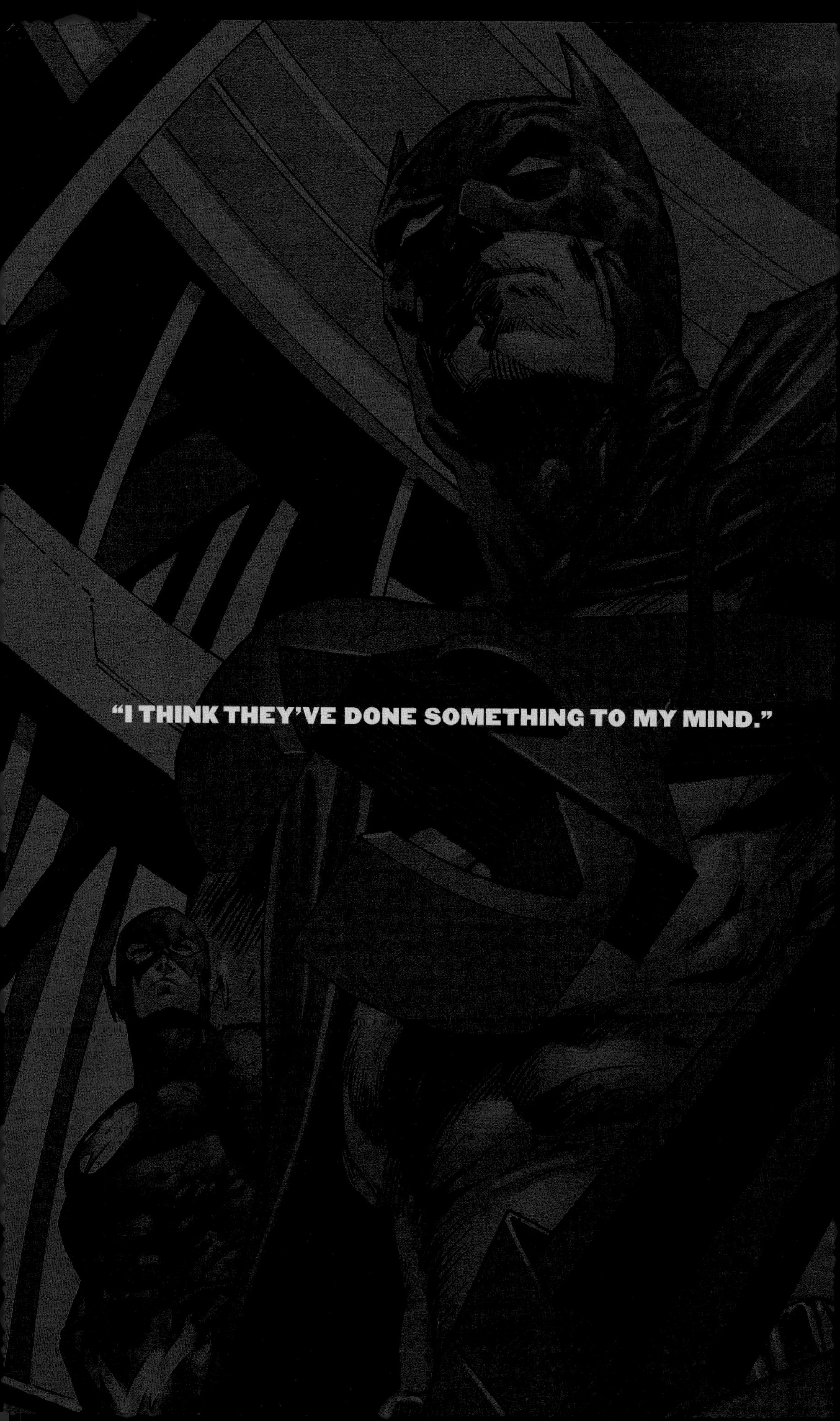
"I THINK THEY'VE DONE SOMETHING TO MY MIND."

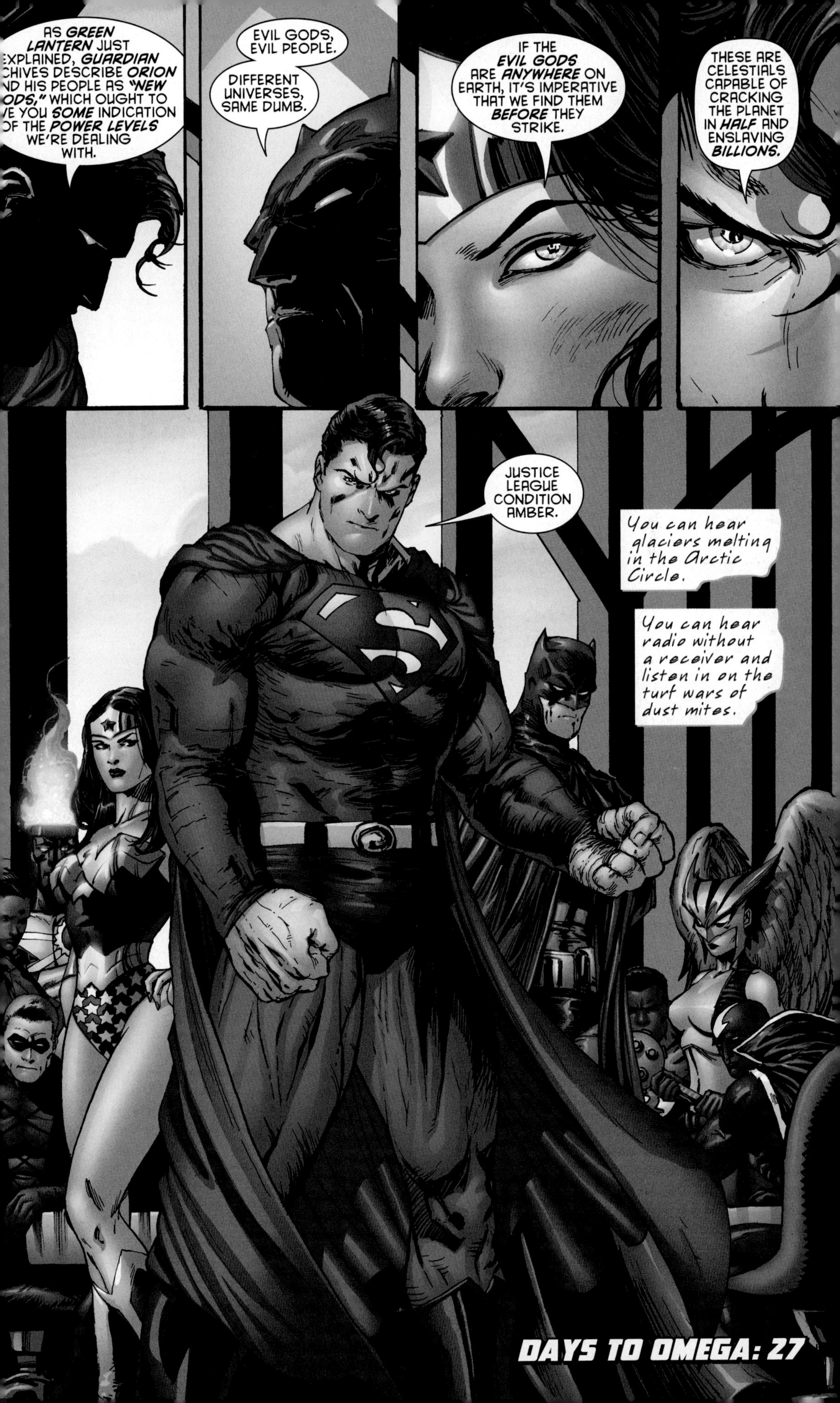
AS GREEN LANTERN JUST EXPLAINED, GUARDIAN CHIVES DESCRIBE ORION ND HIS PEOPLE AS "NEW ODS," WHICH OUGHT TO VE YOU SOME INDICATION OF THE POWER LEVELS WE'RE DEALING WITH.
EVIL GODS, EVIL PEOPLE.
DIFFERENT UNIVERSES, SAME DUMB.
IF THE EVIL GODS ARE ANYWHERE ON EARTH, IT'S IMPERATIVE THAT WE FIND THEM BEFORE THEY STRIKE.
THESE ARE CELESTIALS CAPABLE OF CRACKING THE PLANET IN HALF AND ENSLAVING BILLIONS.
JUSTICE LEAGUE CONDITION AMBER.
You can hear glaciers melting in the Arctic Circle.
You can hear radio without a receiver and listen in on the turf wars of dust mites.
DAYS TO OMEGA: 27

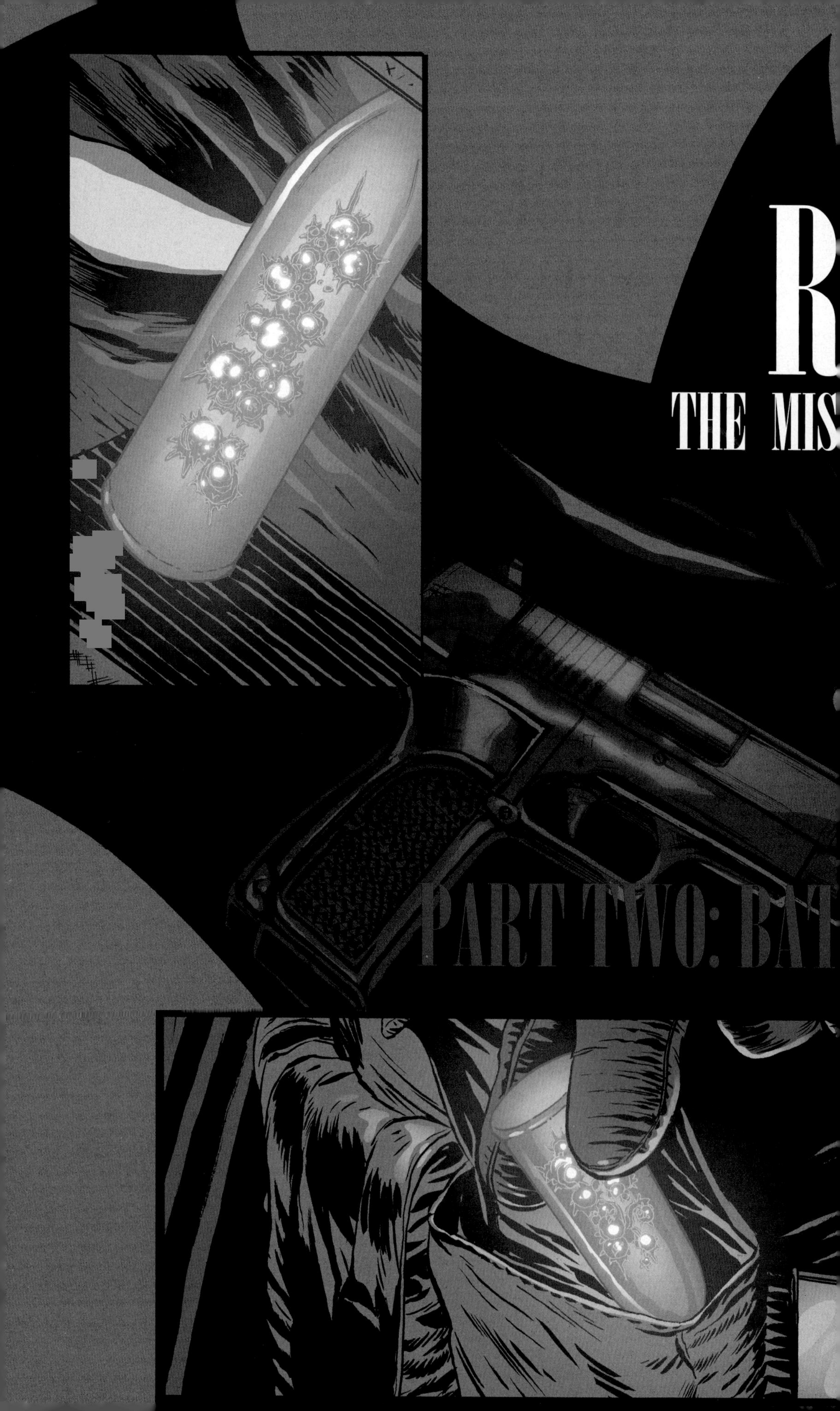

R
THE MIS
PART TWO: BAT

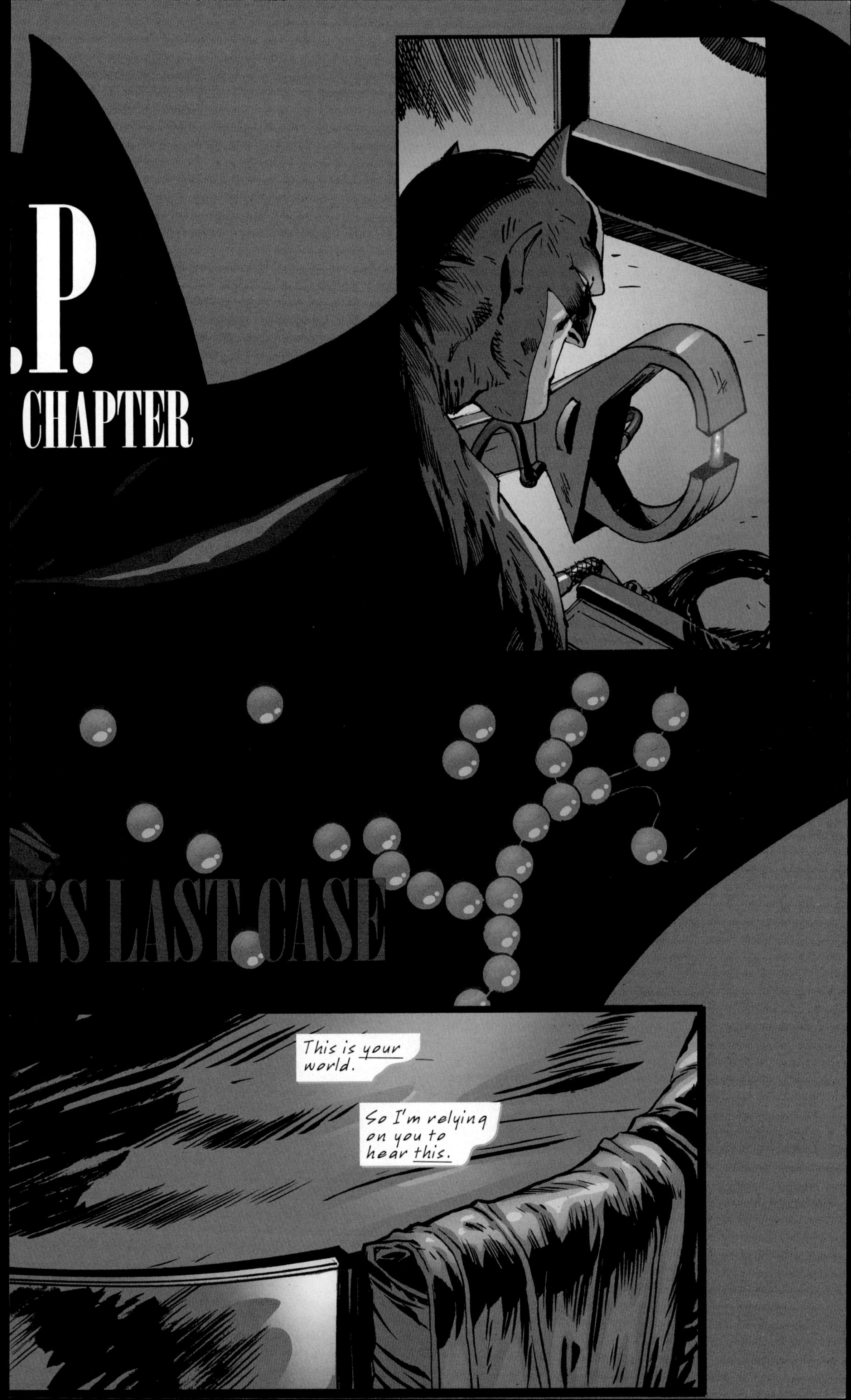

.P.
CHAPTER
N'S LAST CASE
This is your world.
So I'm relying on you to hear this.

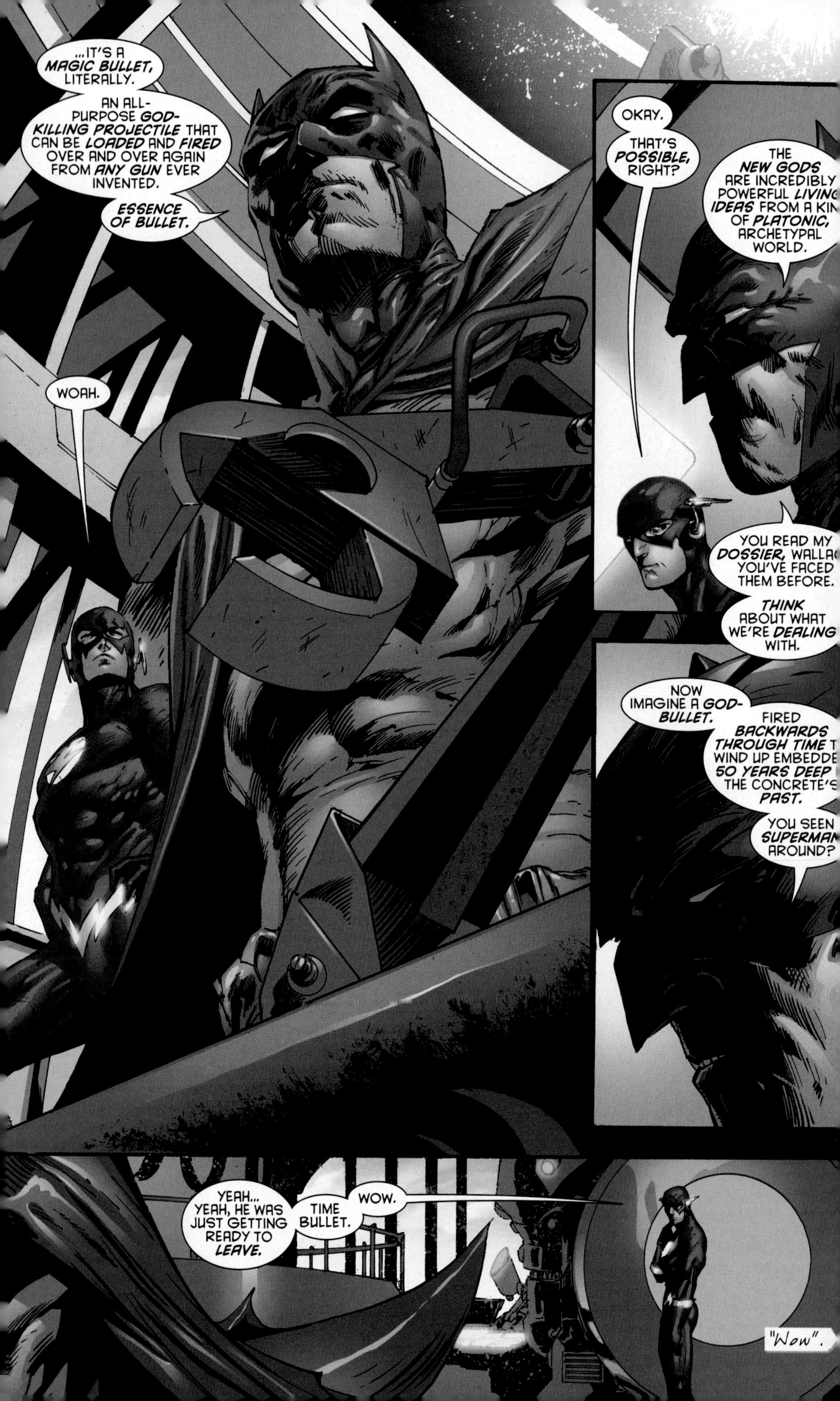
...IT'S A MAGIC BULLET, LITERALLY.
AN ALL-PURPOSE GOD-KILLING PROJECTILE THAT CAN BE LOADED AND FIRED OVER AND OVER AGAIN FROM ANY GUN EVER INVENTED.
ESSENCE OF BULLET.
WOAH.
OKAY.
THAT'S POSSIBLE, RIGHT?
THE NEW GODS ARE INCREDIBLY POWERFUL LIVING IDEAS FROM A KIN OF PLATONIC, ARCHETYPAL WORLD.
YOU READ MY DOSSIER, WALLAC YOU'VE FACED THEM BEFORE.
THINK ABOUT WHAT WE'RE DEALING WITH.
NOW IMAGINE A GOD-BULLET.
FIRED BACKWARDS THROUGH TIME T WIND UP EMBEDDE 50 YEARS DEEP THE CONCRETE'S PAST.
YOU SEEN SUPERMAN AROUND?
YEAH... YEAH, HE WAS JUST GETTING READY TO LEAVE.
TIME BULLET.
WOW.
"Wow".

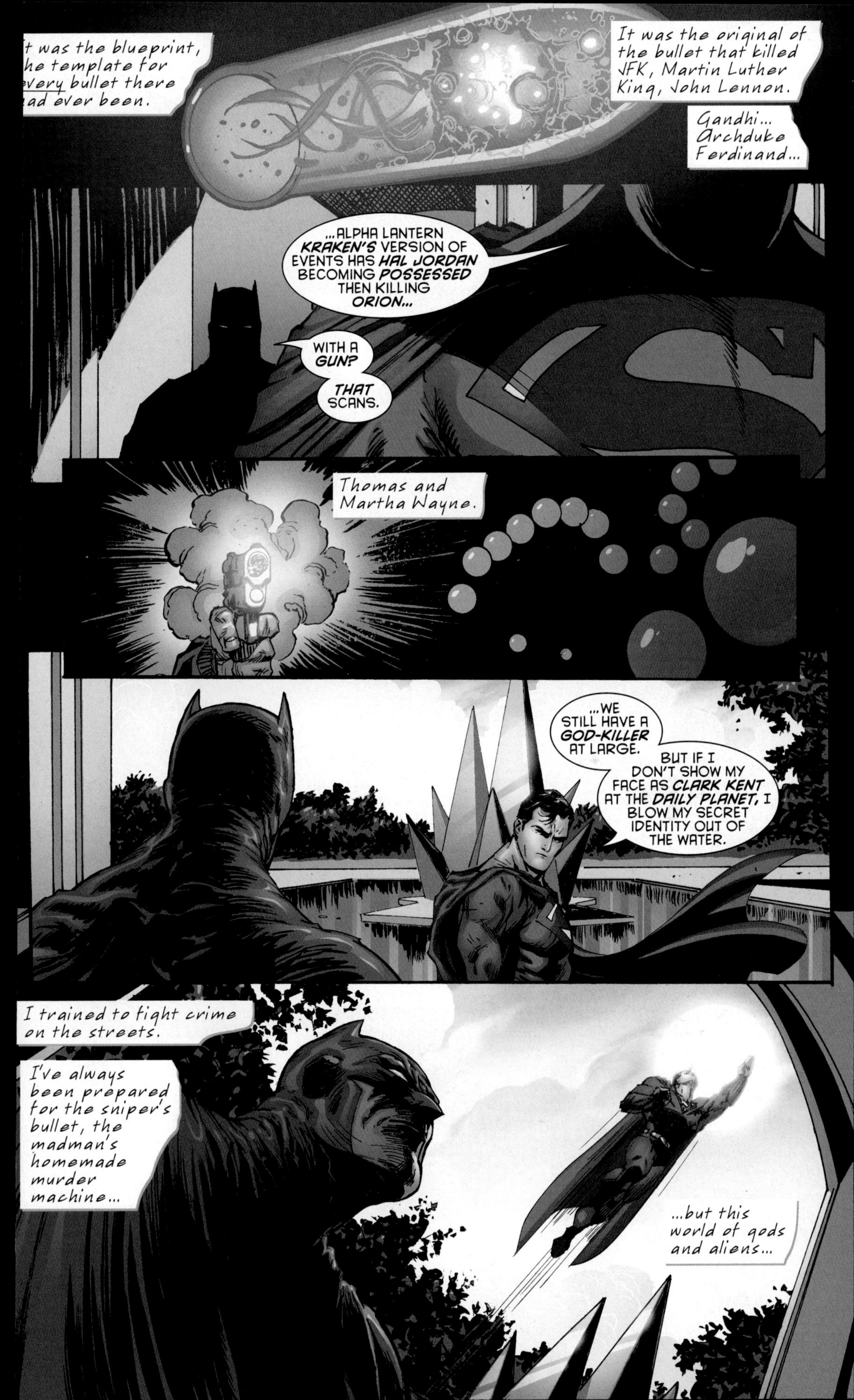
It was the blueprint, the template for every bullet there had ever been.
It was the original of the bullet that killed JFK, Martin Luther King, John Lennon.
Gandhi... Archduke Ferdinand...
...ALPHA LANTERN KRAKEN'S VERSION OF EVENTS HAS HAL JORDAN BECOMING POSSESSED THEN KILLING ORION...
WITH A GUN?
THAT SCANS.
Thomas and Martha Wayne.
...WE STILL HAVE A GOD-KILLER AT LARGE.
BUT IF I DON'T SHOW MY FACE AS CLARK KENT AT THE DAILY PLANET, I BLOW MY SECRET IDENTITY OUT OF THE WATER.
I trained to fight crime on the streets.
I've always been prepared for the sniper's bullet, the madman's homemade murder machine...
...but this world of gods and aliens...

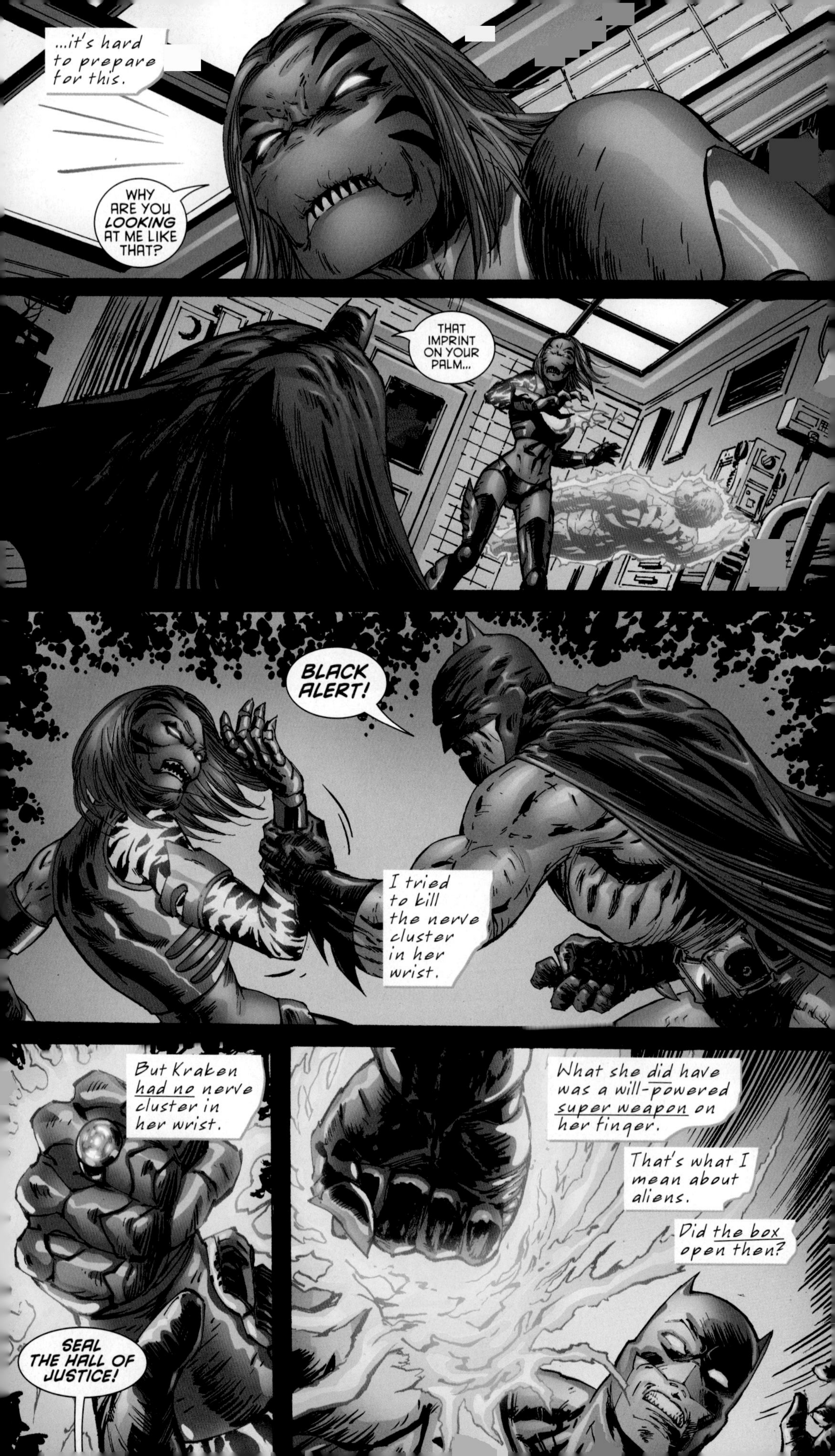
...it's hard to prepare for this.
WHY ARE YOU LOOKING AT ME LIKE THAT?
THAT IMPRINT ON YOUR PALM...
BLACK ALERT!
I tried to kill the nerve cluster in her wrist.
But Kraken had no nerve cluster in her wrist.
SEAL THE HALL OF JUSTICE!
What she did have was a will-powered super weapon on her finger.
That's what I mean about aliens.
Did the box open then?

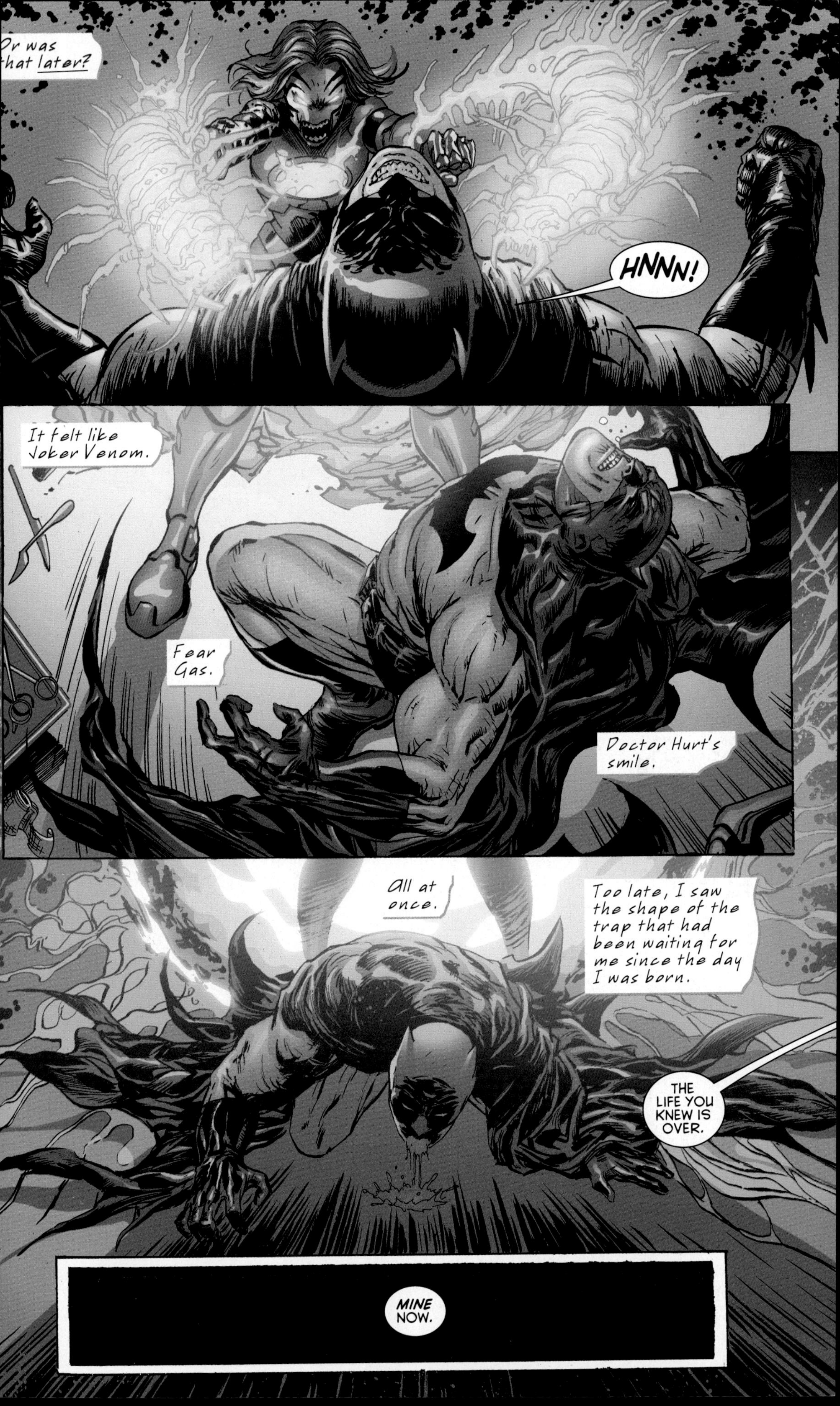

Or was that later?
HNNN!
It felt like Joker Venom.
Fear Gas.
Doctor Hurt's smile.
All at once.
Too late, I saw the shape of the trap that had been waiting for me since the day I was born.
THE LIFE YOU KNEW IS OVER.
MINE NOW.

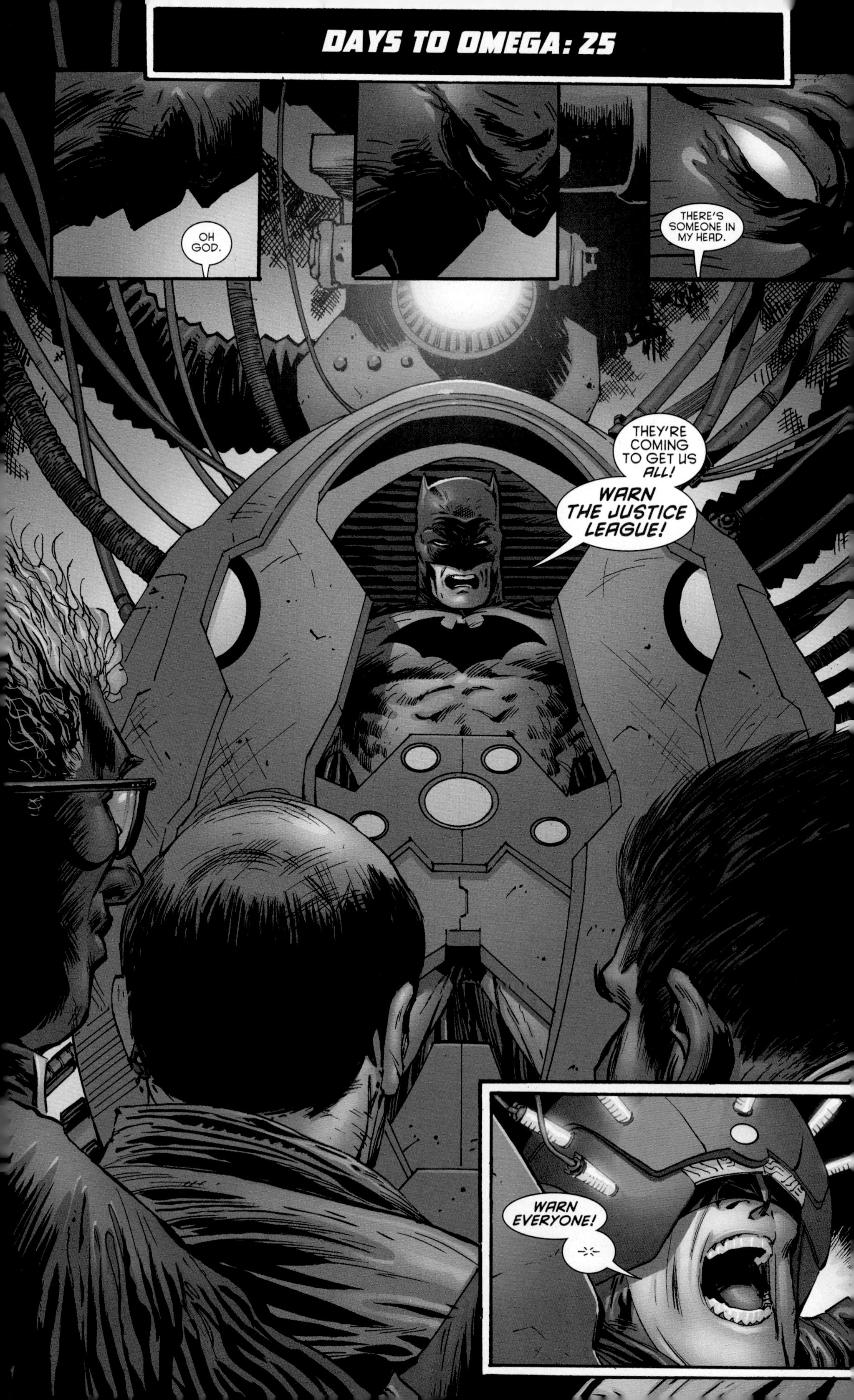
DAYS TO OMEGA: 25
OH GOD.
THERE'S SOMEONE IN MY HEAD.
THEY'RE COMING TO GET US ALL!
WARN THE JUSTICE LEAGUE!
WARN EVERYONE!

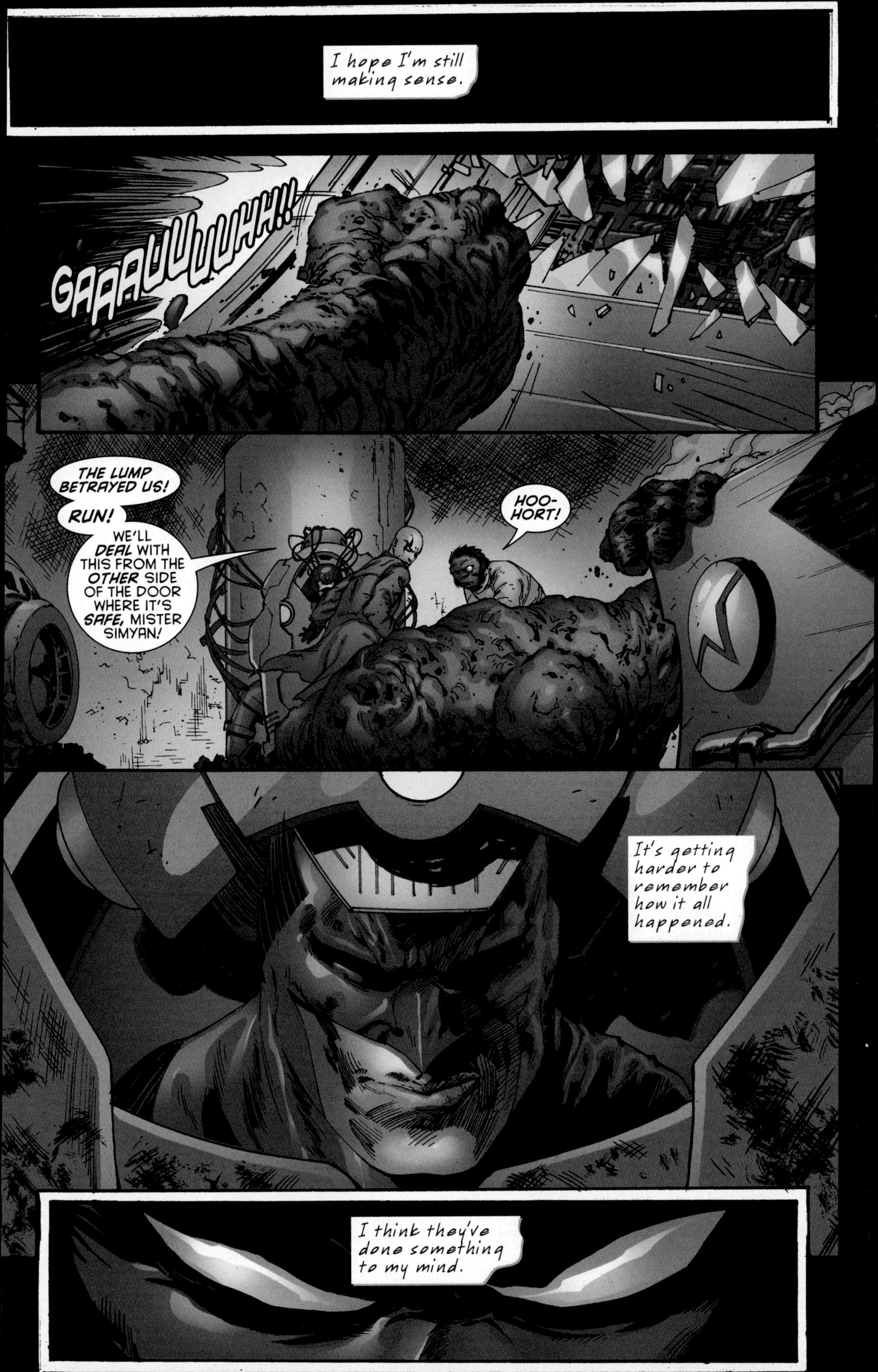
I hope I'm still making sense.
GAAAUUUUHH!!
THE LUMP BETRAYED US!
RUN!
WE'LL DEAL WITH THIS FROM THE OTHER SIDE OF THE DOOR WHERE IT'S SAFE, MISTER SIMYAN!
HOO-HORT!
It's getting harder to remember how it all happened.
I think they've done something to my mind.

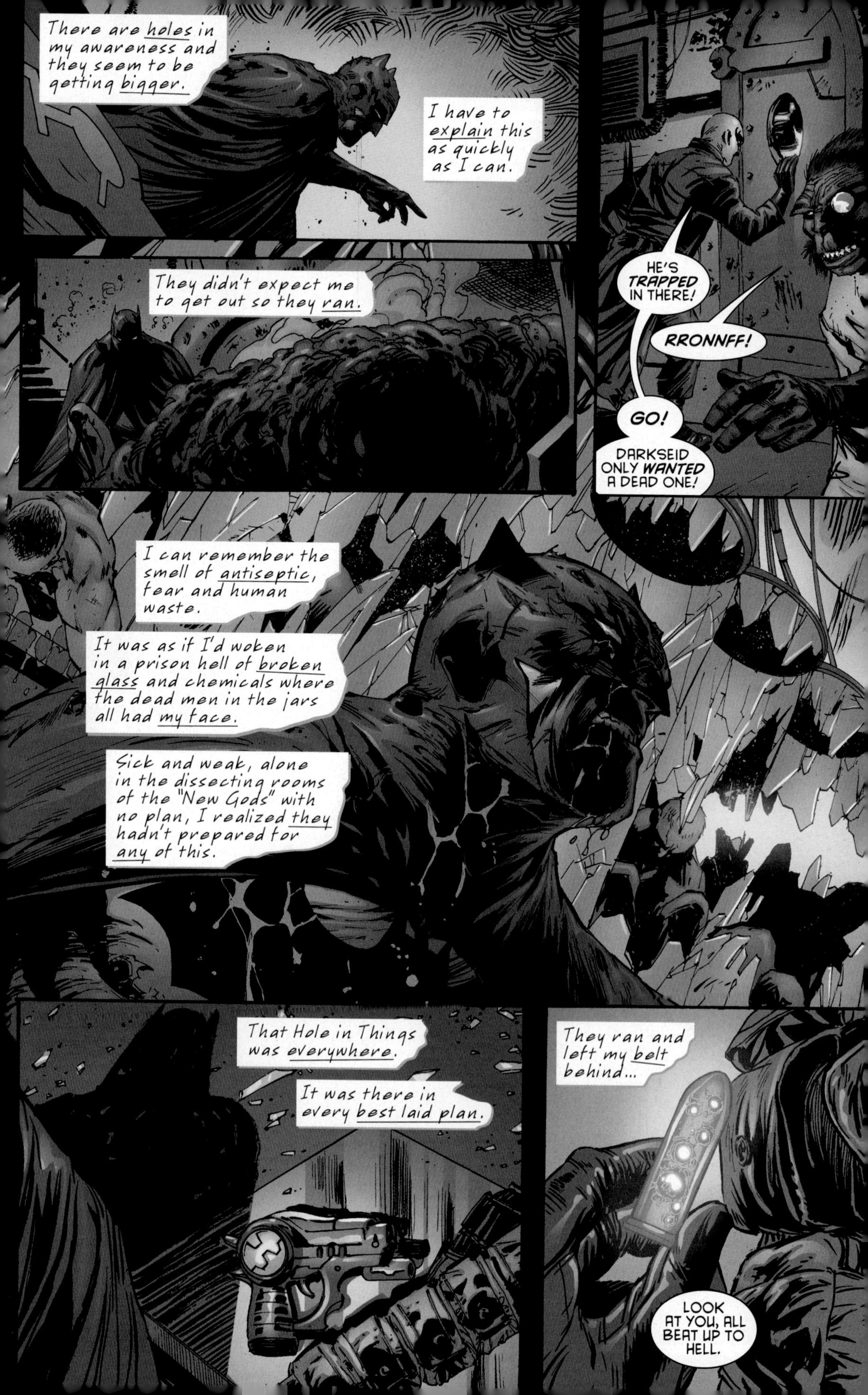

There are holes in my awareness and they seem to be getting bigger.
I have to explain this as quickly as I can.
HE'S TRAPPED IN THERE!
RRONNFF!
GO!
DARKSEID ONLY WANTED A DEAD ONE!
They didn't expect me to get out so they ran.
I can remember the smell of antiseptic, fear and human waste.
It was as if I'd woken in a prison hell of broken glass and chemicals where the dead men in the jars all had my face.
Sick and weak, alone in the dissecting rooms of the "New Gods" with no plan, I realized they hadn't prepared for any of this.
That Hole in Things was everywhere.
It was there in every best laid plan.
They ran and left my belt behind...
LOOK AT YOU, ALL BEAT UP TO HELL.

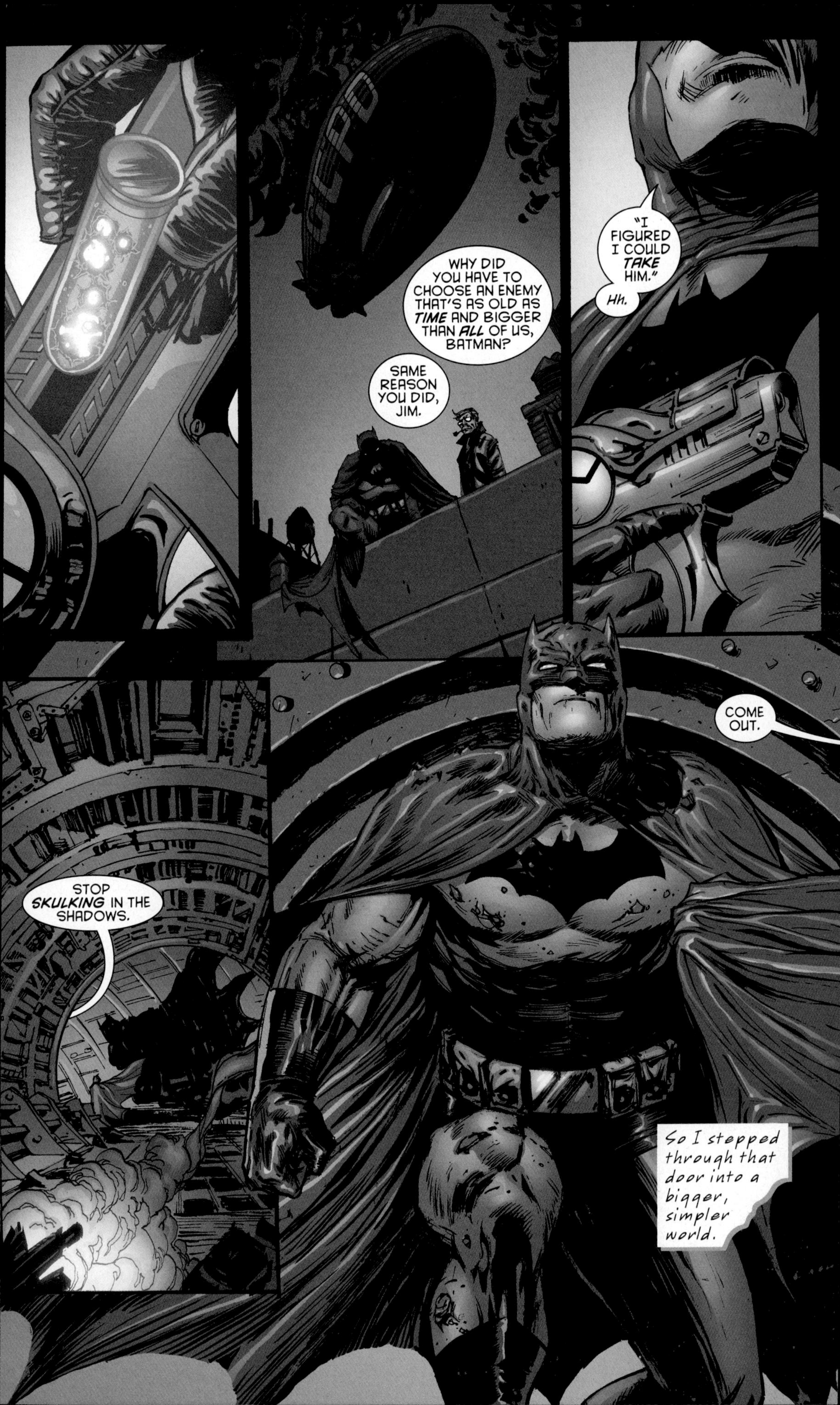
WHY DID YOU HAVE TO CHOOSE AN ENEMY THAT'S AS OLD AS *TIME* AND BIGGER THAN *ALL* OF US, BATMAN?
SAME REASON YOU DID, JIM.
"I FIGURED I COULD *TAKE* HIM."
Hh.
COME OUT.
STOP *SKULKING* IN THE SHADOWS.
So I stepped through that door into a bigger, simpler world.

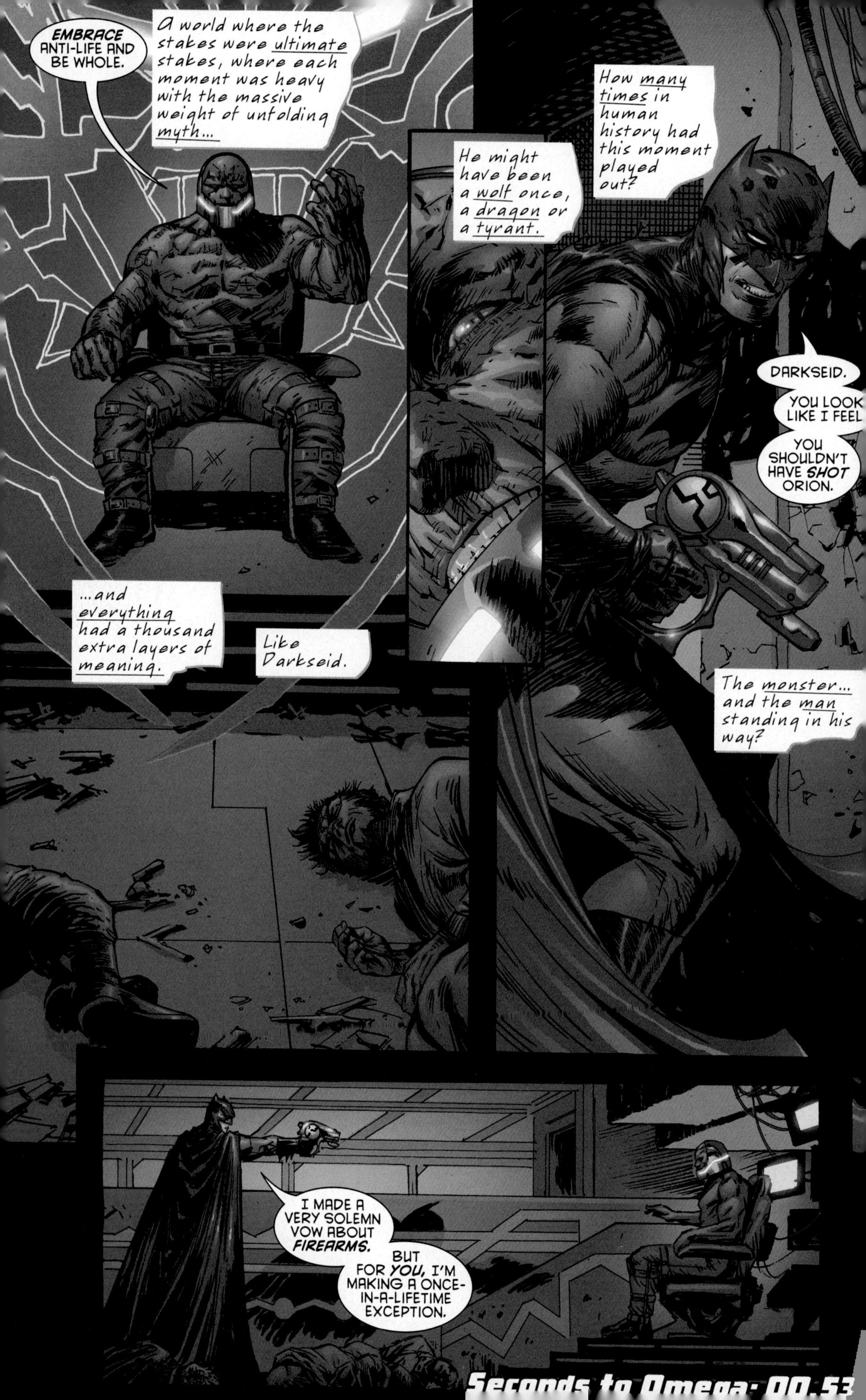

EMBRACE ANTI-LIFE AND BE WHOLE.
A world where the stakes were ultimate stakes, where each moment was heavy with the massive weight of unfolding myth...
...and everything had a thousand extra layers of meaning.
Like Darkseid.
He might have been a wolf once, a dragon or a tyrant.
How many times in human history had this moment played out?
DARKSEID.
YOU LOOK LIKE I FEEL.
YOU SHOULDN'T HAVE SHOT ORION.
The monster... and the man standing in his way?
I MADE A VERY SOLEMN VOW ABOUT FIREARMS.
BUT FOR YOU, I'M MAKING A ONCE-IN-A-LIFETIME EXCEPTION.
Seconds to Omega: 00.53

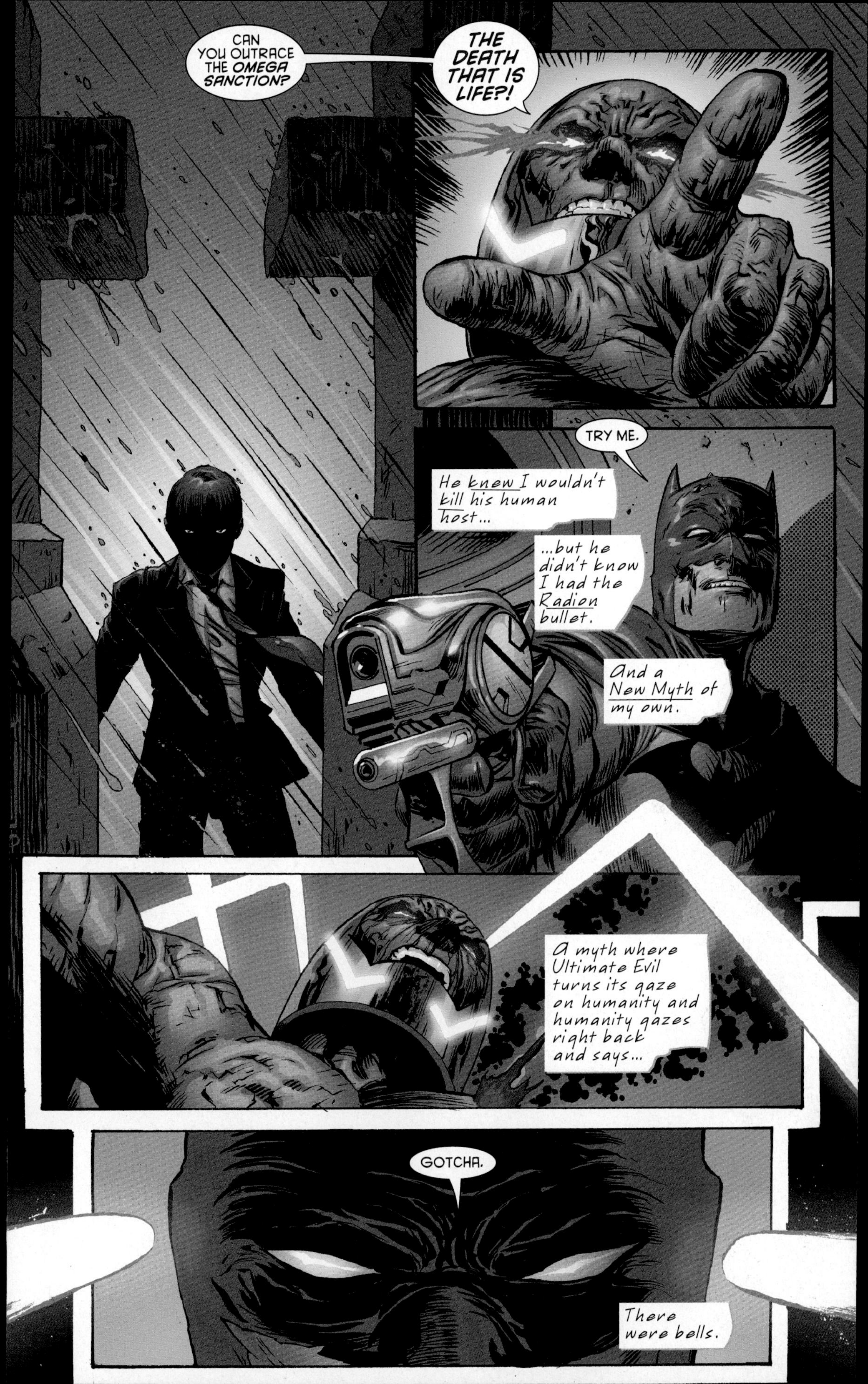
CAN YOU OUTRACE THE OMEGA SANCTION?
THE DEATH THAT IS LIFE?!
TRY ME.
He knew I wouldn't kill his human host...
...but he didn't know I had the Radion bullet.
And a New Myth of my own.
A myth where Ultimate Evil turns its gaze on humanity and humanity gazes right back and says...
GOTCHA.
There were bells.

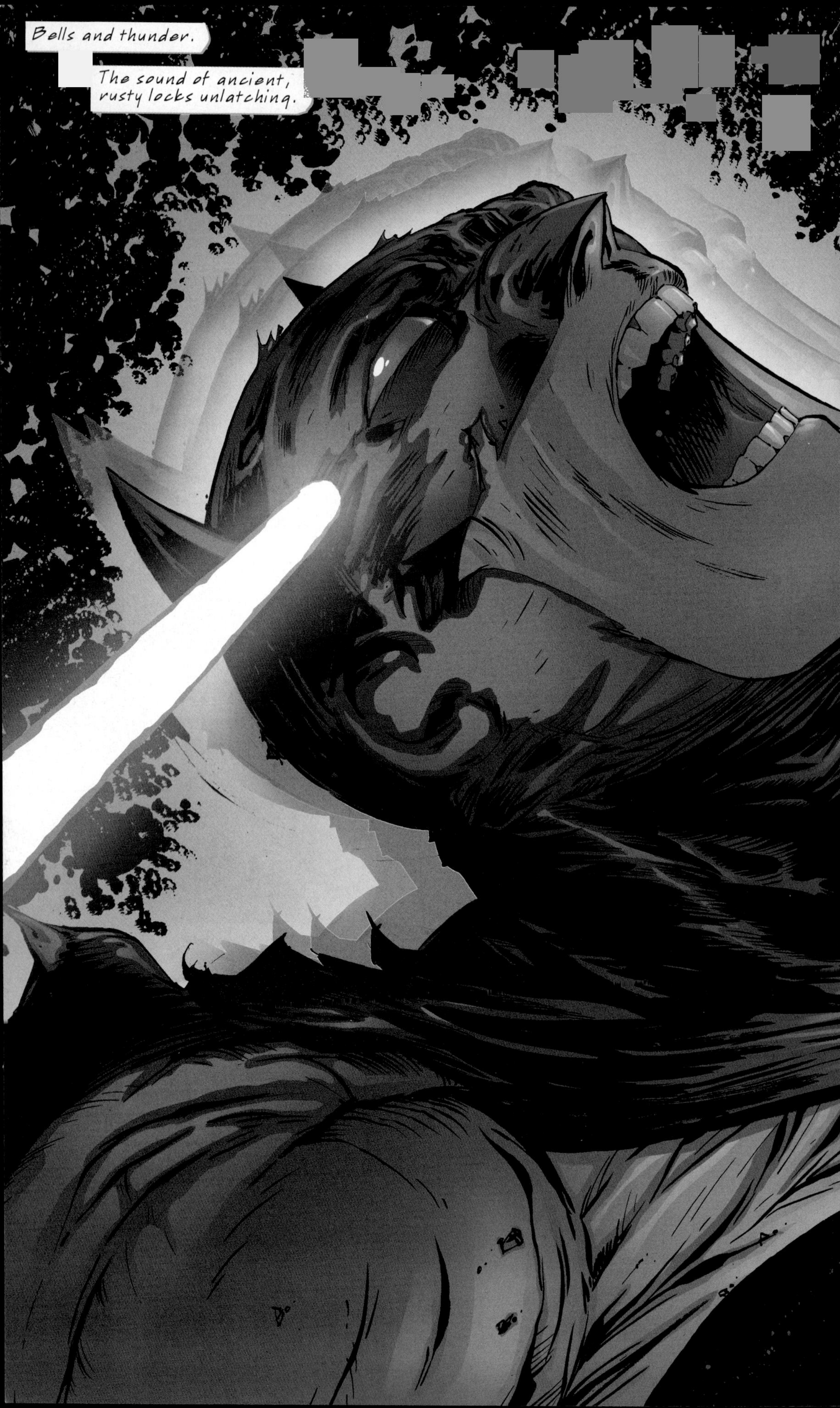
Bells and thunder.
The sound of ancient, rusty locks unlatching.

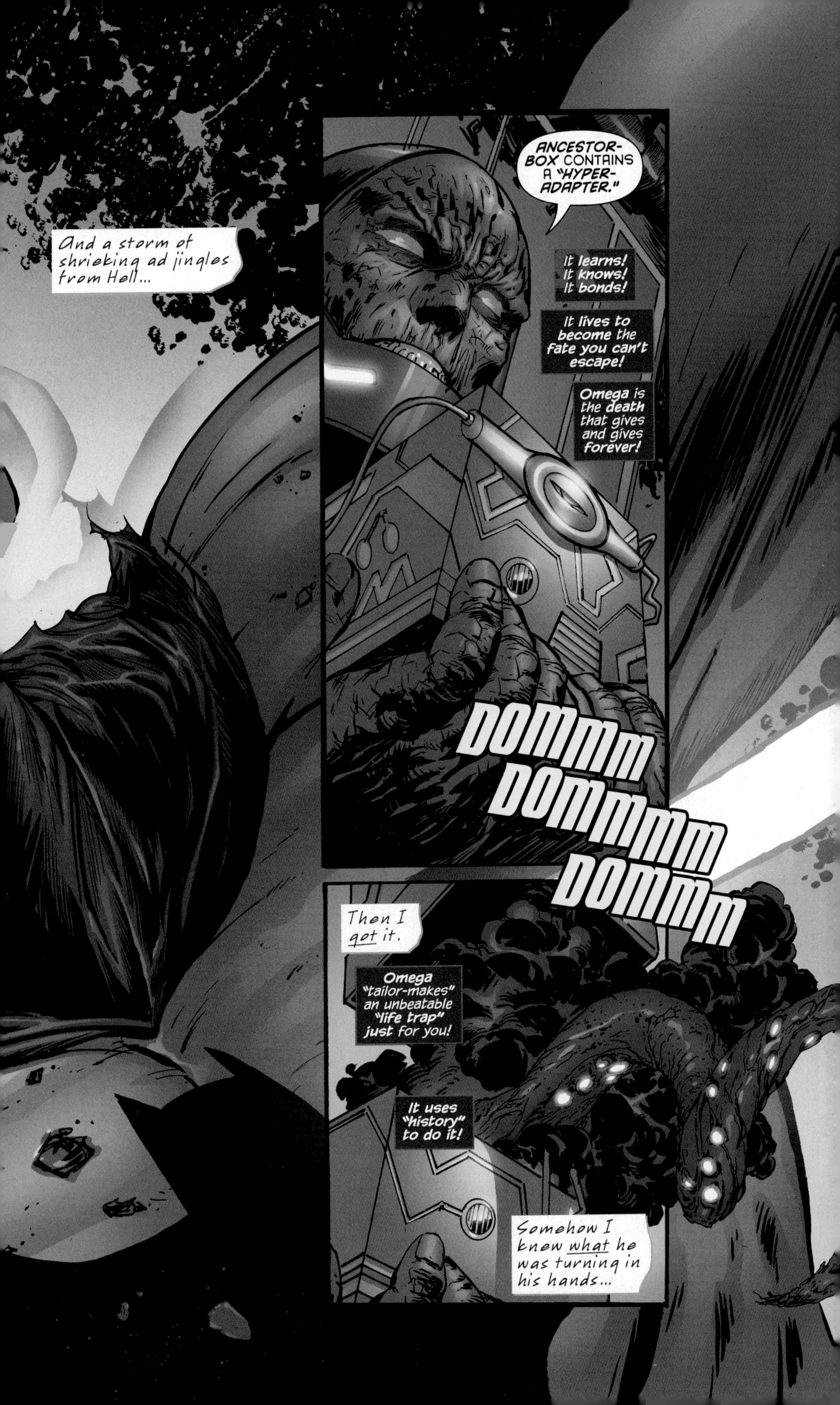

And a storm of shrieking ad jingles from Hell...
ANCESTOR-BOX CONTAINS A "HYPER-ADAPTER."
It learns! It knows! It bonds!
It lives to become the fate you can't escape!
Omega is the death that gives and gives forever!
DOMMM DOMMMMM DOMMM
Then I got it.
Omega "tailor-makes" an unbeatable "life trap" just for you!
It uses "history" to do it!
Somehow I knew what he was turning in his hands...

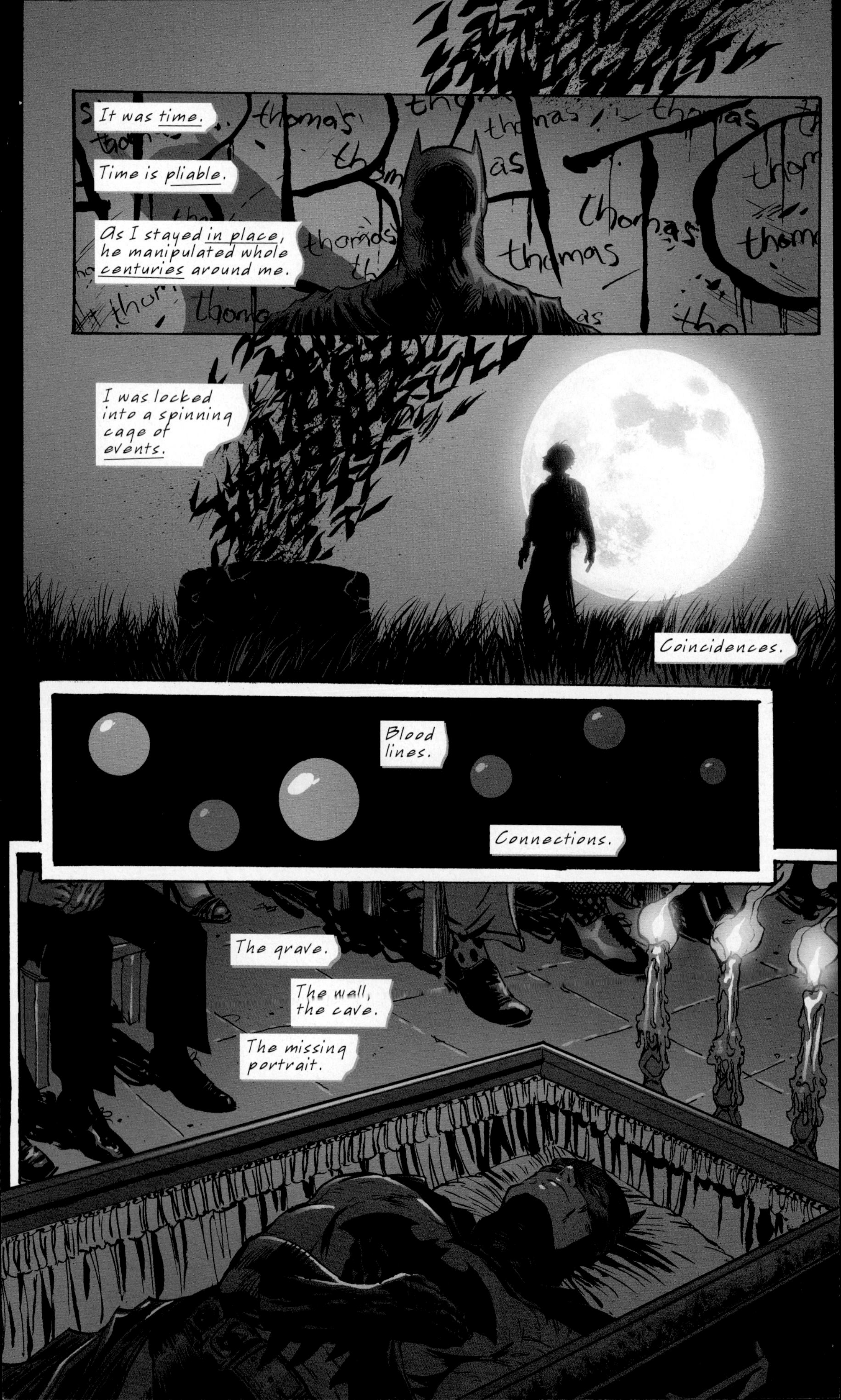

It was time.
Time is pliable.
As I stayed in place, he manipulated whole centuries around me.
I was locked into a spinning cage of events.
Coincidences.
Blood lines.
Connections.
The grave.
The wall, the cave.
The missing portrait.

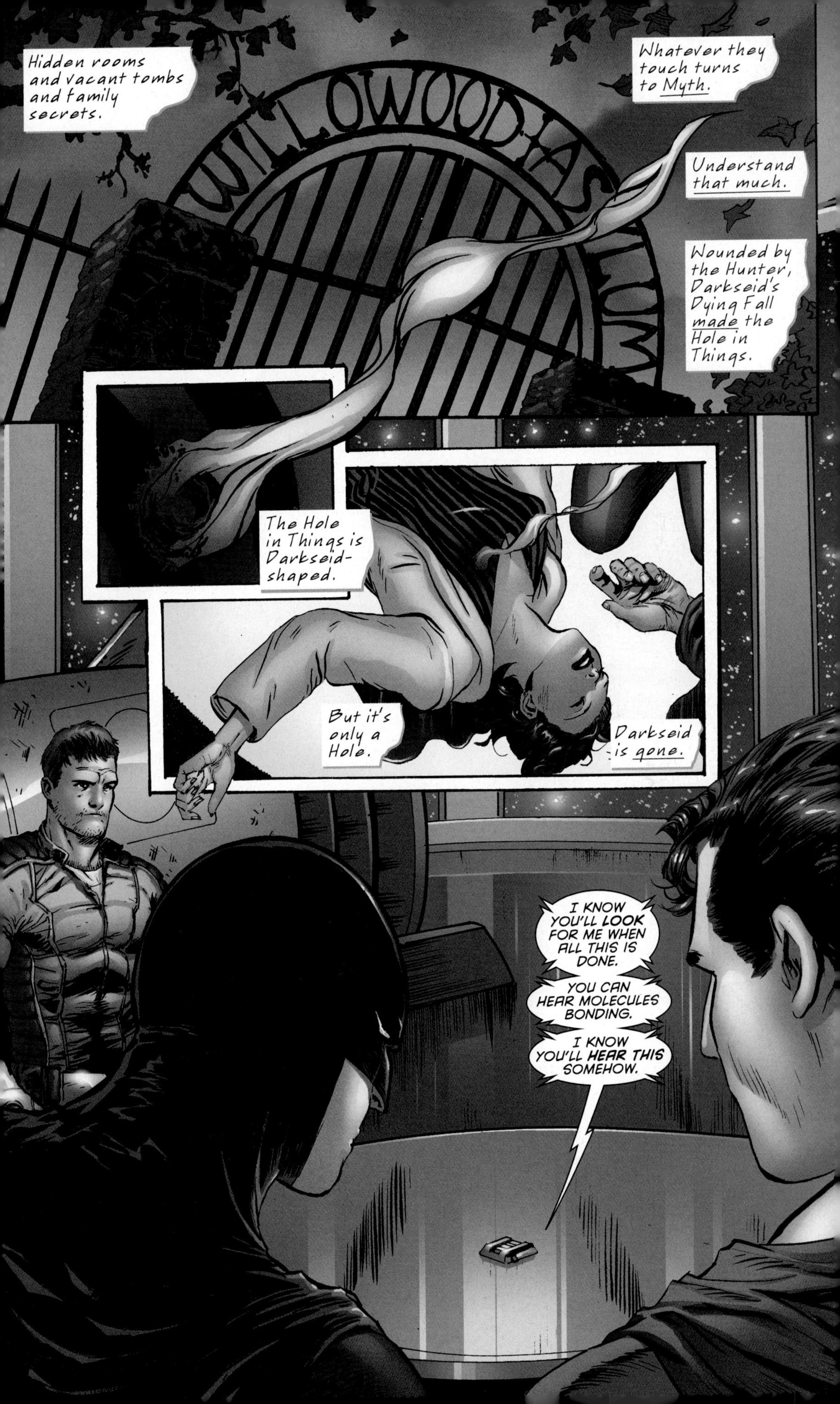

WILLOWOOD ASYLUM
Hidden rooms and vacant tombs and family secrets.
Whatever they touch turns to Myth.
Understand that much.
Wounded by the Hunter, Darkseid's Dying Fall made the Hole in Things.
The Hole in Things is Darkseid-shaped.
But it's only a Hole.
Darkseid is gone.
I KNOW YOU'LL LOOK FOR ME WHEN ALL THIS IS DONE.
YOU CAN HEAR MOLECULES BONDING.
I KNOW YOU'LL HEAR THIS SOMEHOW.

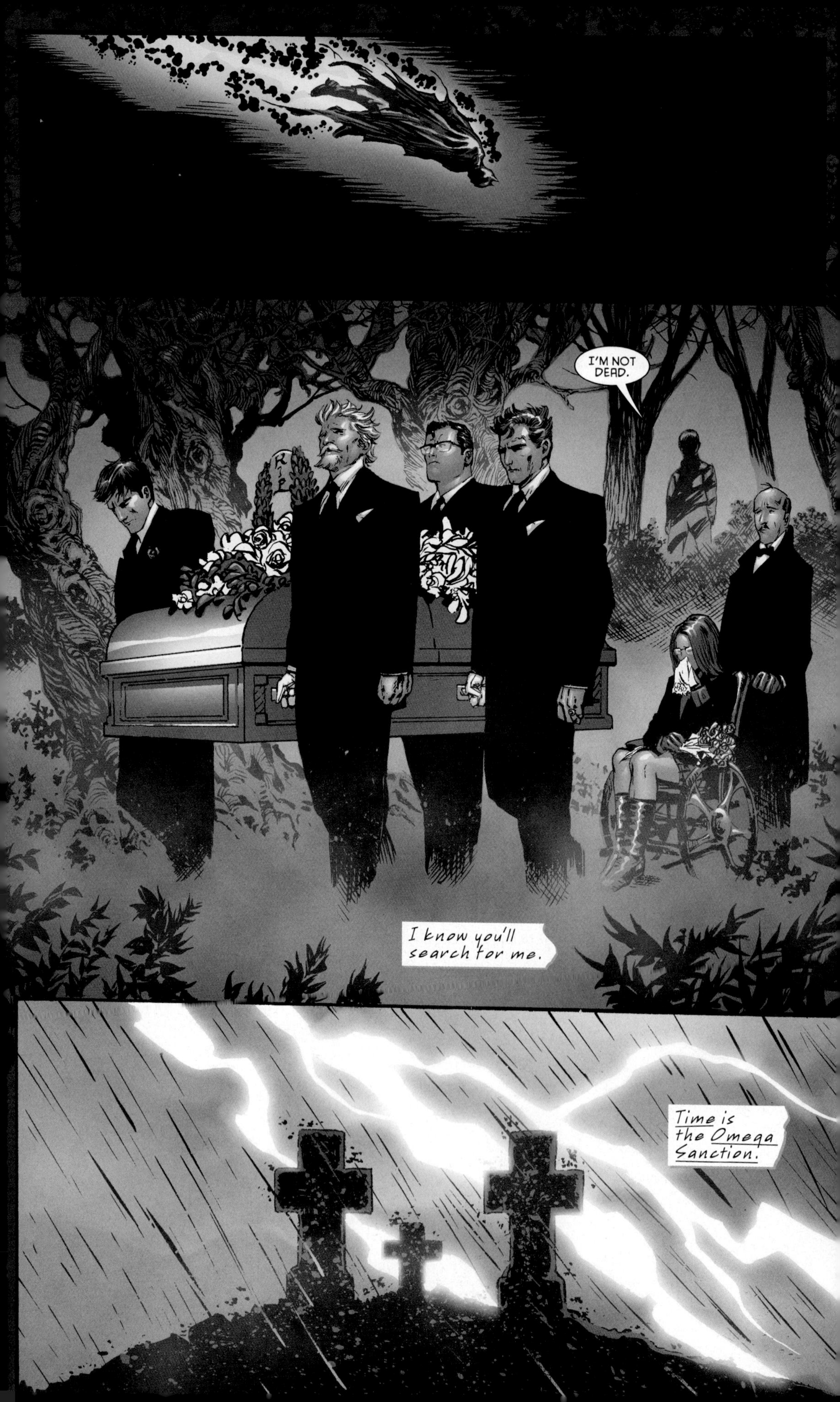
I'M NOT DEAD.
I know you'll search for me.
Time is the Omega Sanction.

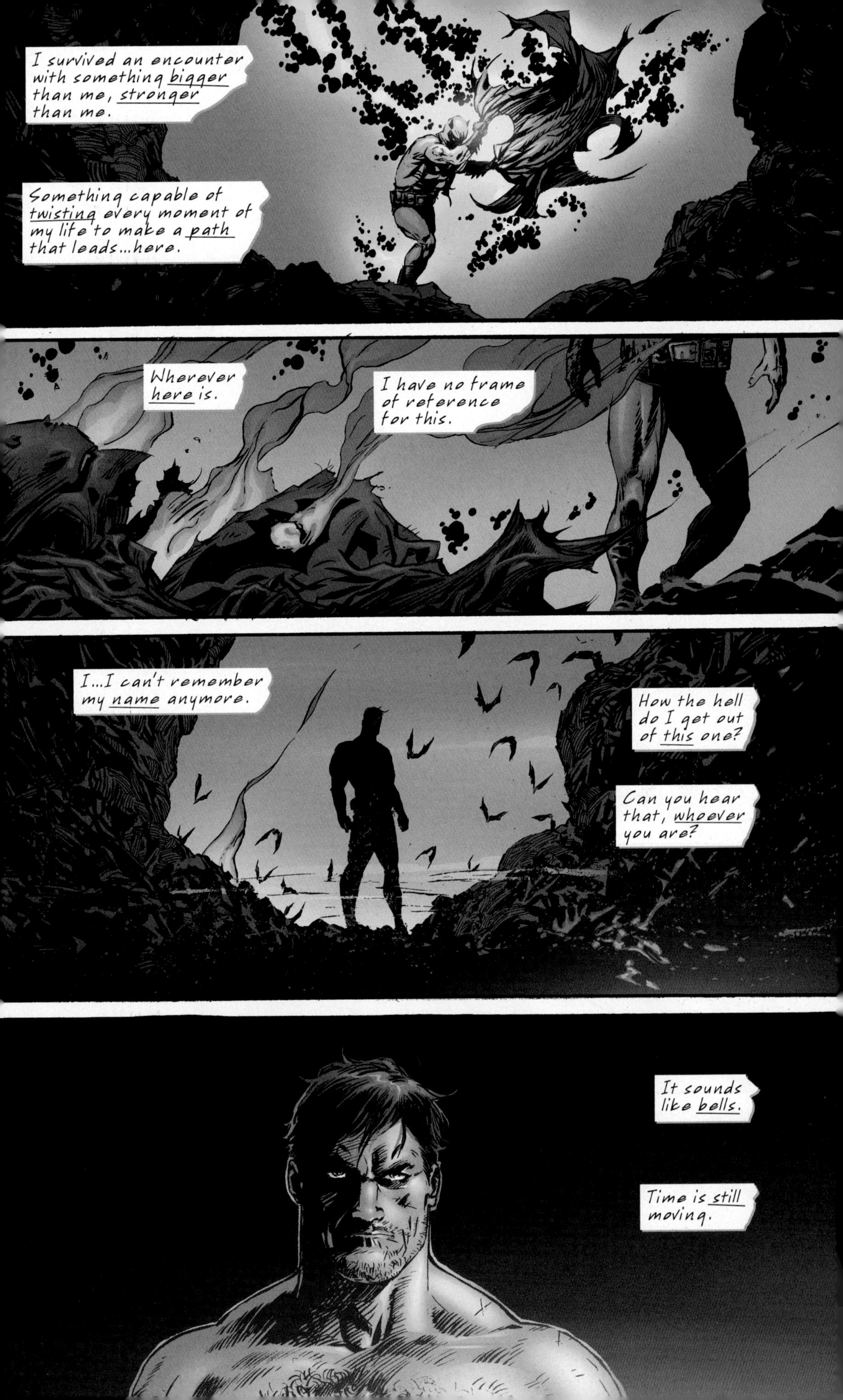

I survived an encounter with something bigger than me, stronger than me.
Something capable of twisting every moment of my life to make a path that leads...here.
Wherever here is.
I have no frame of reference for this.
I...I can't remember my name anymore.
How the hell do I get out of this one?
Can you hear that, whoever you are?
It sounds like bells.
Time is still moving.

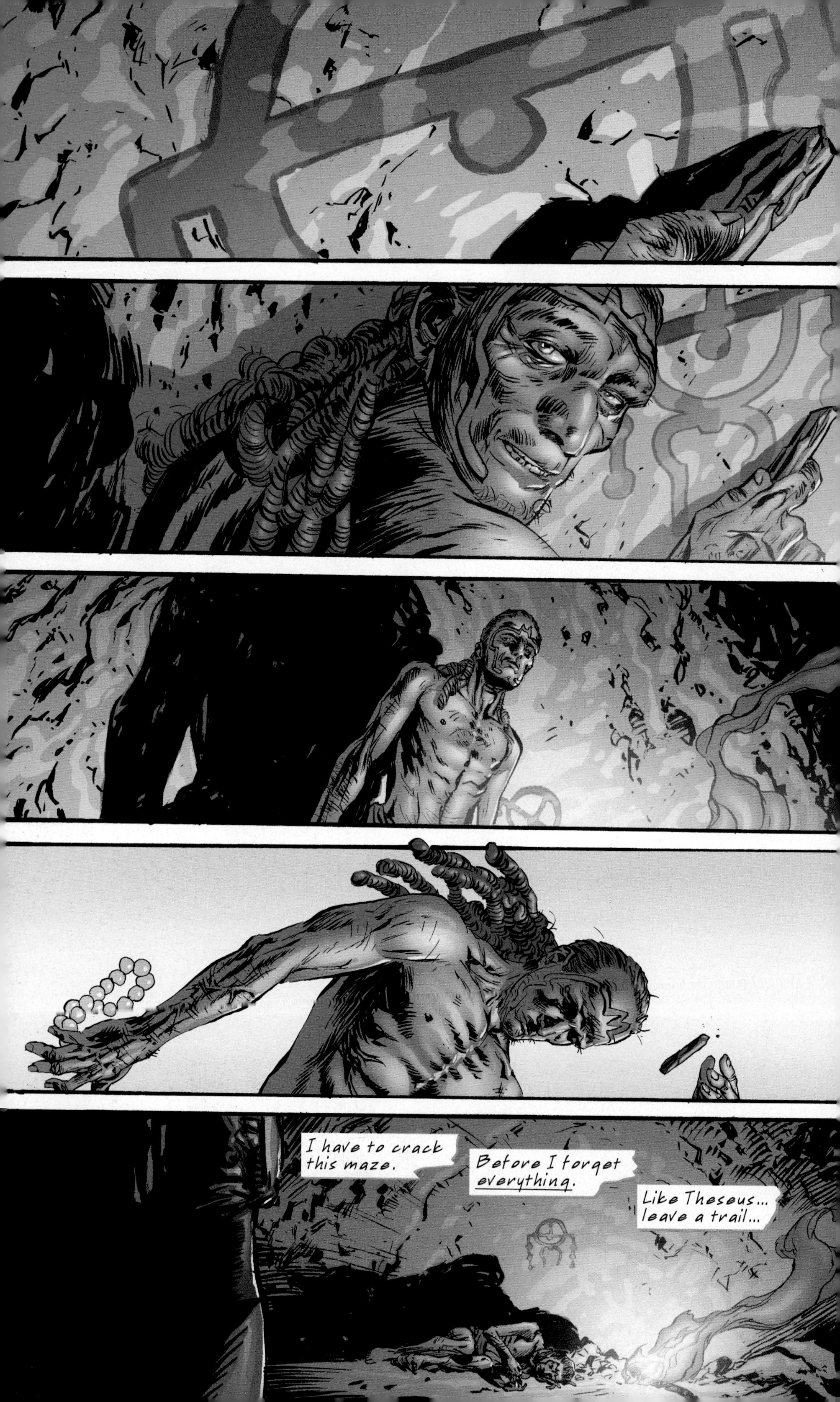
I have to crack this maze.
Before I forget everything.
Like Theseus... leave a trail...

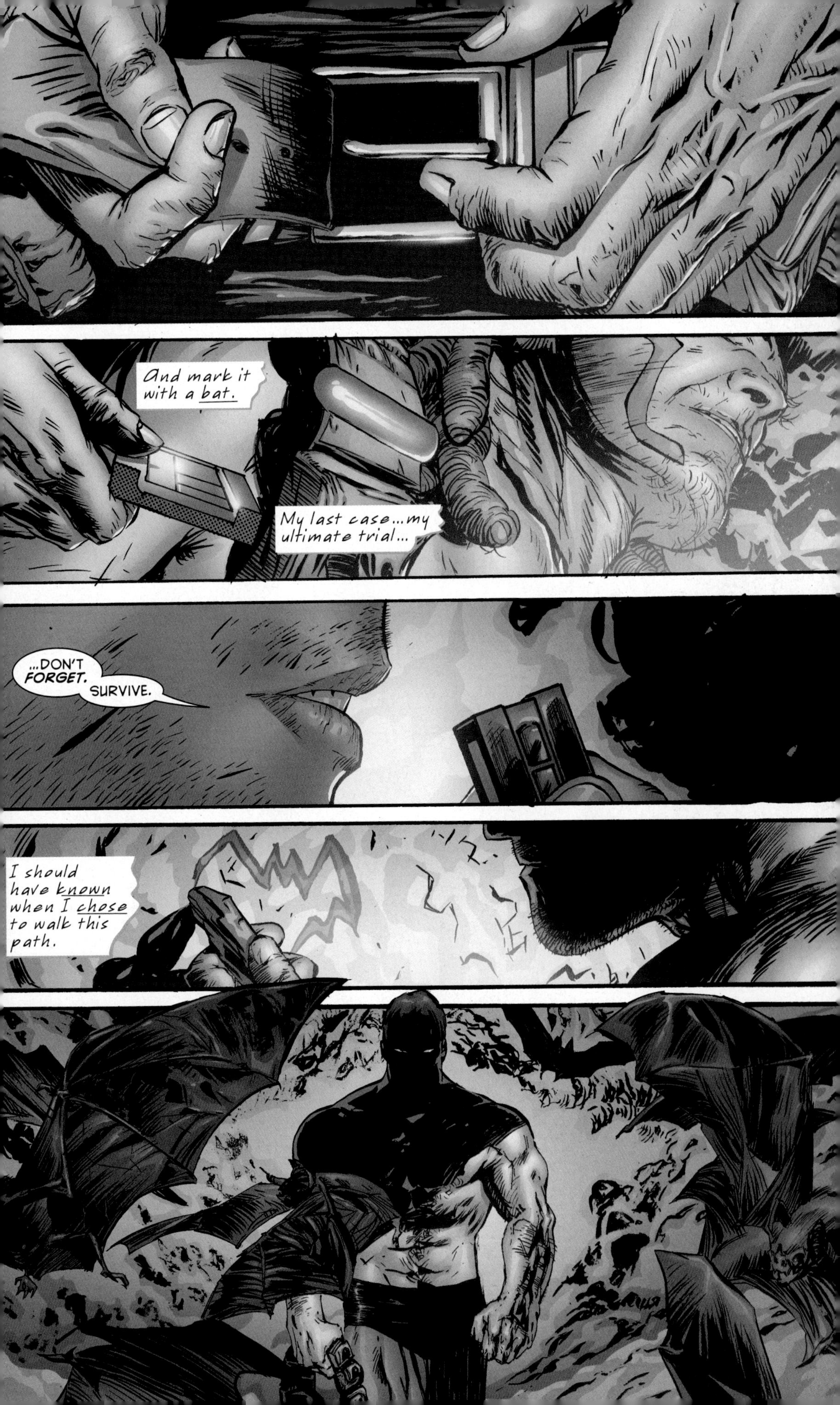
And mark it with a bat.
My last case...my ultimate trial...
...DON'T FORGET. SURVIVE.
I should have known when I chose to walk this path.

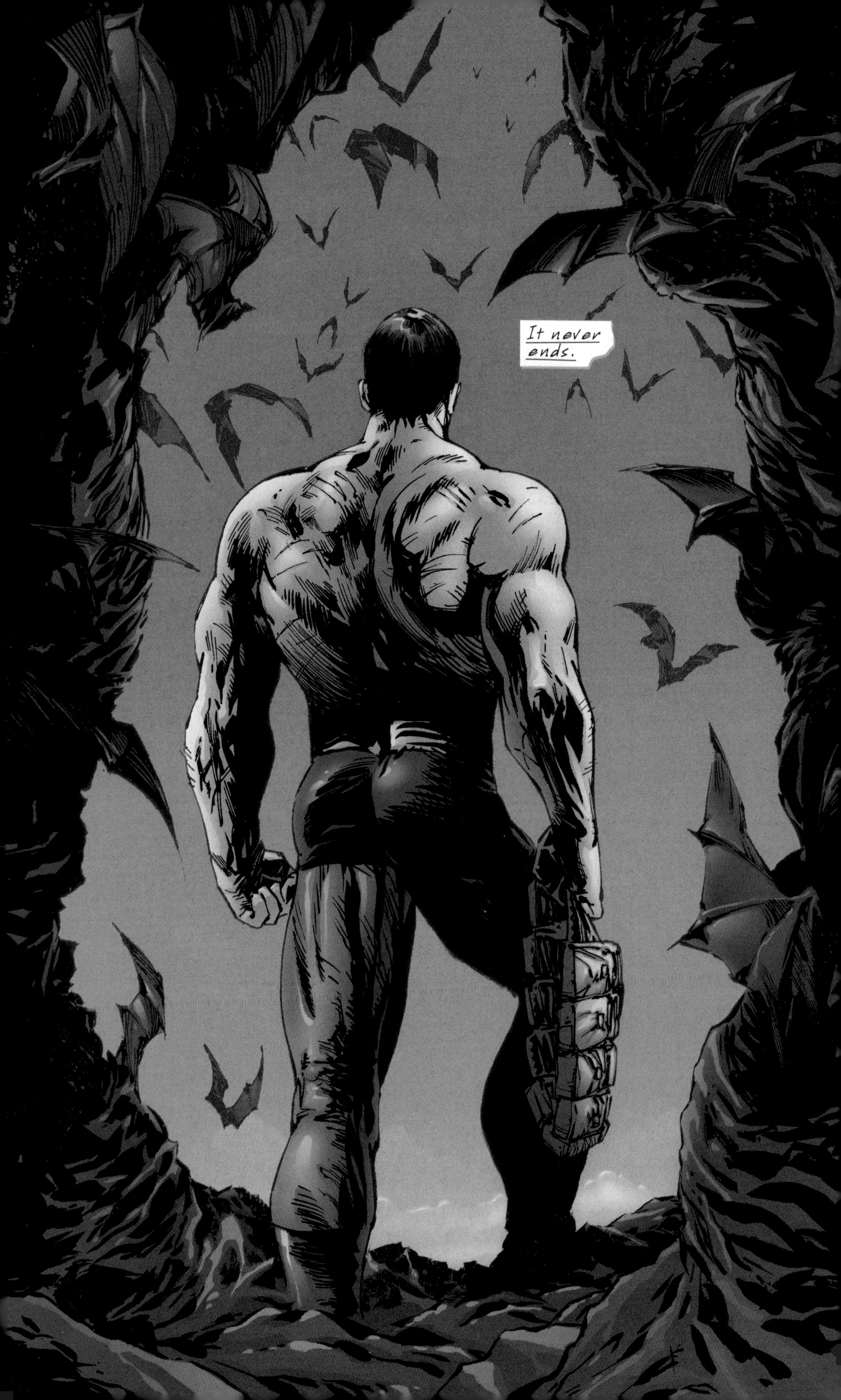
It never ends.

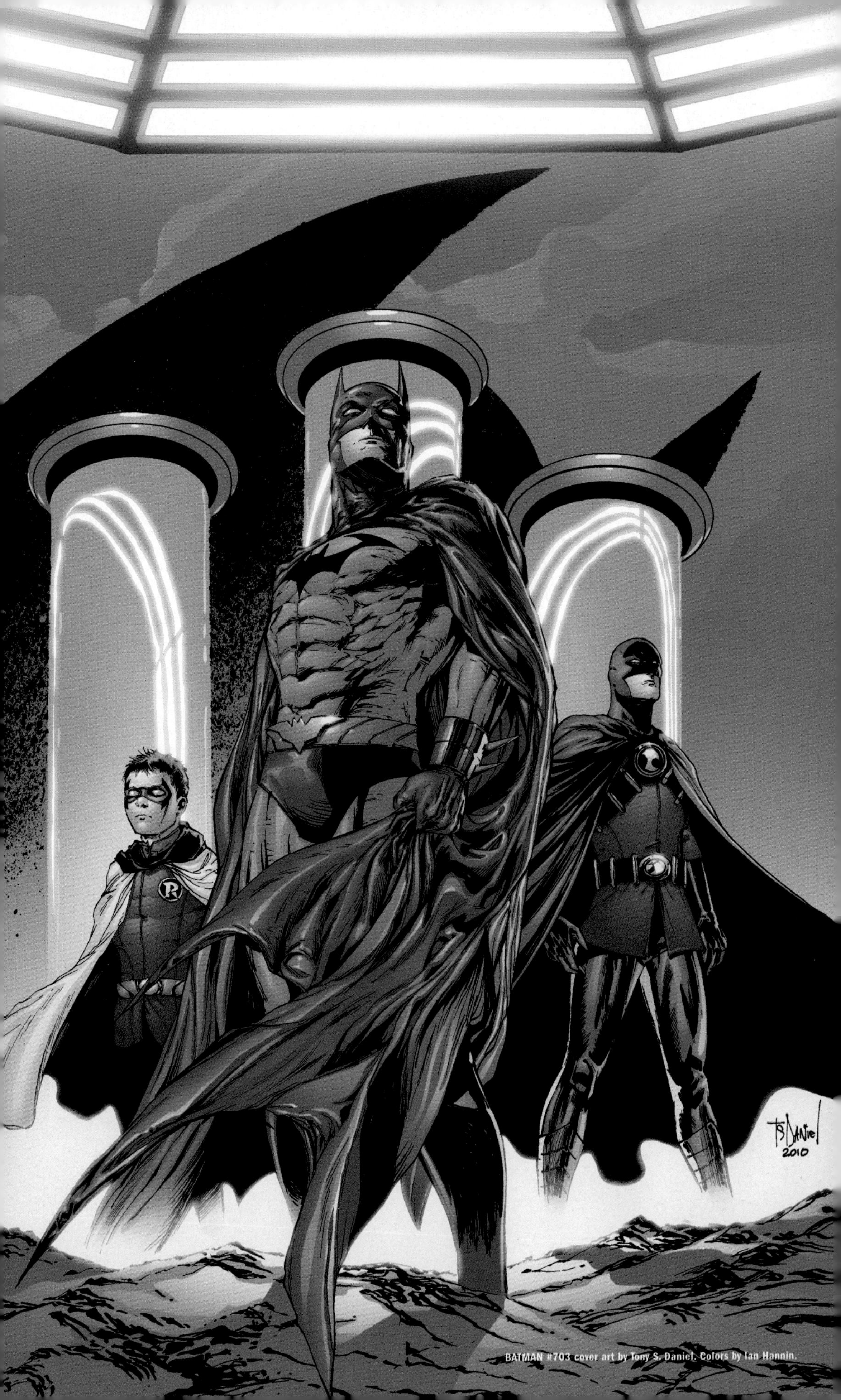
TS Daniel
2010

BATMAN #703 cover art by Tony S. Daniel. Colors by Ian Hannin.

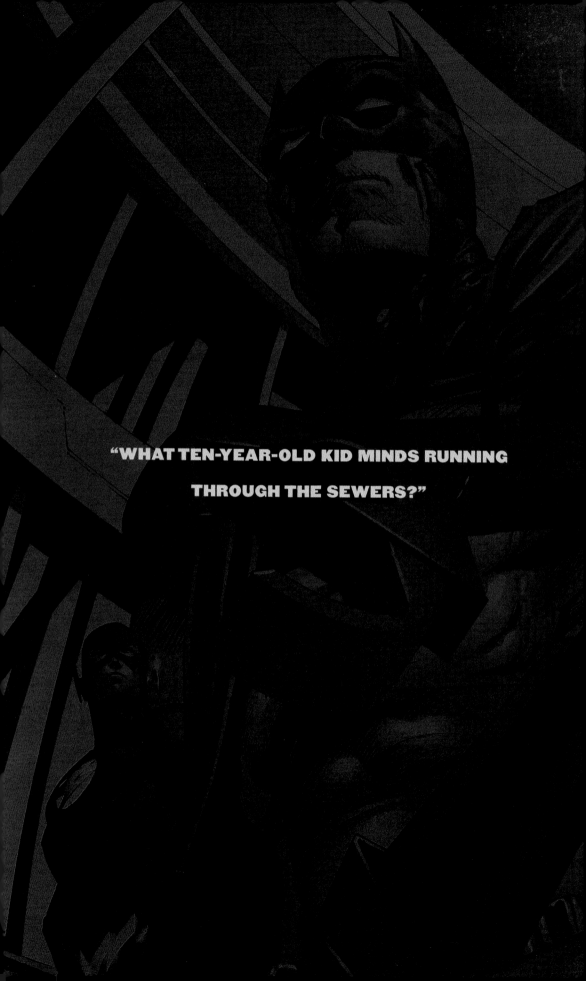

"WHAT TEN-YEAR-OLD KID MINDS RUNNING

THROUGH THE SEWERS?"

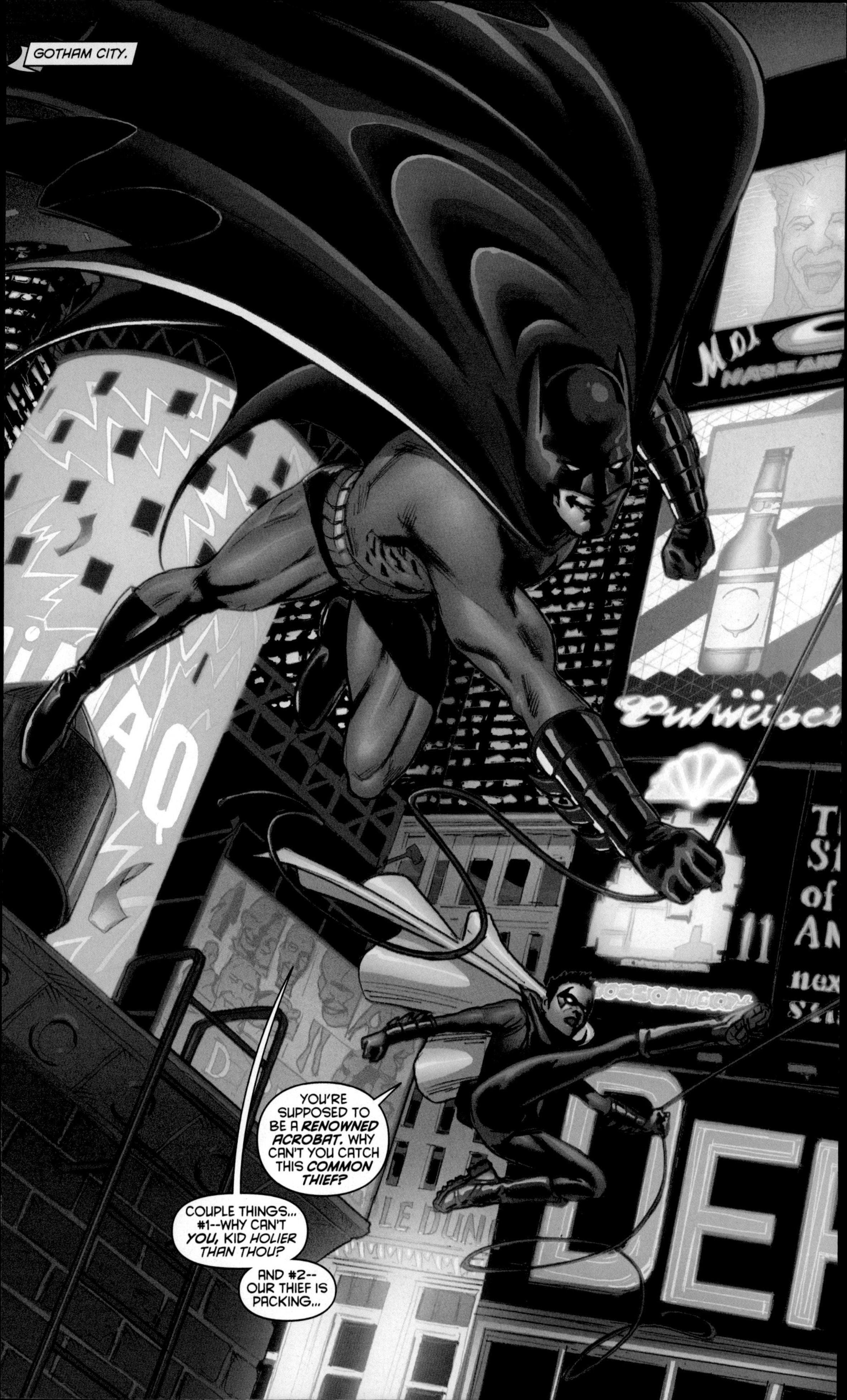
GOTHAM CITY.
YOU'RE SUPPOSED TO BE A RENOWNED ACROBAT. WHY CAN'T YOU CATCH THIS COMMON THIEF?
COUPLE THINGS... #1--WHY CAN'T YOU, KID HOLIER THAN THOU?
AND #2-- OUR THIEF IS PACKING...

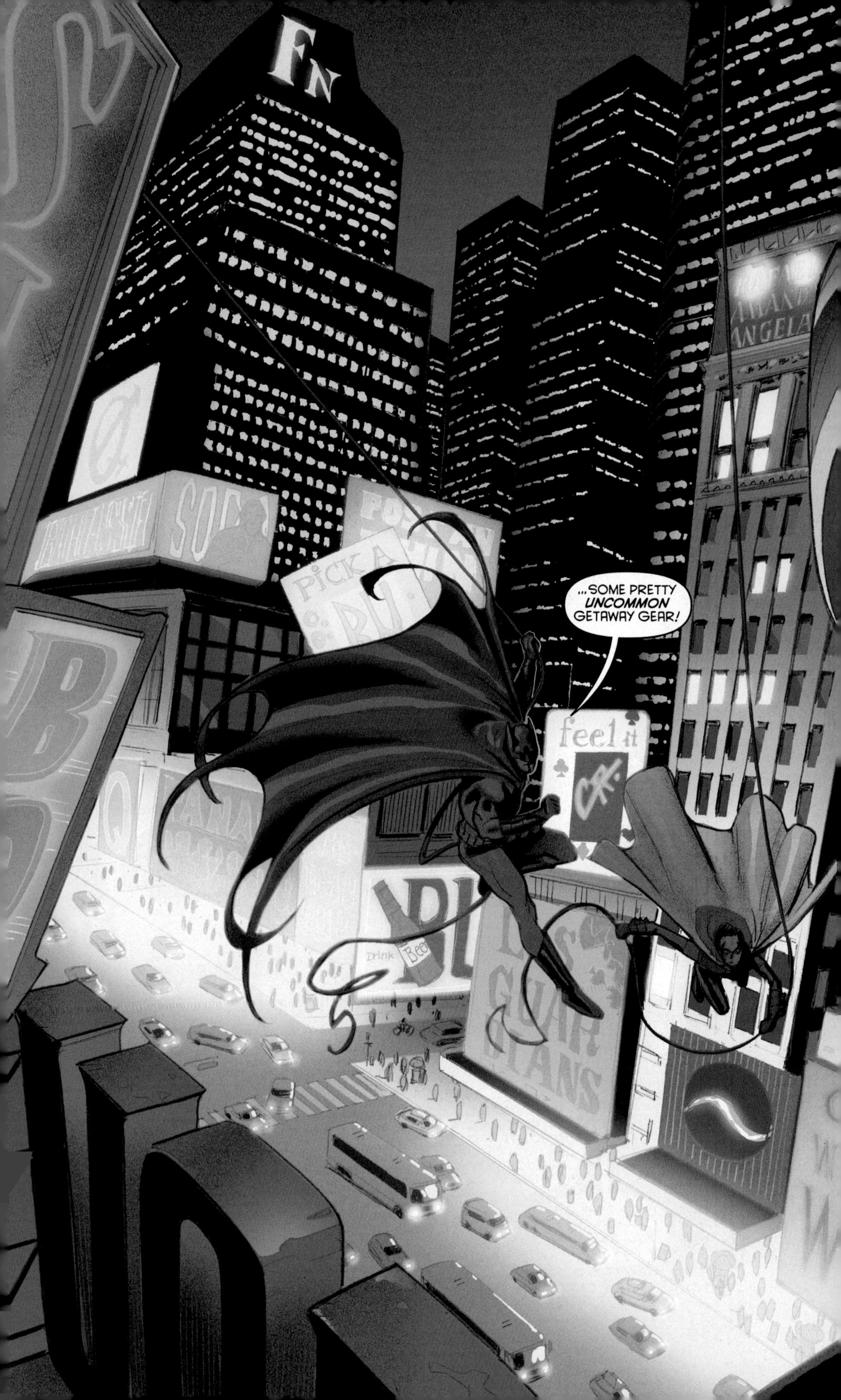
...SOME PRETTY UNCOMMON GETAWAY GEAR!
feel it
PICK A

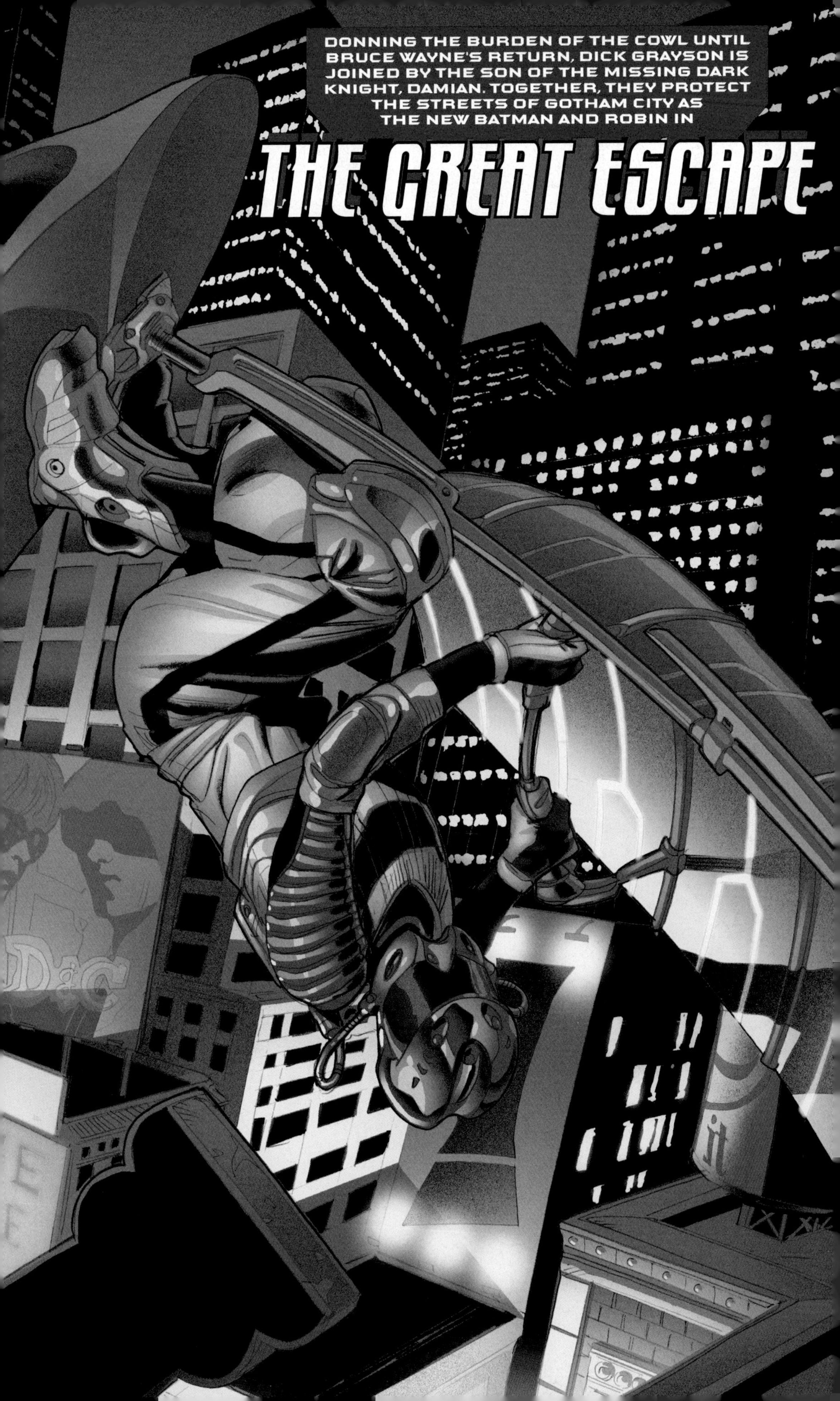
DONNING THE BURDEN OF THE COWL UNTIL BRUCE WAYNE'S RETURN, DICK GRAYSON IS JOINED BY THE SON OF THE MISSING DARK KNIGHT, DAMIAN. TOGETHER, THEY PROTECT THE STREETS OF GOTHAM CITY AS THE NEW BATMAN AND ROBIN IN
THE GREAT ESCAPE

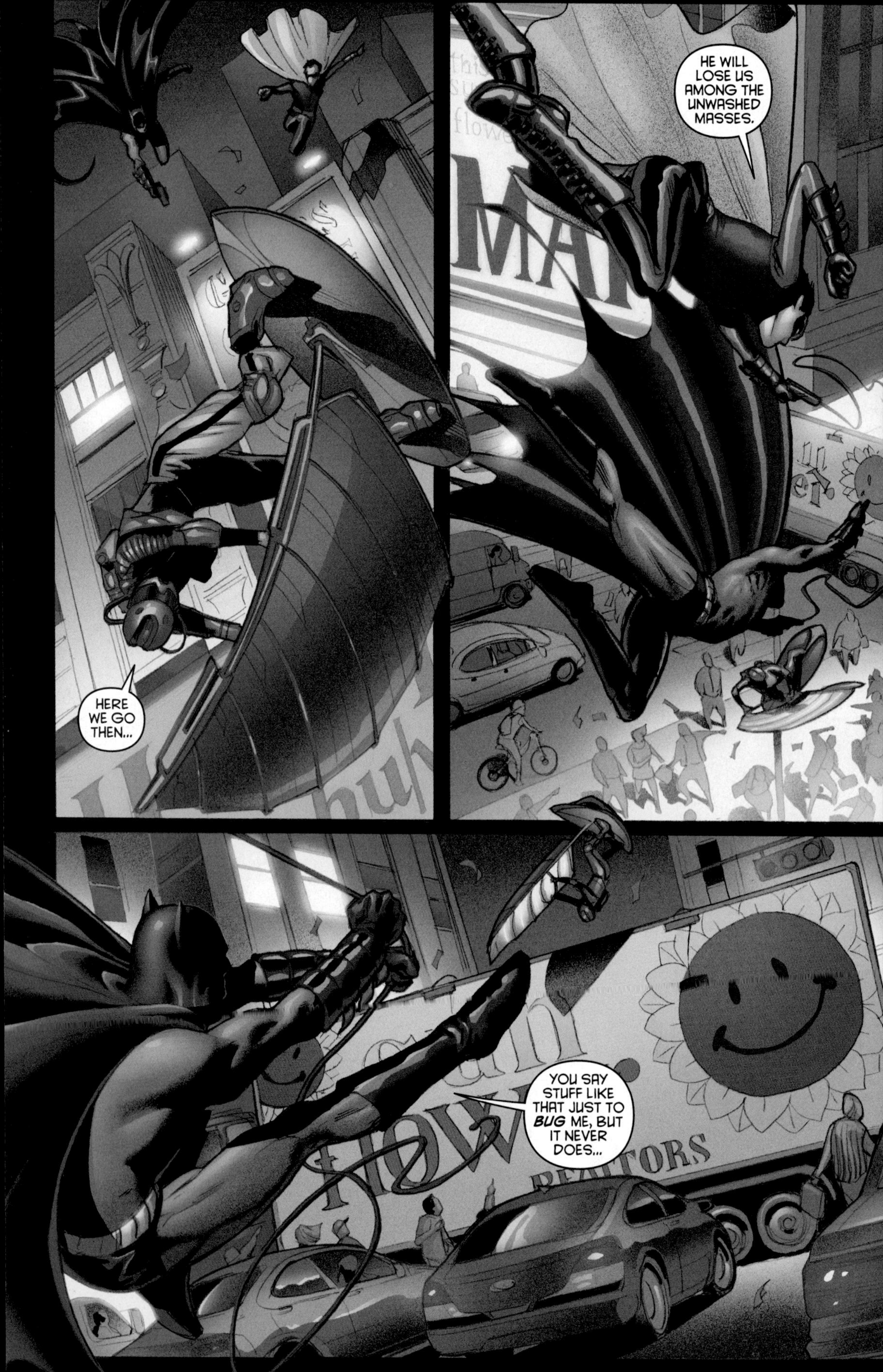
HE WILL LOSE US AMONG THE UNWASHED MASSES.
HERE WE GO THEN...
YOU SAY STUFF LIKE THAT JUST TO BUG ME, BUT IT NEVER DOES...

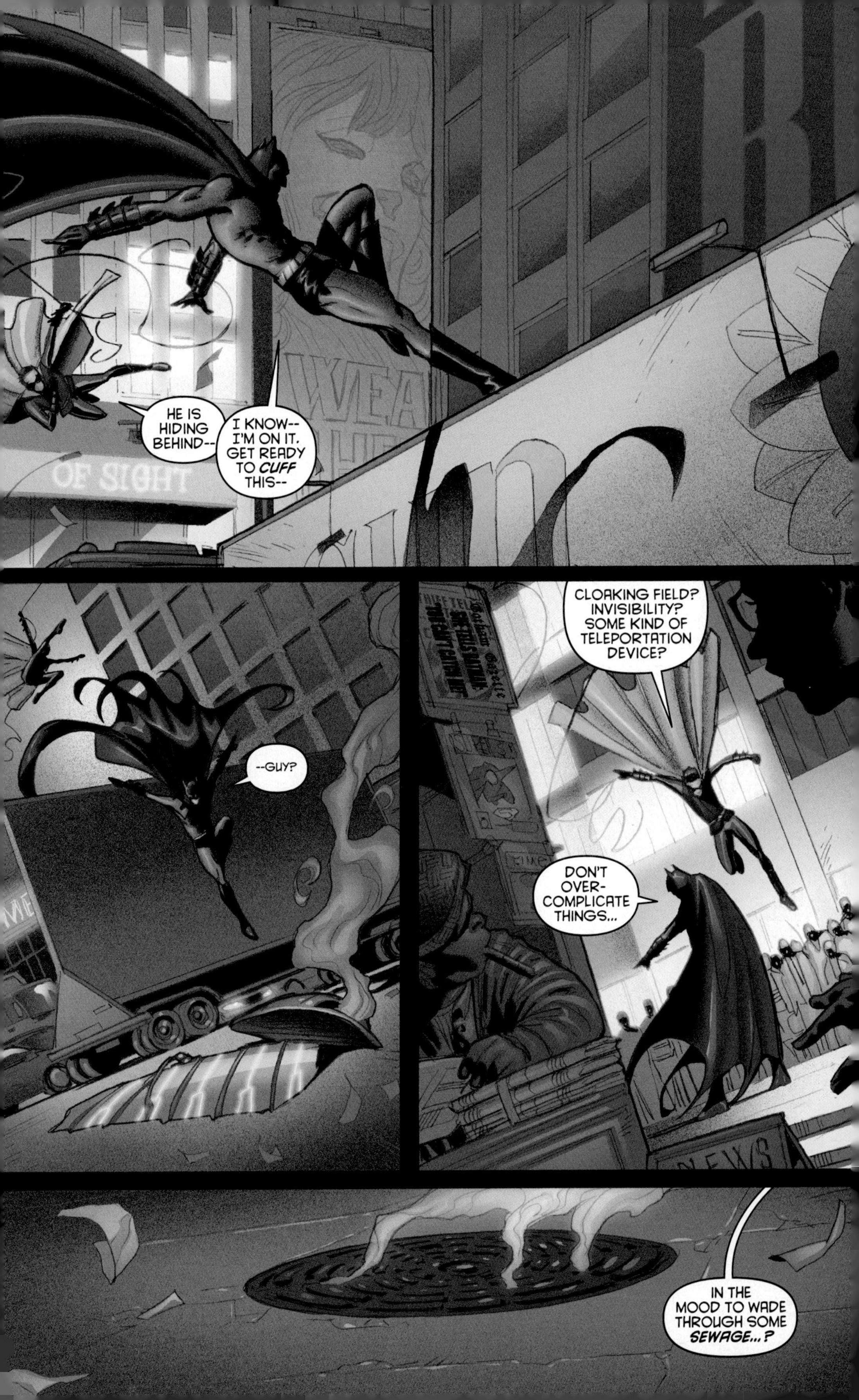

WEA
OF SIGHT
HE IS HIDING BEHIND--
I KNOW-- I'M ON IT. GET READY TO *CUFF* THIS--
--GUY?
CLOAKING FIELD? INVISIBILITY? SOME KIND OF TELEPORTATION DEVICE?
DON'T OVER-COMPLICATE THINGS...
IN THE MOOD TO WADE THROUGH SOME *SEWAGE...?*

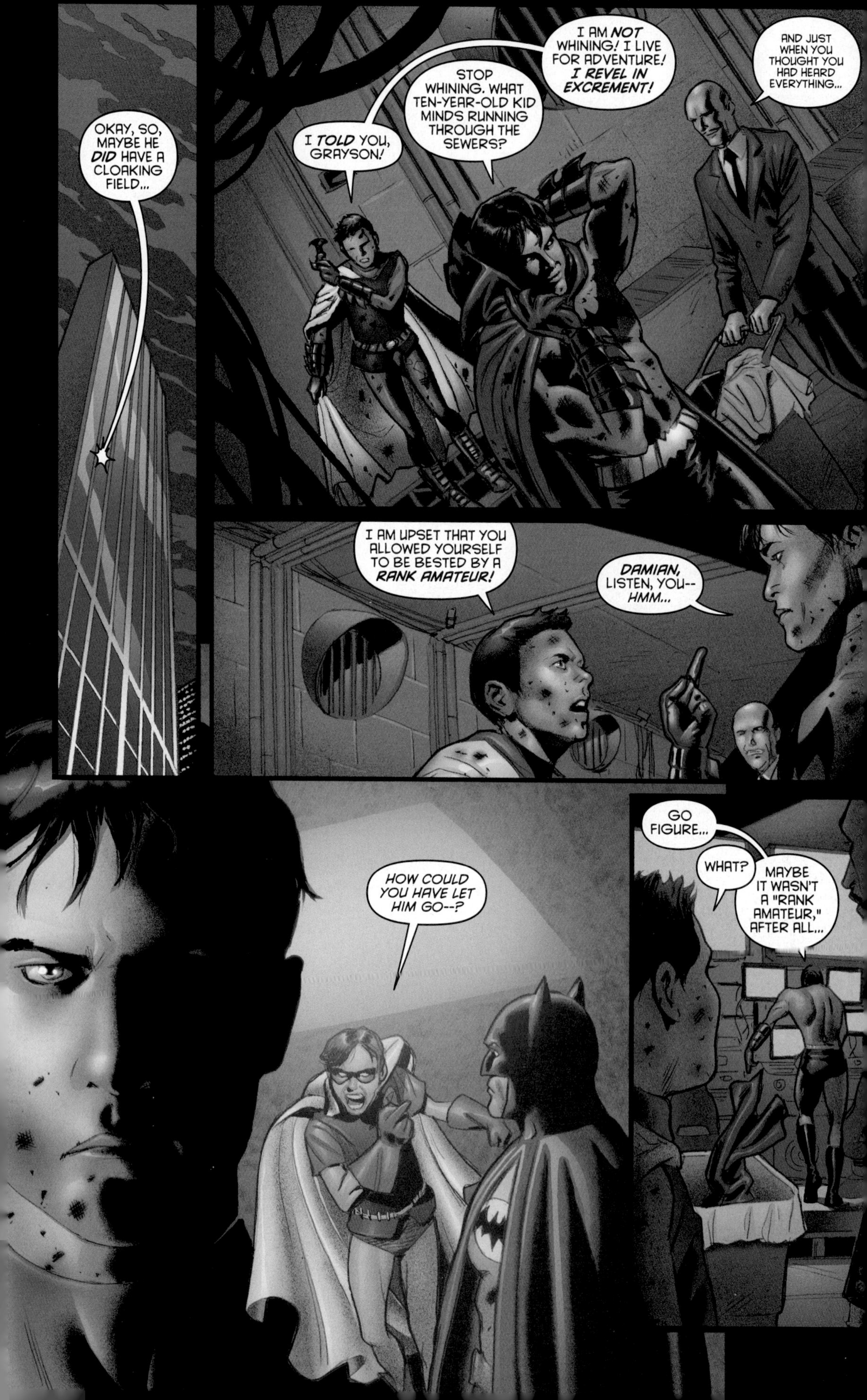

OKAY, SO, MAYBE HE *DID* HAVE A CLOAKING FIELD...
I *TOLD* YOU, GRAYSON!
STOP WHINING. WHAT TEN-YEAR-OLD KID MINDS RUNNING THROUGH THE SEWERS?
I AM *NOT* WHINING! I LIVE FOR ADVENTURE! ***I REVEL IN EXCREMENT!***
AND JUST WHEN YOU THOUGHT YOU HAD HEARD EVERYTHING...
I AM UPSET THAT YOU ALLOWED YOURSELF TO BE BESTED BY A ***RANK AMATEUR!***
DAMIAN, LISTEN, YOU-- HMM...
HOW COULD YOU HAVE LET HIM GO--?
GO FIGURE...
WHAT?
MAYBE IT WASN'T A "RANK AMATEUR," AFTER ALL...

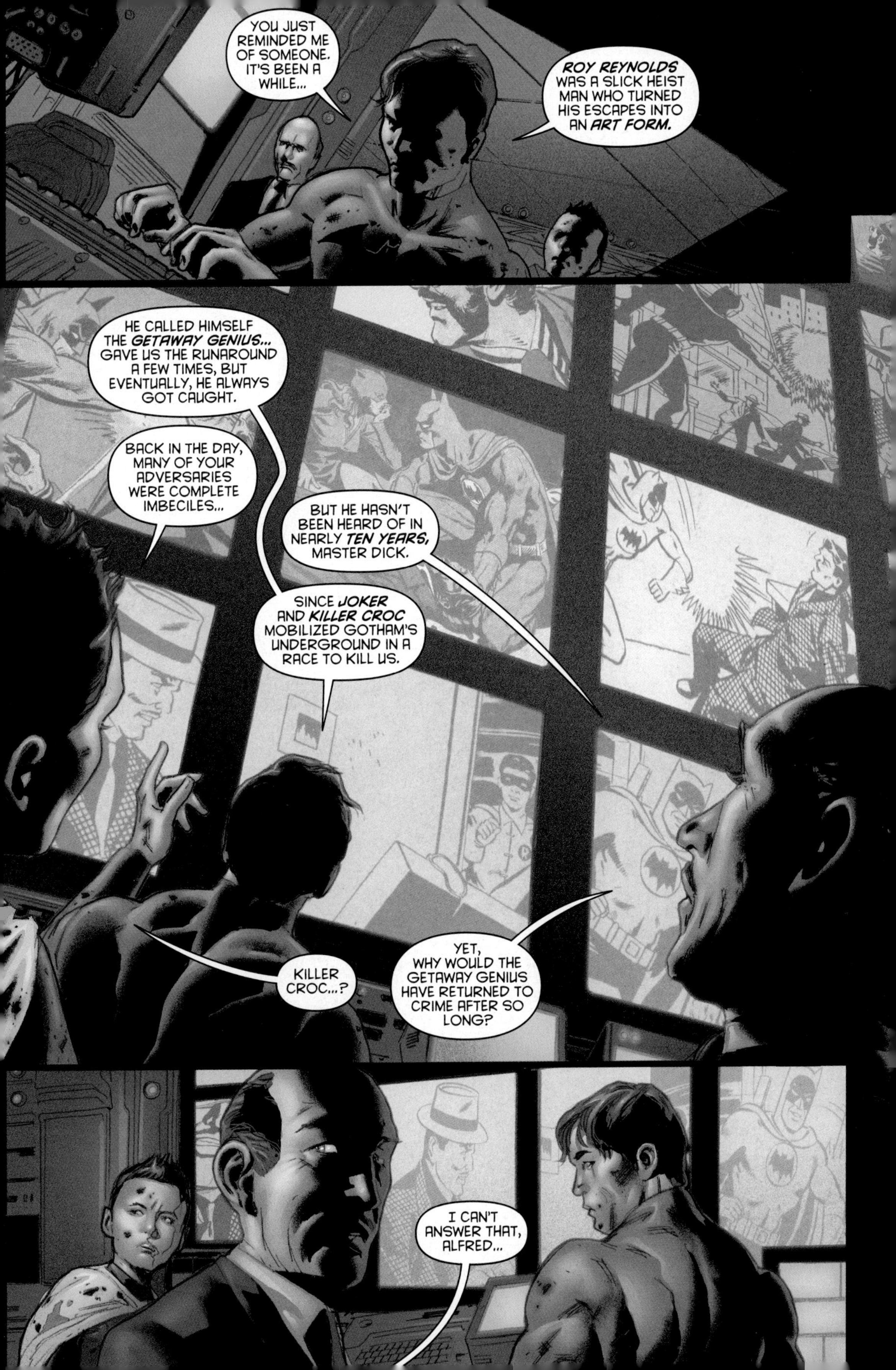
YOU JUST REMINDED ME OF SOMEONE. IT'S BEEN A WHILE...
ROY REYNOLDS WAS A SLICK HEIST MAN WHO TURNED HIS ESCAPES INTO AN ART FORM.
HE CALLED HIMSELF THE GETAWAY GENIUS... GAVE US THE RUNAROUND A FEW TIMES, BUT EVENTUALLY, HE ALWAYS GOT CAUGHT.
BACK IN THE DAY, MANY OF YOUR ADVERSARIES WERE COMPLETE IMBECILES...
BUT HE HASN'T BEEN HEARD OF IN NEARLY TEN YEARS, MASTER DICK.
SINCE JOKER AND KILLER CROC MOBILIZED GOTHAM'S UNDERGROUND IN A RACE TO KILL US.
KILLER CROC...?
YET, WHY WOULD THE GETAWAY GENIUS HAVE RETURNED TO CRIME AFTER SO LONG?
I CAN'T ANSWER THAT, ALFRED...

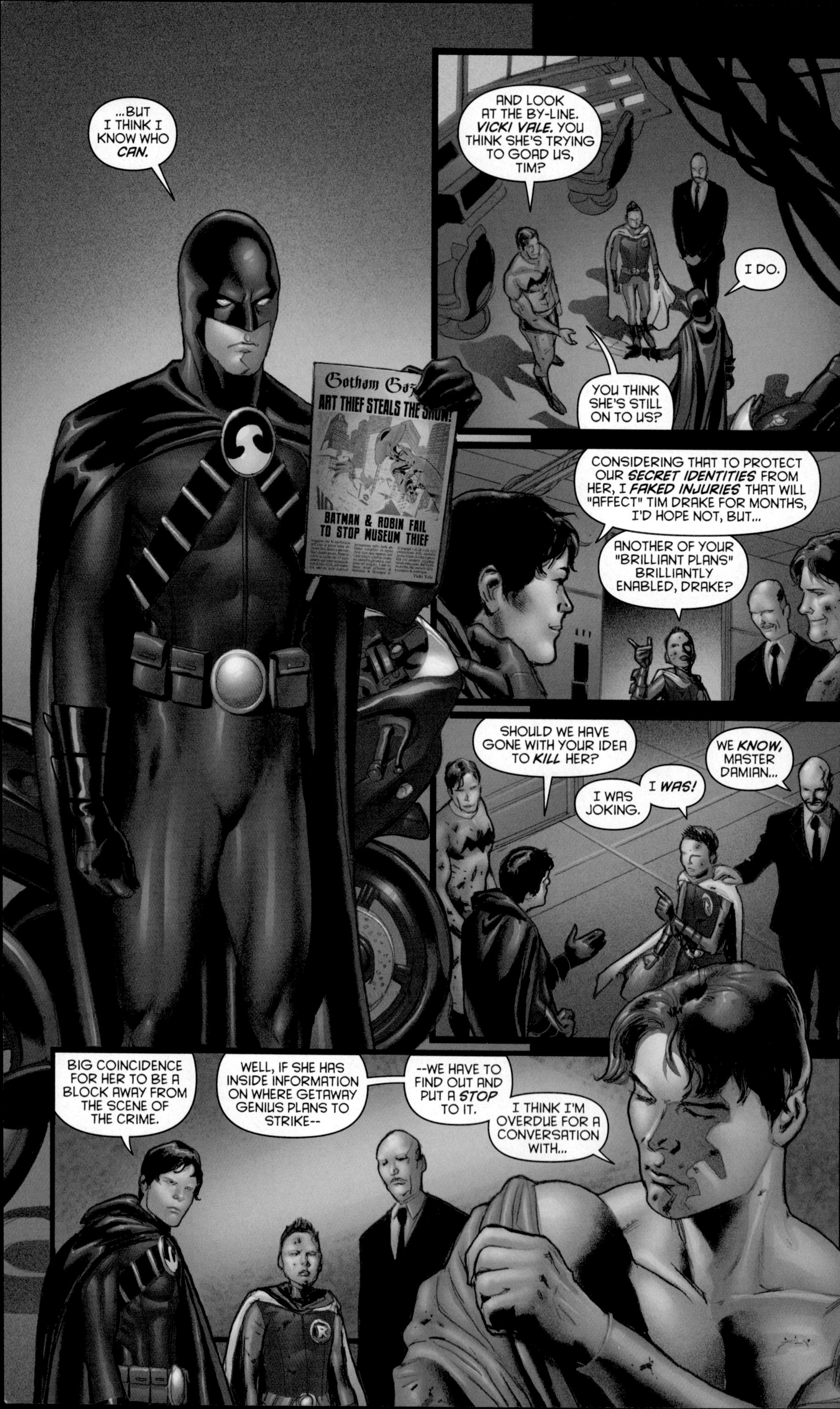
...BUT I THINK I KNOW WHO CAN.
Gotham Gaz
ART THIEF STEALS THE SHOW!
BATMAN & ROBIN FAIL TO STOP MUSEUM THIEF
AND LOOK AT THE BY-LINE. VICKI VALE. YOU THINK SHE'S TRYING TO GOAD US, TIM?
I DO.
YOU THINK SHE'S STILL ON TO US?
CONSIDERING THAT TO PROTECT OUR SECRET IDENTITIES FROM HER, I FAKED INJURIES THAT WILL "AFFECT" TIM DRAKE FOR MONTHS, I'D HOPE NOT, BUT...
ANOTHER OF YOUR "BRILLIANT PLANS" BRILLIANTLY ENABLED, DRAKE?
SHOULD WE HAVE GONE WITH YOUR IDEA TO KILL HER?
I WAS JOKING.
I WAS!
WE KNOW, MASTER DAMIAN...
BIG COINCIDENCE FOR HER TO BE A BLOCK AWAY FROM THE SCENE OF THE CRIME.
WELL, IF SHE HAS INSIDE INFORMATION ON WHERE GETAWAY GENIUS PLANS TO STRIKE--
--WE HAVE TO FIND OUT AND PUT A STOP TO IT.
I THINK I'M OVERDUE FOR A CONVERSATION WITH...

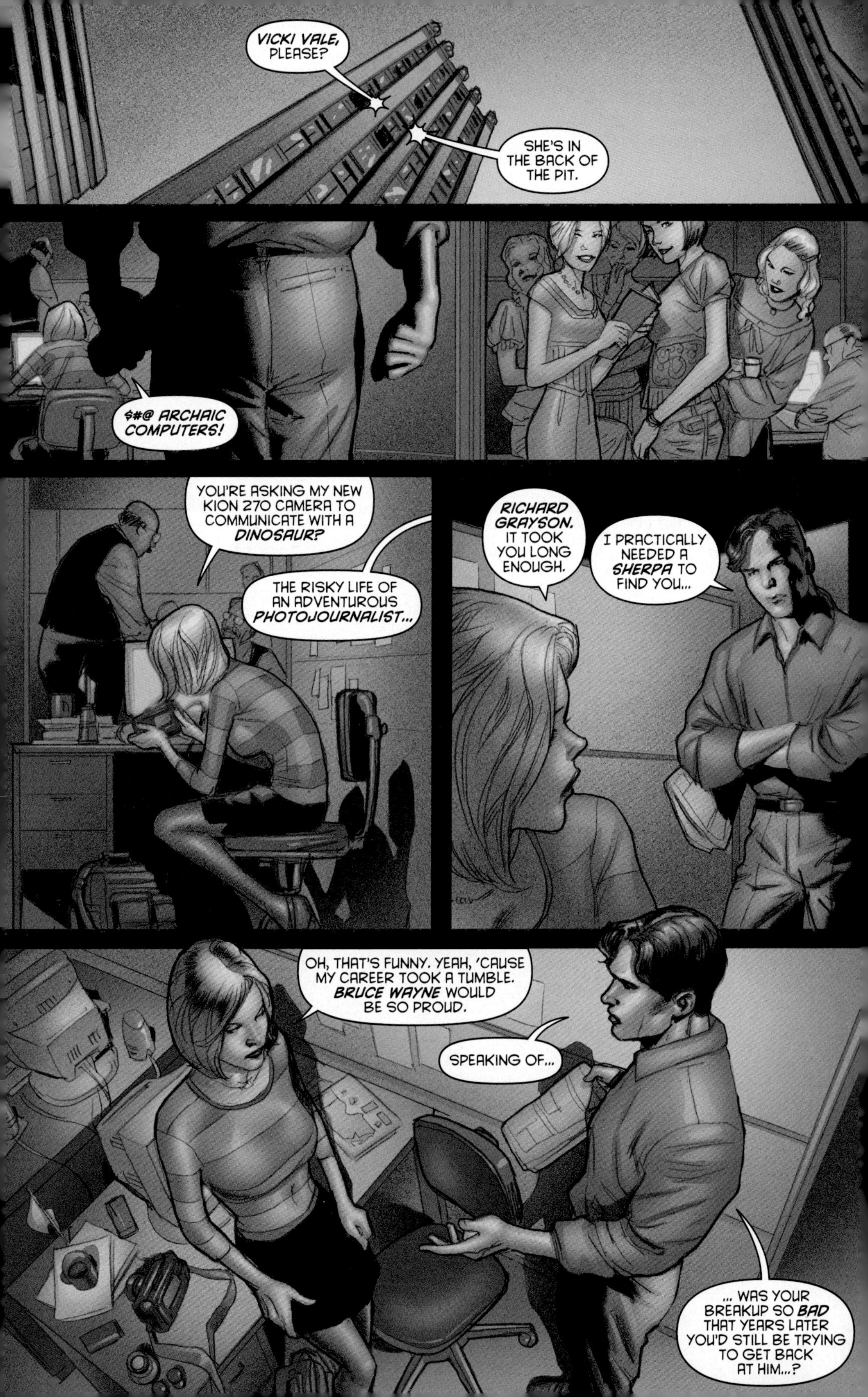
VICKI VALE, PLEASE?
SHE'S IN THE BACK OF THE PIT.
$#@ ARCHAIC COMPUTERS!
YOU'RE ASKING MY NEW KION 270 CAMERA TO COMMUNICATE WITH A DINOSAUR?
THE RISKY LIFE OF AN ADVENTUROUS PHOTOJOURNALIST...
RICHARD GRAYSON. IT TOOK YOU LONG ENOUGH.
I PRACTICALLY NEEDED A SHERPA TO FIND YOU...
OH, THAT'S FUNNY. YEAH, 'CAUSE MY CAREER TOOK A TUMBLE. BRUCE WAYNE WOULD BE SO PROUD.
SPEAKING OF...
... WAS YOUR BREAKUP SO BAD THAT YEARS LATER YOU'D STILL BE TRYING TO GET BACK AT HIM...?

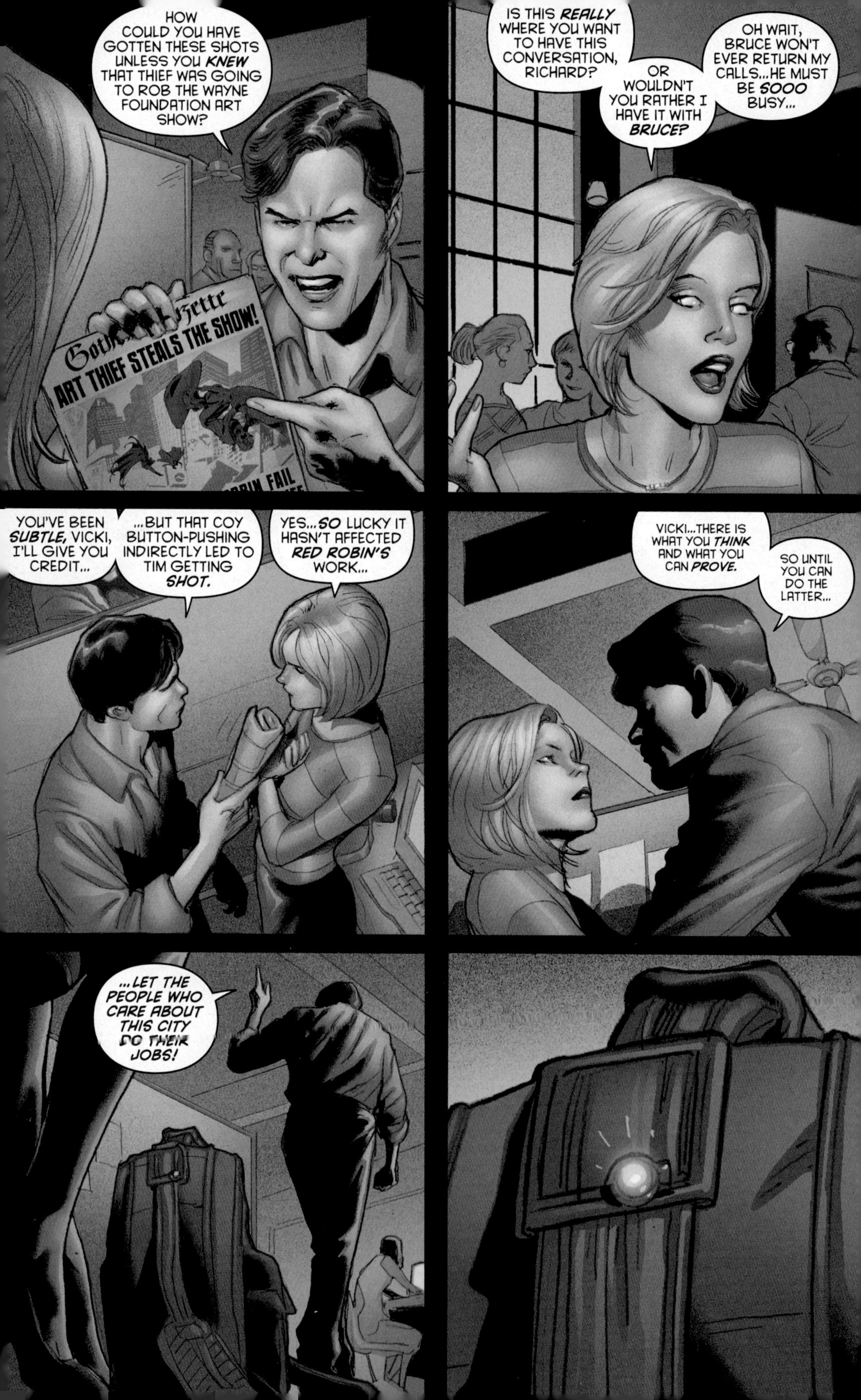
HOW COULD YOU HAVE GOTTEN THESE SHOTS UNLESS YOU KNEW THAT THIEF WAS GOING TO ROB THE WAYNE FOUNDATION ART SHOW?
ART THIEF STEALS THE SHOW!
IS THIS REALLY WHERE YOU WANT TO HAVE THIS CONVERSATION, RICHARD?
OR WOULDN'T YOU RATHER I HAVE IT WITH BRUCE?
OH WAIT, BRUCE WON'T EVER RETURN MY CALLS...HE MUST BE SOOO BUSY...
YOU'VE BEEN SUBTLE, VICKI, I'LL GIVE YOU CREDIT...
...BUT THAT COY BUTTON-PUSHING INDIRECTLY LED TO TIM GETTING SHOT.
YES...SO LUCKY IT HASN'T AFFECTED RED ROBIN'S WORK...
VICKI...THERE IS WHAT YOU THINK AND WHAT YOU CAN PROVE.
SO UNTIL YOU CAN DO THE LATTER...
...LET THE PEOPLE WHO CARE ABOUT THIS CITY DO THEIR JOBS!

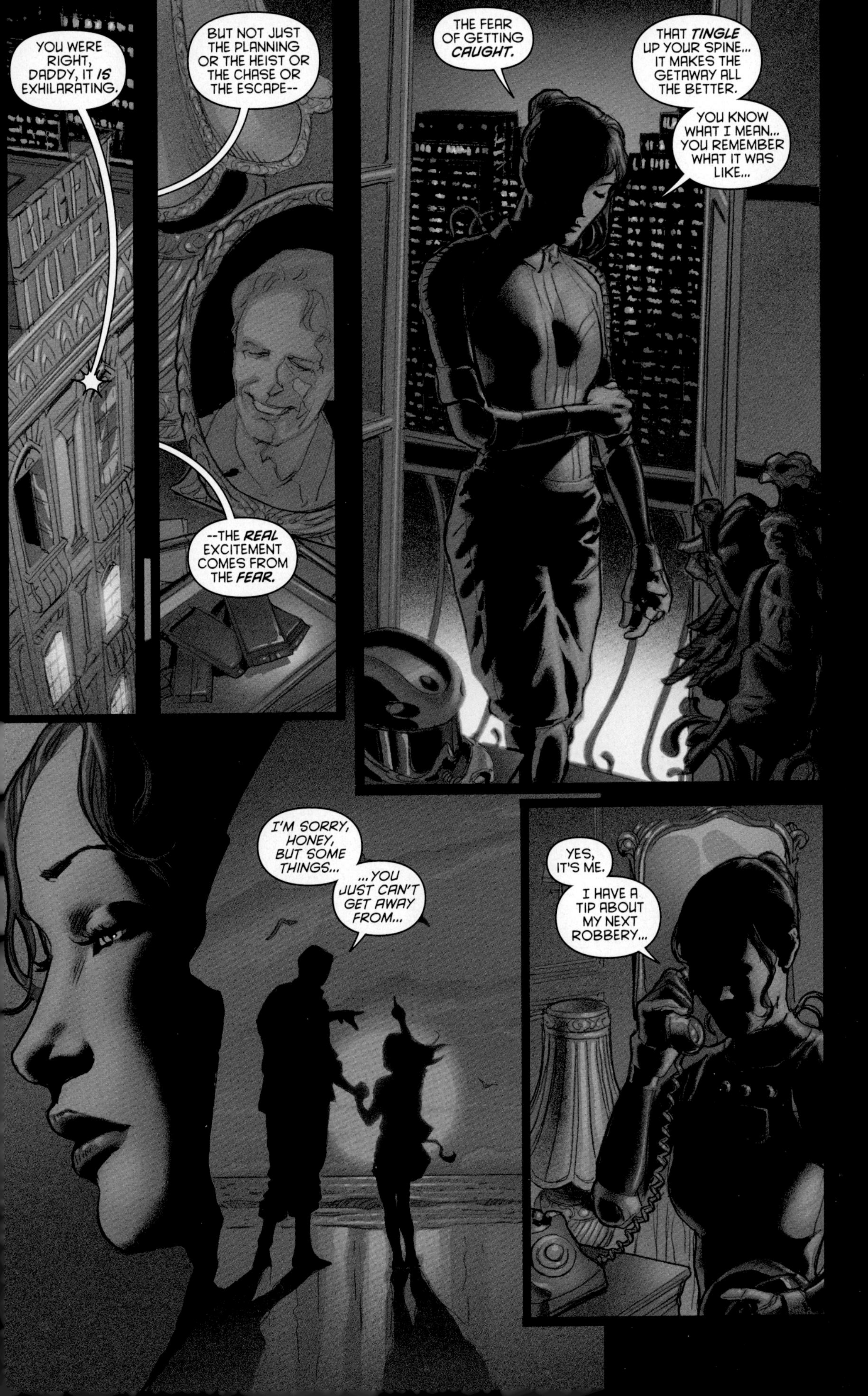
YOU WERE RIGHT, DADDY, IT IS EXHILARATING.
BUT NOT JUST THE PLANNING OR THE HEIST OR THE CHASE OR THE ESCAPE--
--THE REAL EXCITEMENT COMES FROM THE FEAR.
THE FEAR OF GETTING CAUGHT.
THAT TINGLE UP YOUR SPINE... IT MAKES THE GETAWAY ALL THE BETTER.
YOU KNOW WHAT I MEAN... YOU REMEMBER WHAT IT WAS LIKE...
I'M SORRY, HONEY, BUT SOME THINGS...
...YOU JUST CAN'T GET AWAY FROM...
YES, IT'S ME.
I HAVE A TIP ABOUT MY NEXT ROBBERY...

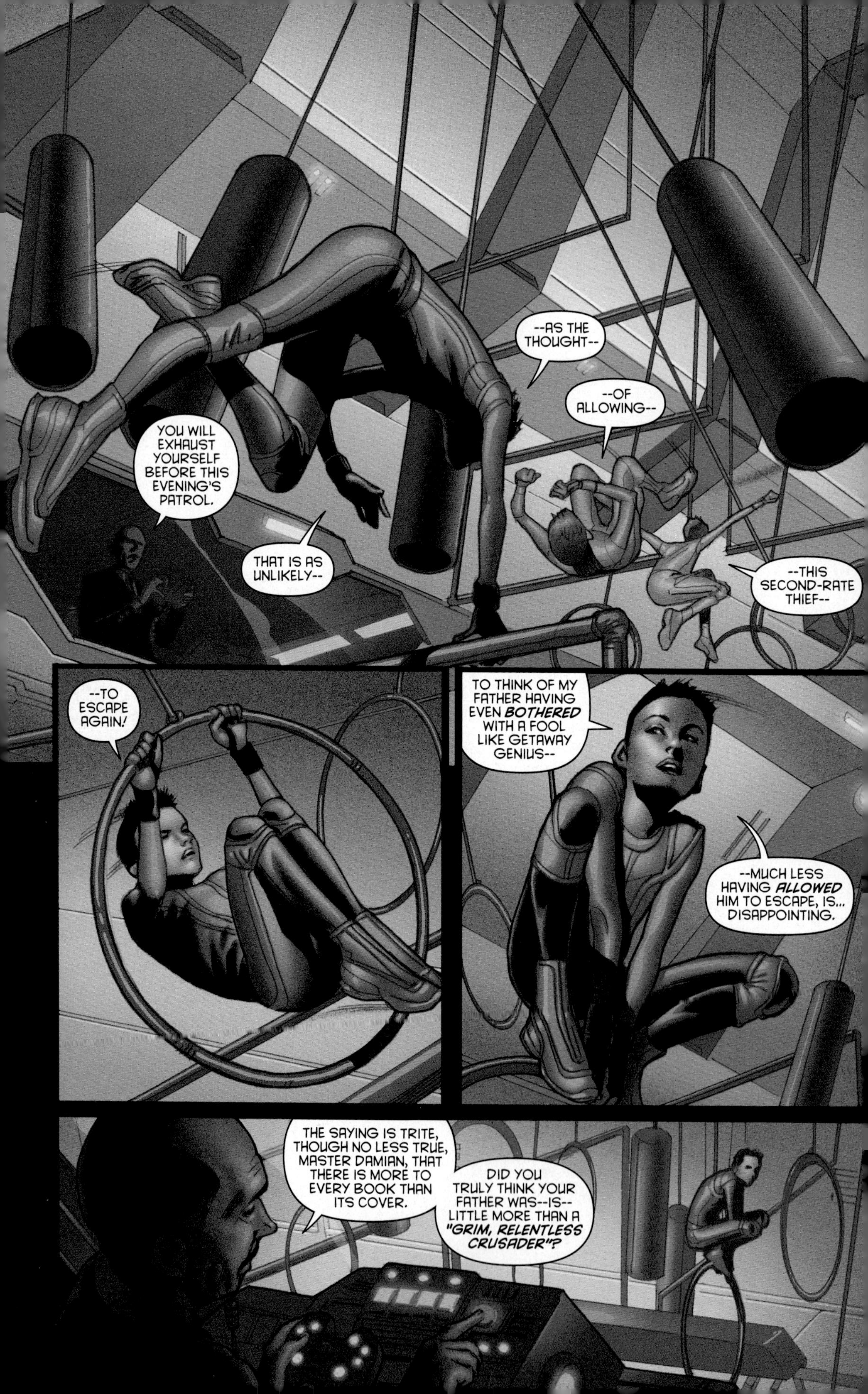
YOU WILL EXHAUST YOURSELF BEFORE THIS EVENING'S PATROL.
THAT IS AS UNLIKELY--
--AS THE THOUGHT--
--OF ALLOWING--
--THIS SECOND-RATE THIEF--
--TO ESCAPE AGAIN!
TO THINK OF MY FATHER HAVING EVEN BOTHERED WITH A FOOL LIKE GETAWAY GENIUS--
--MUCH LESS HAVING ALLOWED HIM TO ESCAPE, IS... DISAPPOINTING.
THE SAYING IS TRITE, THOUGH NO LESS TRUE, MASTER DAMIAN, THAT THERE IS MORE TO EVERY BOOK THAN ITS COVER.
DID YOU TRULY THINK YOUR FATHER WAS--IS-- LITTLE MORE THAN A "GRIM, RELENTLESS CRUSADER"?

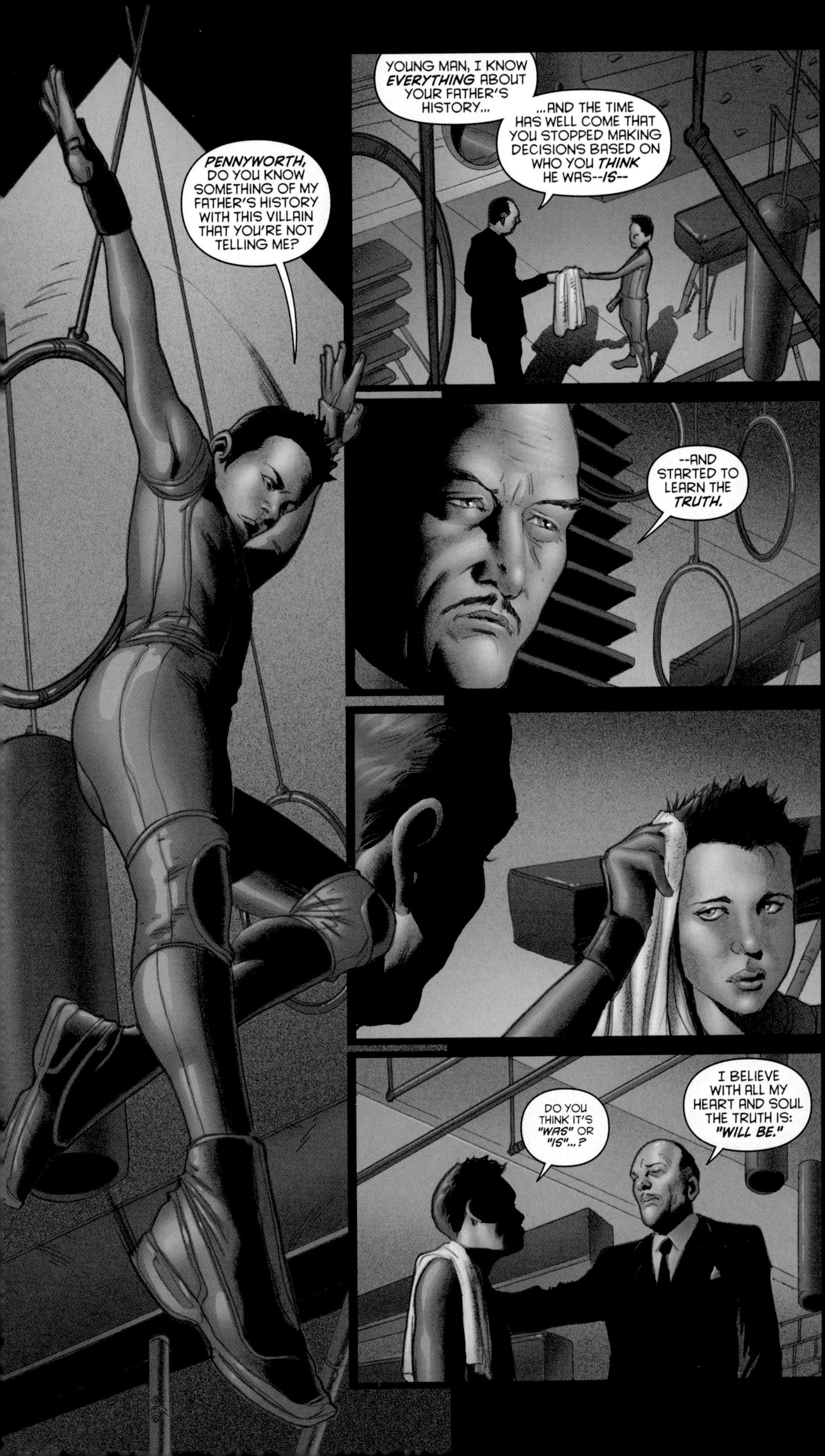
PENNYWORTH, DO YOU KNOW SOMETHING OF MY FATHER'S HISTORY WITH THIS VILLAIN THAT YOU'RE NOT TELLING ME?
YOUNG MAN, I KNOW EVERYTHING ABOUT YOUR FATHER'S HISTORY...
...AND THE TIME HAS WELL COME THAT YOU STOPPED MAKING DECISIONS BASED ON WHO YOU THINK HE WAS--IS--
--AND STARTED TO LEARN THE TRUTH.
DO YOU THINK IT'S "WAS" OR "IS"...?
I BELIEVE WITH ALL MY HEART AND SOUL THE TRUTH IS: "WILL BE."

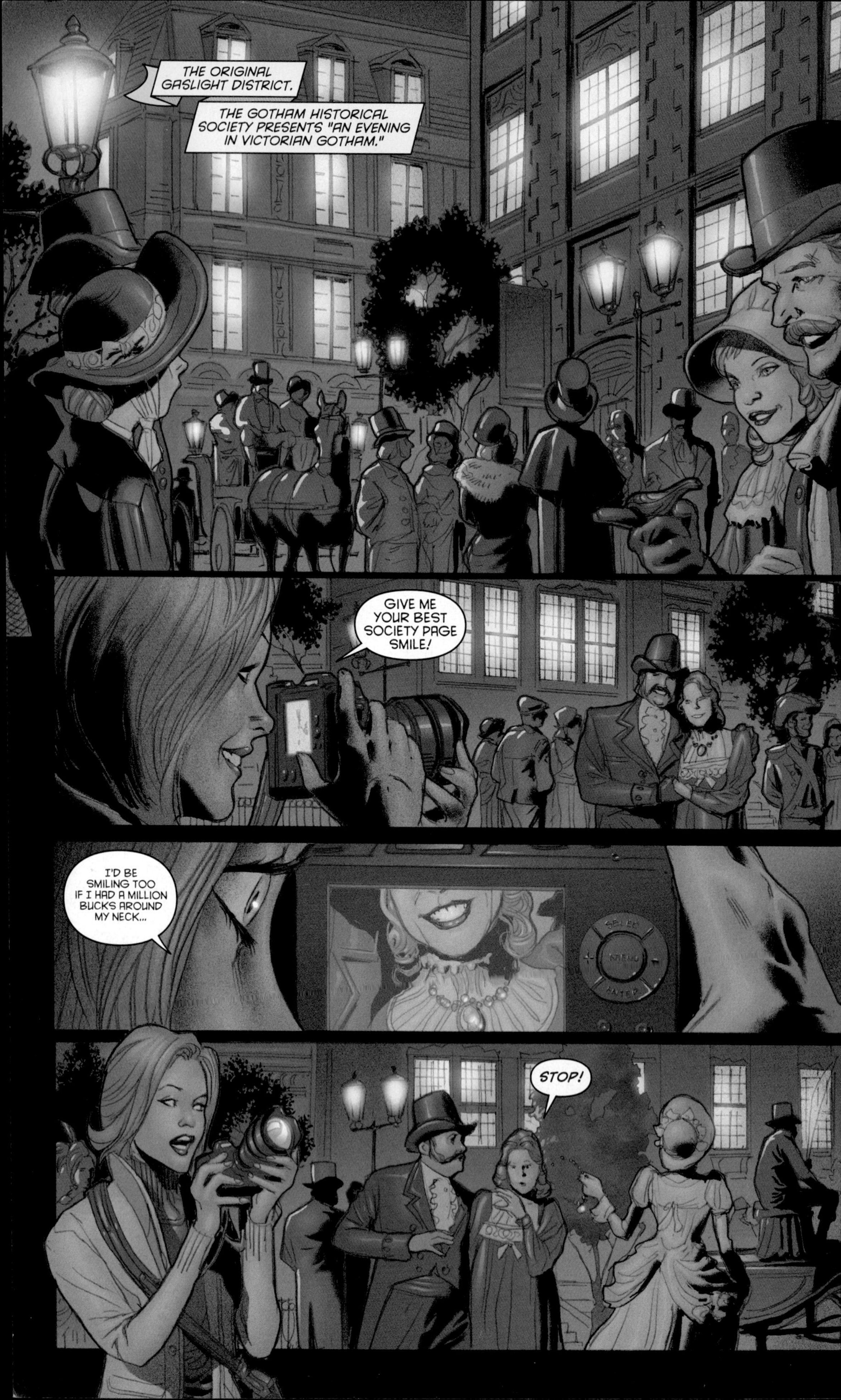
THE ORIGINAL GASLIGHT DISTRICT.
THE GOTHAM HISTORICAL SOCIETY PRESENTS "AN EVENING IN VICTORIAN GOTHAM."
GIVE ME YOUR BEST SOCIETY PAGE SMILE!
I'D BE SMILING TOO IF I HAD A MILLION BUCKS AROUND MY NECK...
STOP!

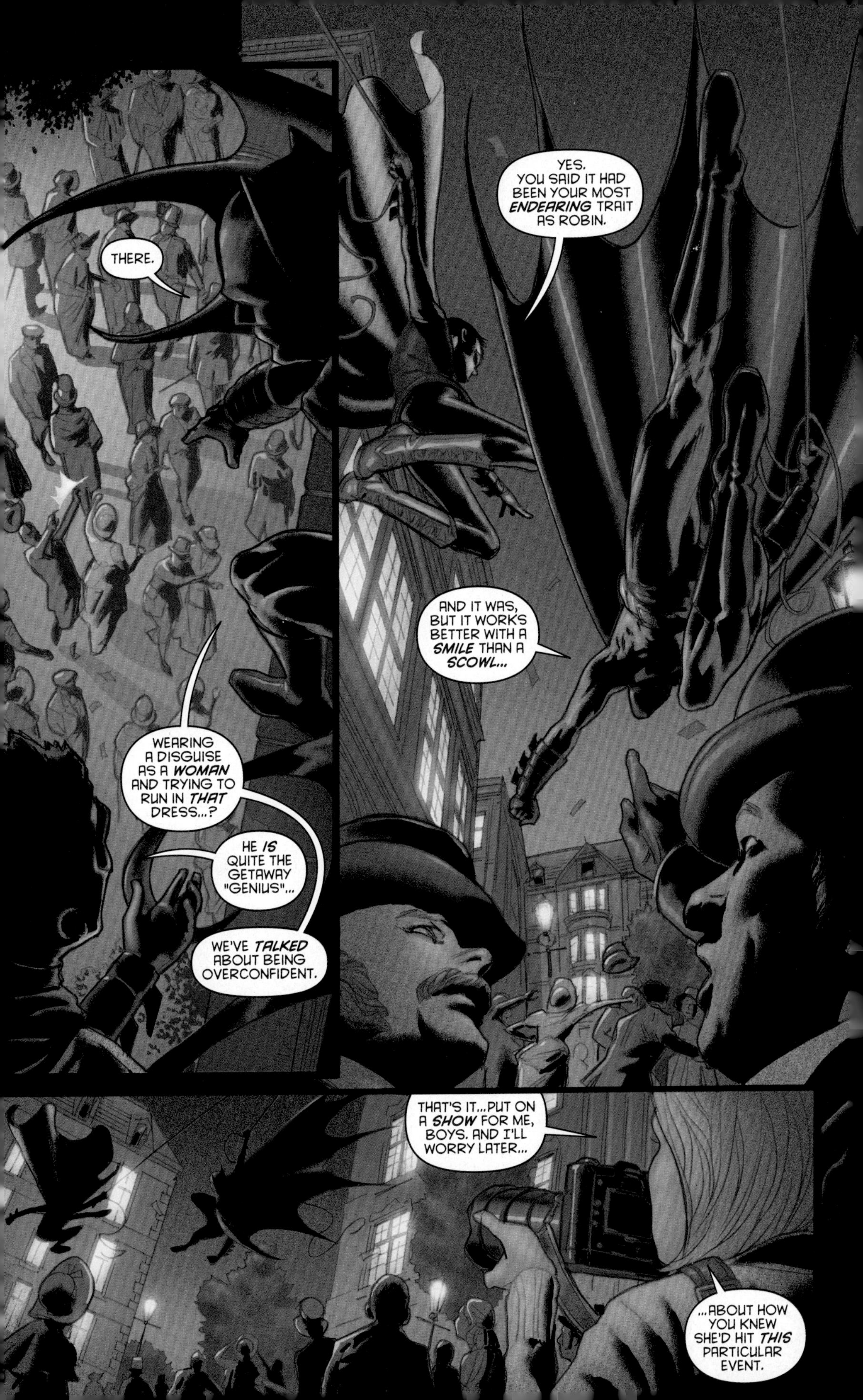
THERE.
YES. YOU SAID IT HAD BEEN YOUR MOST ENDEARING TRAIT AS ROBIN.
AND IT WAS, BUT IT WORKS BETTER WITH A SMILE THAN A SCOWL...
WEARING A DISGUISE AS A WOMAN AND TRYING TO RUN IN THAT DRESS...?
HE IS QUITE THE GETAWAY "GENIUS"...
WE'VE TALKED ABOUT BEING OVERCONFIDENT.
THAT'S IT...PUT ON A SHOW FOR ME, BOYS. AND I'LL WORRY LATER...
...ABOUT HOW YOU KNEW SHE'D HIT THIS PARTICULAR EVENT.

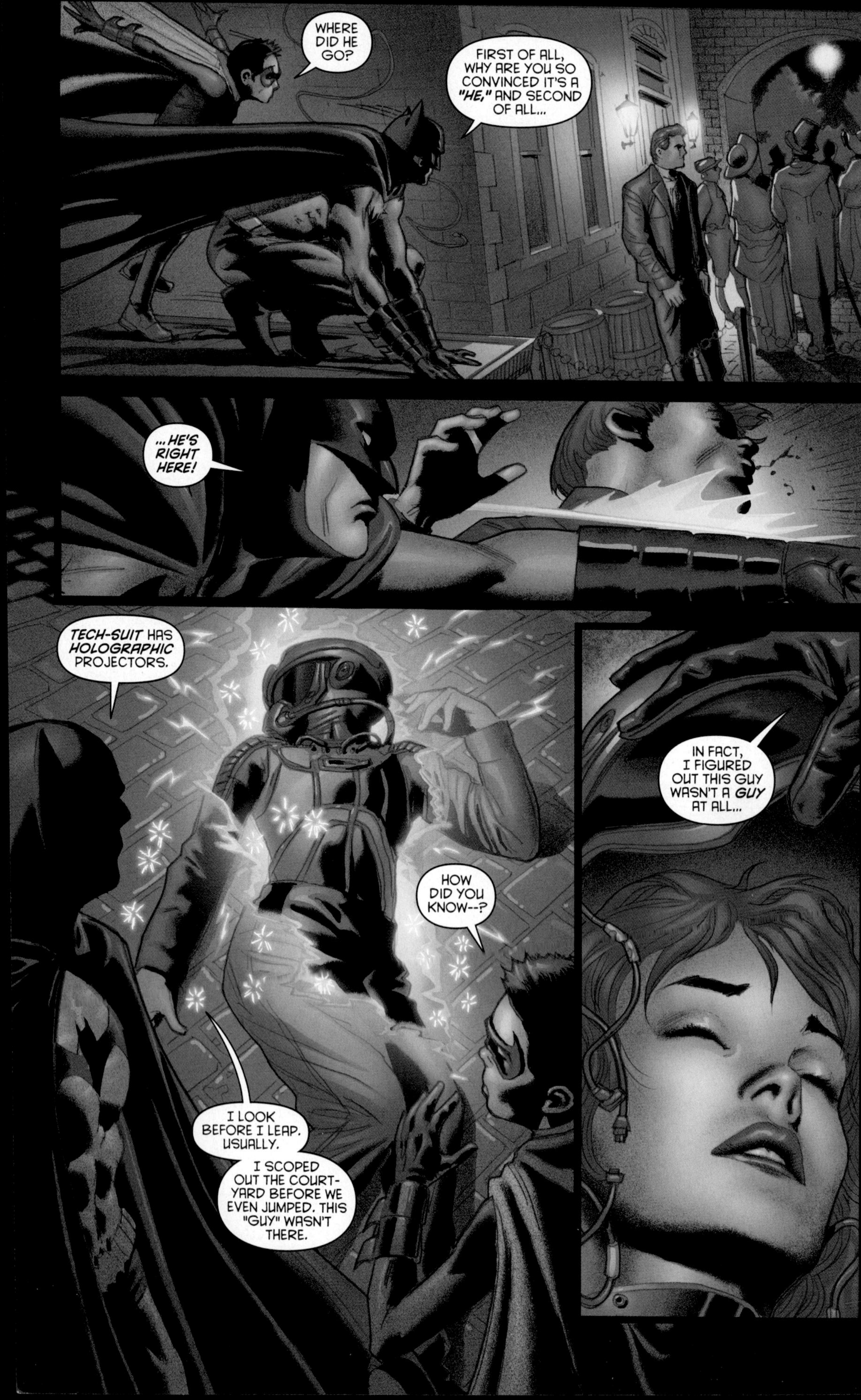
WHERE DID HE GO?
FIRST OF ALL, WHY ARE YOU SO CONVINCED IT'S A "HE," AND SECOND OF ALL...
...HE'S RIGHT HERE!
TECH-SUIT HAS HOLOGRAPHIC PROJECTORS.
HOW DID YOU KNOW--?
I LOOK BEFORE I LEAP. USUALLY.
I SCOPED OUT THE COURT-YARD BEFORE WE EVEN JUMPED. THIS "GUY" WASN'T THERE.
IN FACT, I FIGURED OUT THIS GUY WASN'T A GUY AT ALL...

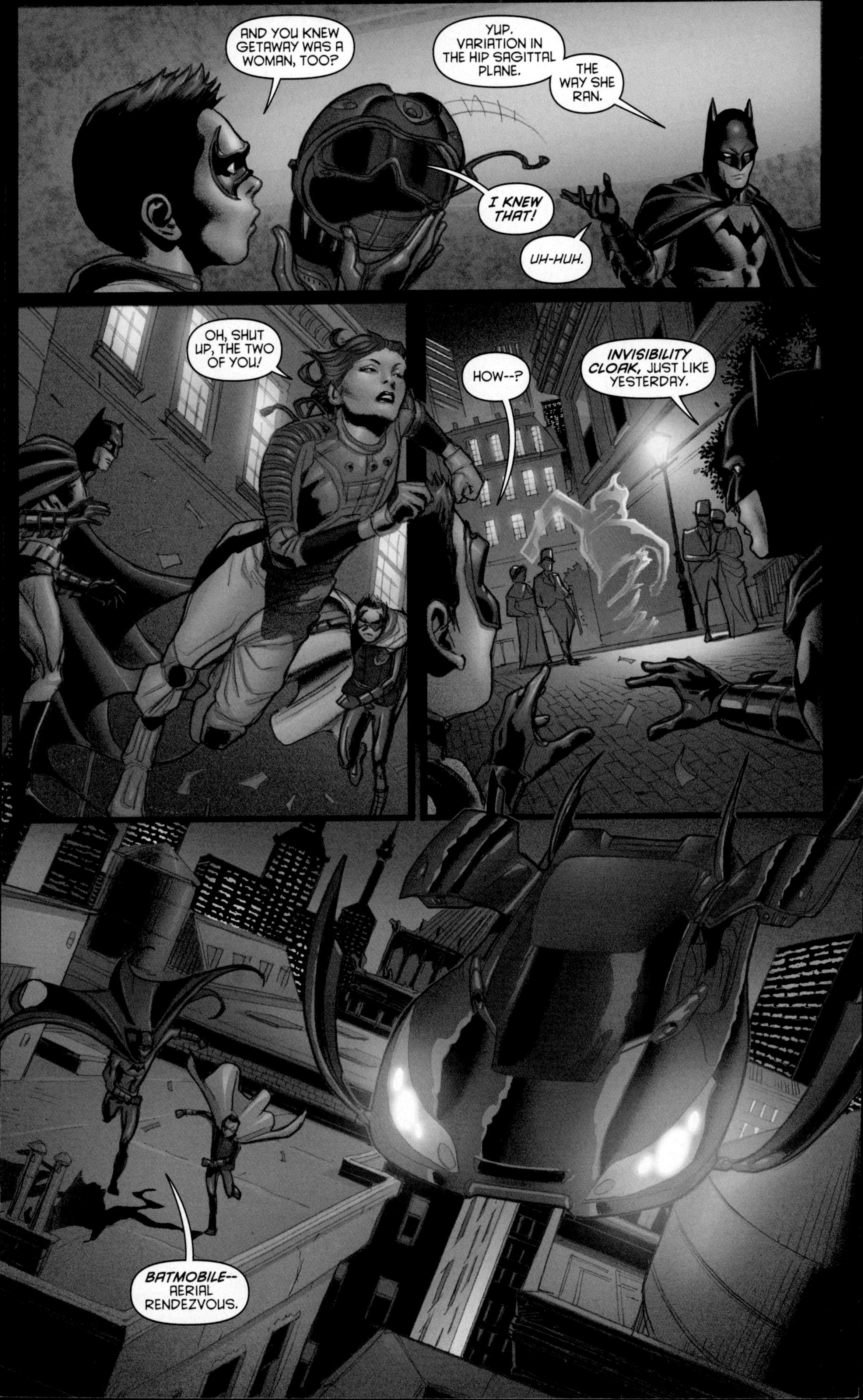
AND YOU KNEW GETAWAY WAS A WOMAN, TOO?
YUP. VARIATION IN THE HIP SAGITTAL PLANE.
THE WAY SHE RAN.
I KNEW THAT!
UH-HUH.
OH, SHUT UP, THE TWO OF YOU!
HOW--?
INVISIBILITY CLOAK, JUST LIKE YESTERDAY.
BATMOBILE-- AERIAL RENDEZVOUS.

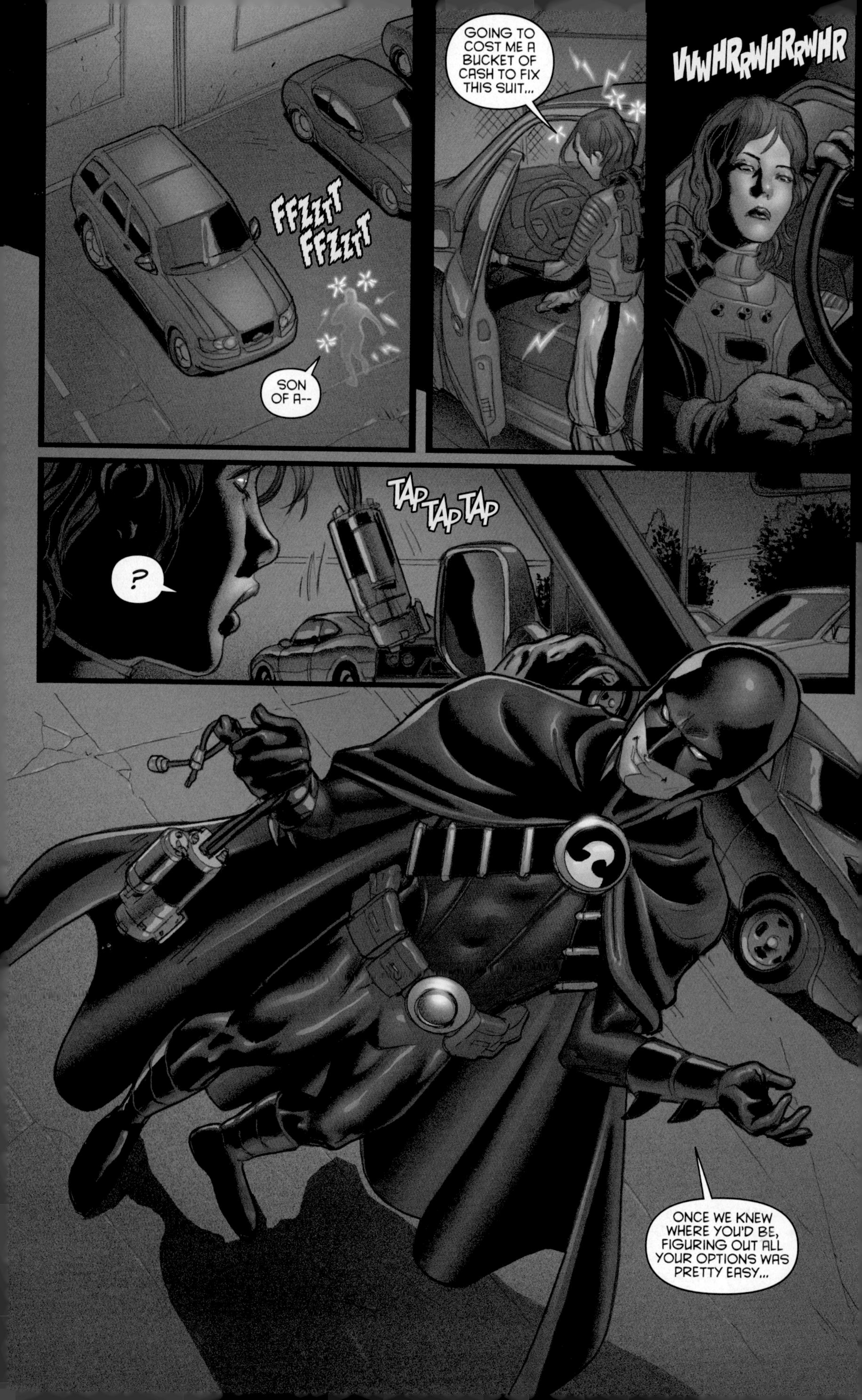
FFZZZTT
FFZZZTT
SON OF A--
GOING TO COST ME A BUCKET OF CASH TO FIX THIS SUIT...
VVWHRRWHRRWHR
TAP TAP TAP
?
ONCE WE KNEW WHERE YOU'D BE, FIGURING OUT ALL YOUR OPTIONS WAS PRETTY EASY...

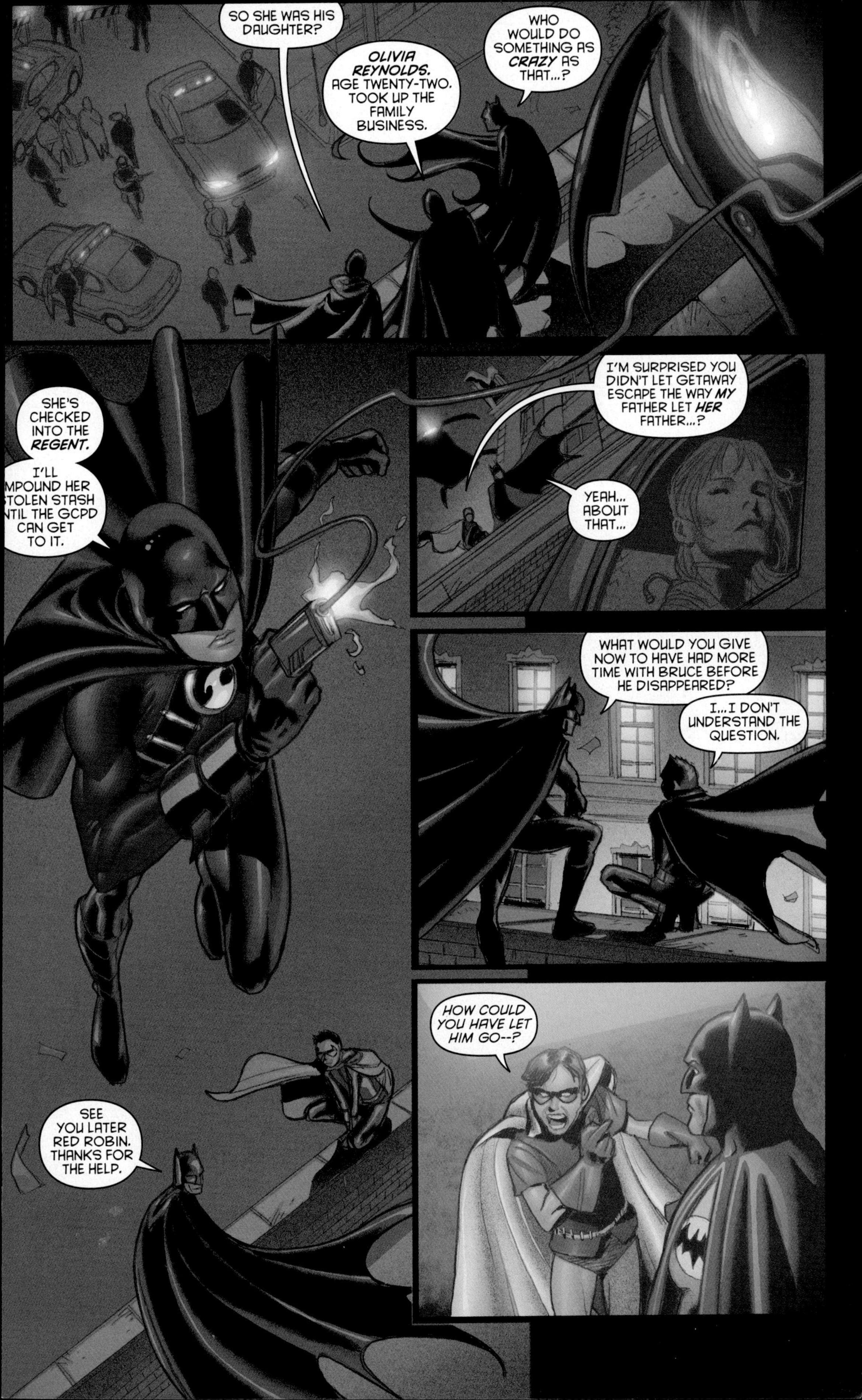
SO SHE WAS HIS DAUGHTER?
OLIVIA REYNOLDS. AGE TWENTY-TWO. TOOK UP THE FAMILY BUSINESS.
WHO WOULD DO SOMETHING AS CRAZY AS THAT...?
SHE'S CHECKED INTO THE REGENT.
I'LL MPOUND HER TOLEN STASH NTIL THE GCPD CAN GET TO IT.
I'M SURPRISED YOU DIDN'T LET GETAWAY ESCAPE THE WAY MY FATHER LET HER FATHER...?
YEAH... ABOUT THAT...
WHAT WOULD YOU GIVE NOW TO HAVE HAD MORE TIME WITH BRUCE BEFORE HE DISAPPEARED?
I... I DON'T UNDERSTAND THE QUESTION.
HOW COULD YOU HAVE LET HIM GO--?
SEE YOU LATER RED ROBIN. THANKS FOR THE HELP.

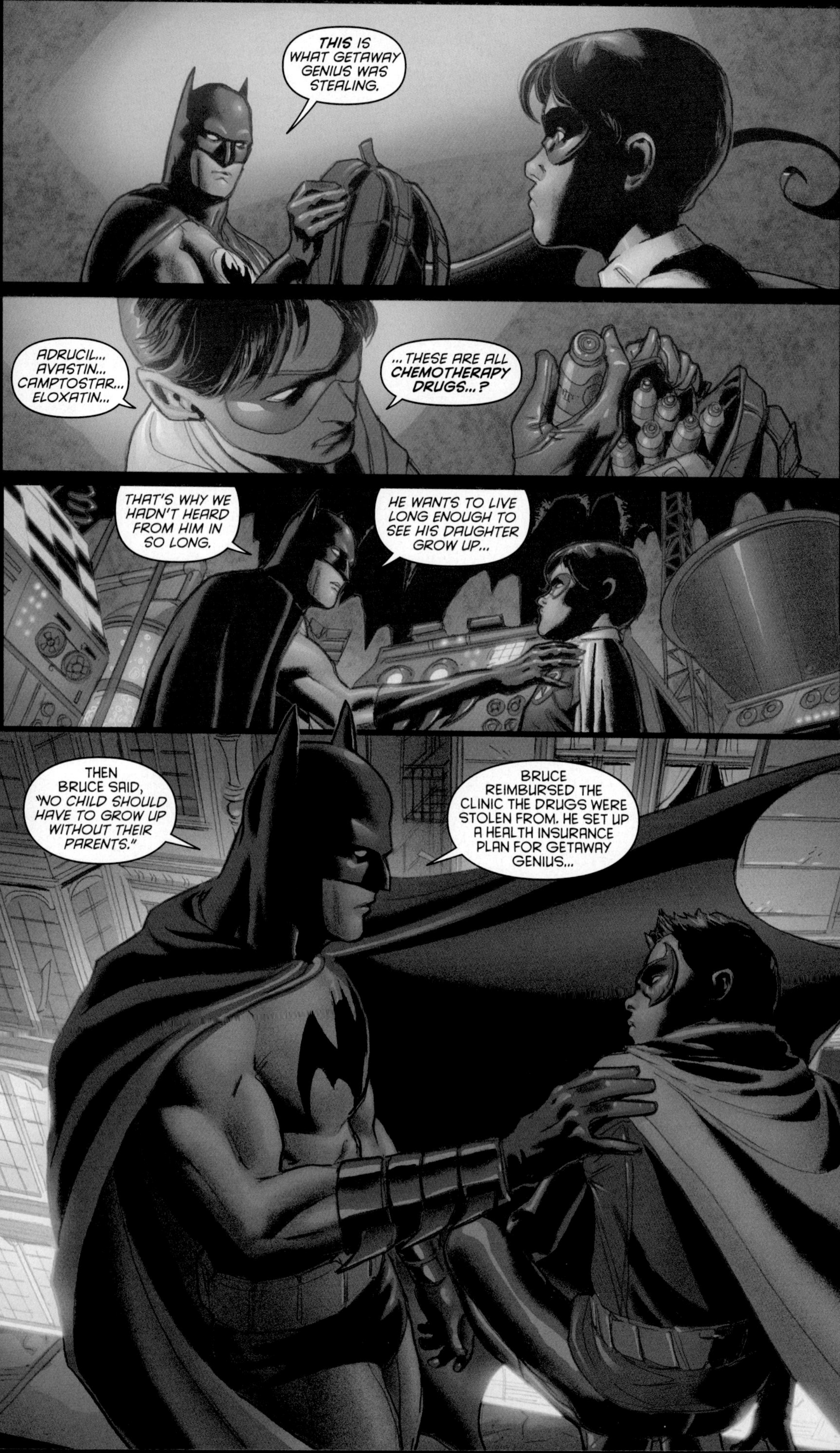

THIS IS WHAT GETAWAY GENIUS WAS STEALING.
ADRUCIL... AVASTIN... CAMPTOSTAR... ELOXATIN...
...THESE ARE ALL **CHEMOTHERAPY DRUGS...?**
THAT'S WHY WE HADN'T HEARD FROM HIM IN SO LONG.
HE WANTS TO LIVE LONG ENOUGH TO SEE HIS DAUGHTER GROW UP...
THEN BRUCE SAID, "NO CHILD SHOULD HAVE TO GROW UP WITHOUT THEIR PARENTS."
BRUCE REIMBURSED THE CLINIC THE DRUGS WERE STOLEN FROM. HE SET UP A HEALTH INSURANCE PLAN FOR GETAWAY GENIUS...

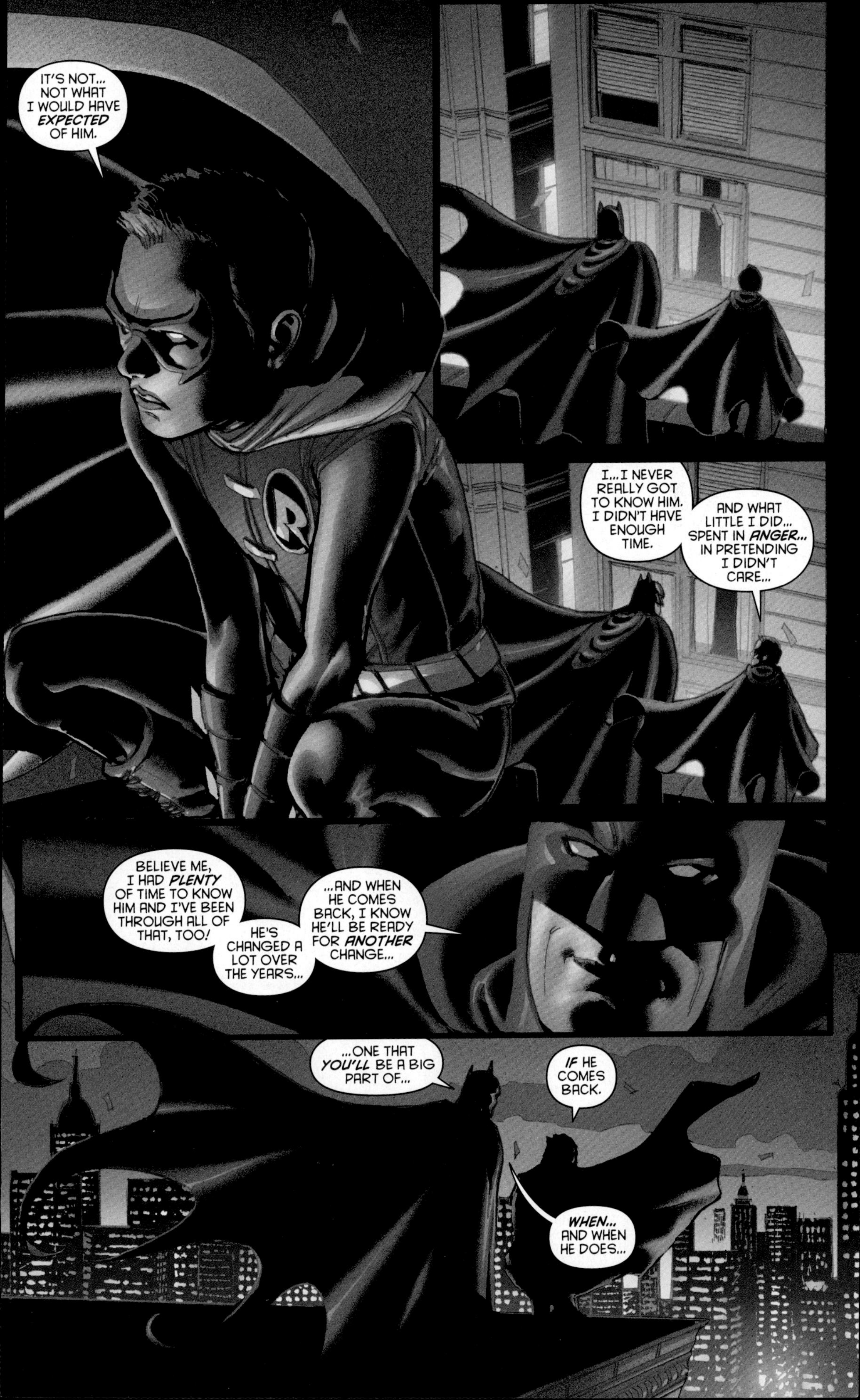
IT'S NOT... NOT WHAT I WOULD HAVE *EXPECTED* OF HIM.
I...I NEVER REALLY GOT TO KNOW HIM. I DIDN'T HAVE ENOUGH TIME.
AND WHAT LITTLE I DID... SPENT IN *ANGER...* IN PRETENDING I DIDN'T CARE...
BELIEVE ME, I HAD *PLENTY* OF TIME TO KNOW HIM AND I'VE BEEN THROUGH ALL OF THAT, TOO!
HE'S CHANGED A LOT OVER THE YEARS...
...AND WHEN HE COMES BACK, I KNOW HE'LL BE READY FOR *ANOTHER* CHANGE...
...ONE THAT *YOU'LL* BE A BIG PART OF...
IF HE COMES BACK.
WHEN... AND WHEN HE DOES...

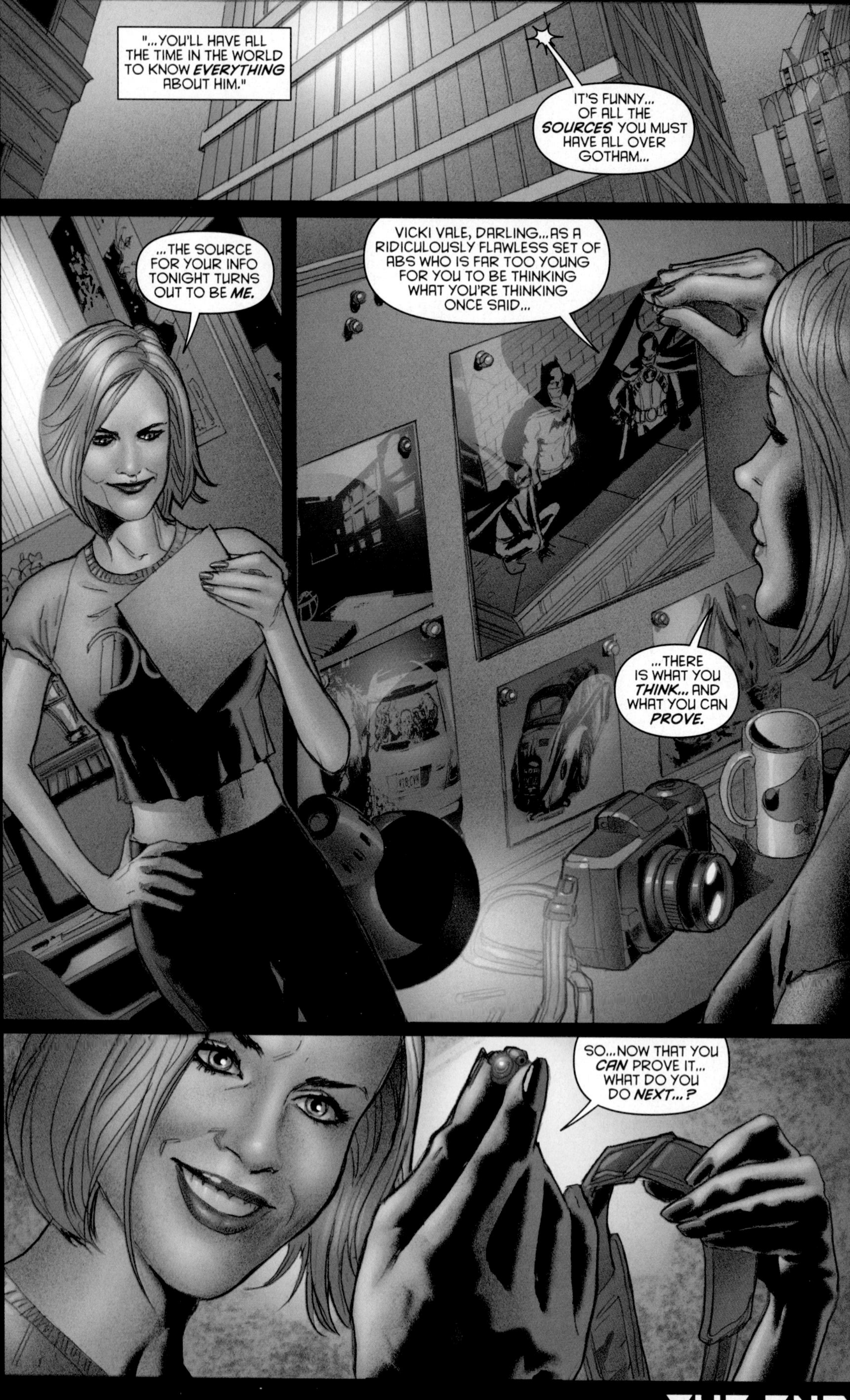

"...YOU'LL HAVE ALL THE TIME IN THE WORLD TO KNOW *EVERYTHING* ABOUT HIM."
IT'S FUNNY... OF ALL THE *SOURCES* YOU MUST HAVE ALL OVER GOTHAM...
...THE SOURCE FOR YOUR INFO TONIGHT TURNS OUT TO BE *ME.*
VICKI VALE, DARLING...AS A RIDICULOUSLY FLAWLESS SET OF ABS WHO IS FAR TOO YOUNG FOR YOU TO BE THINKING WHAT YOU'RE THINKING ONCE SAID...
...THERE IS WHAT YOU *THINK...* AND WHAT YOU CAN *PROVE.*
SO...NOW THAT YOU *CAN* PROVE IT... WHAT DO YOU DO *NEXT...?*

THE END

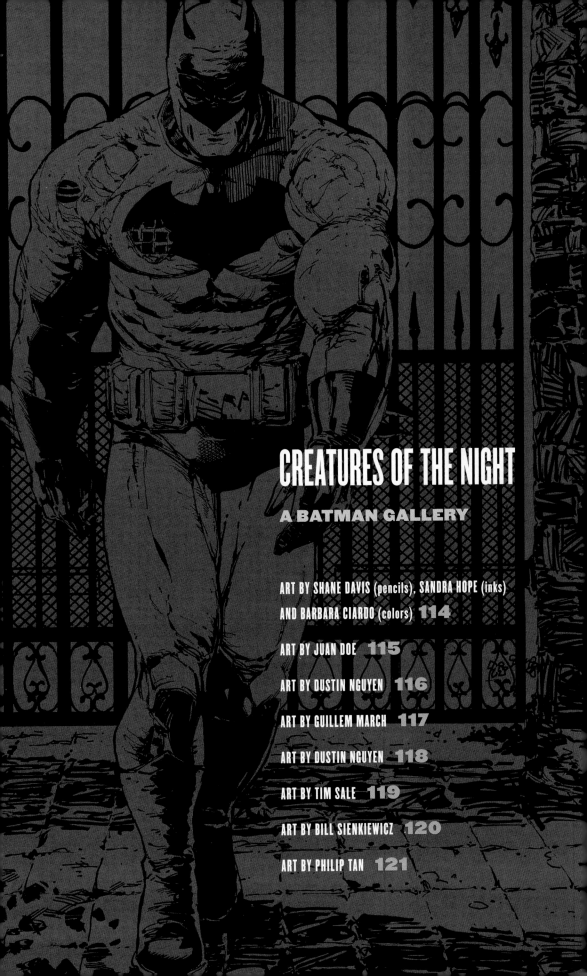

CREATURES OF THE NIGHT

A BATMAN GALLERY

ART BY SHANE DAVIS (pencils), SANDRA HOPE (inks)
AND BARBARA CIARDO (colors) 114

ART BY JUAN DOE 115

ART BY DUSTIN NGUYEN 116

ART BY GUILLEM MARCH 117

ART BY DUSTIN NGUYEN 118

ART BY TIM SALE 119

ART BY BILL SIENKIEWICZ 120

ART BY PHILIP TAN 121

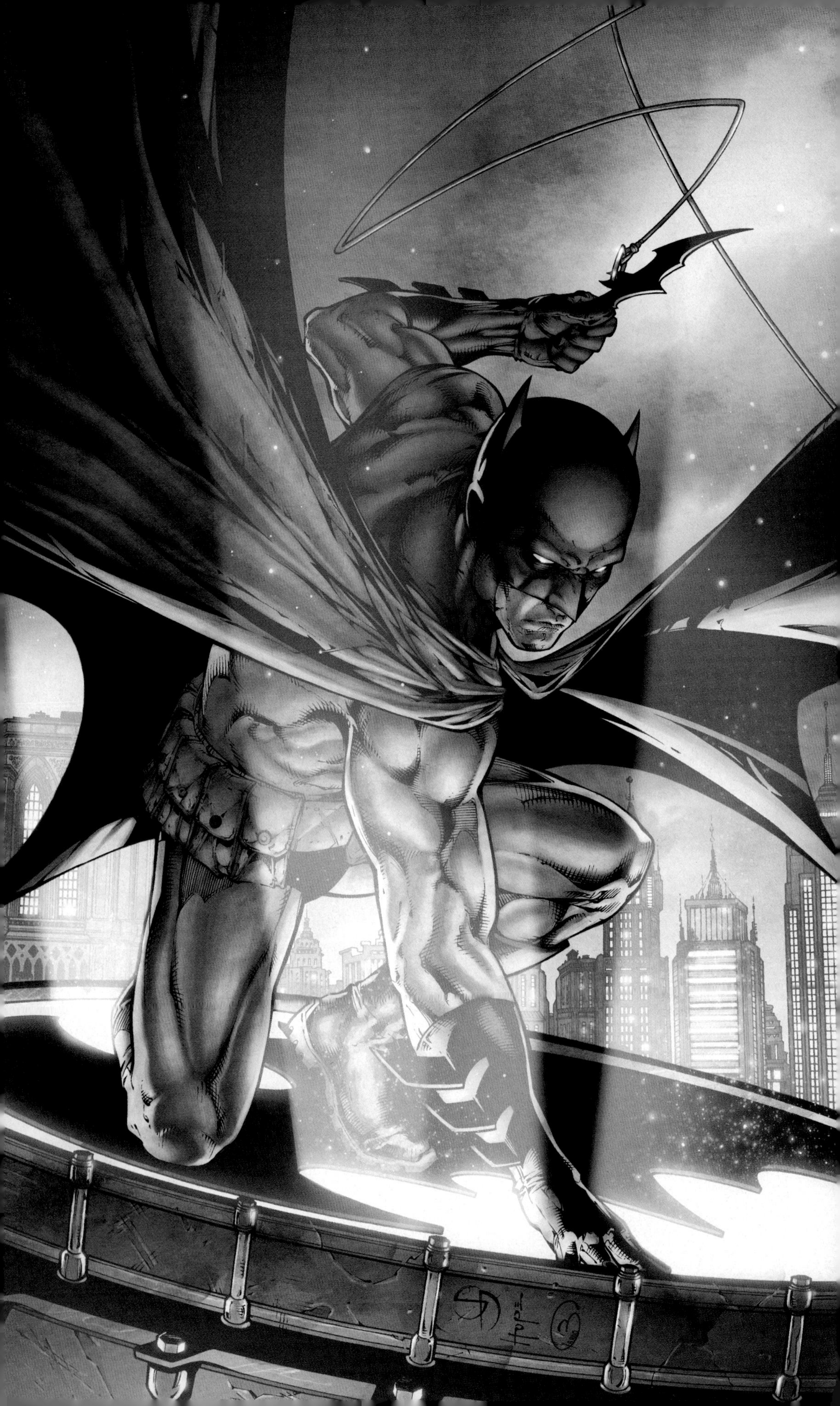

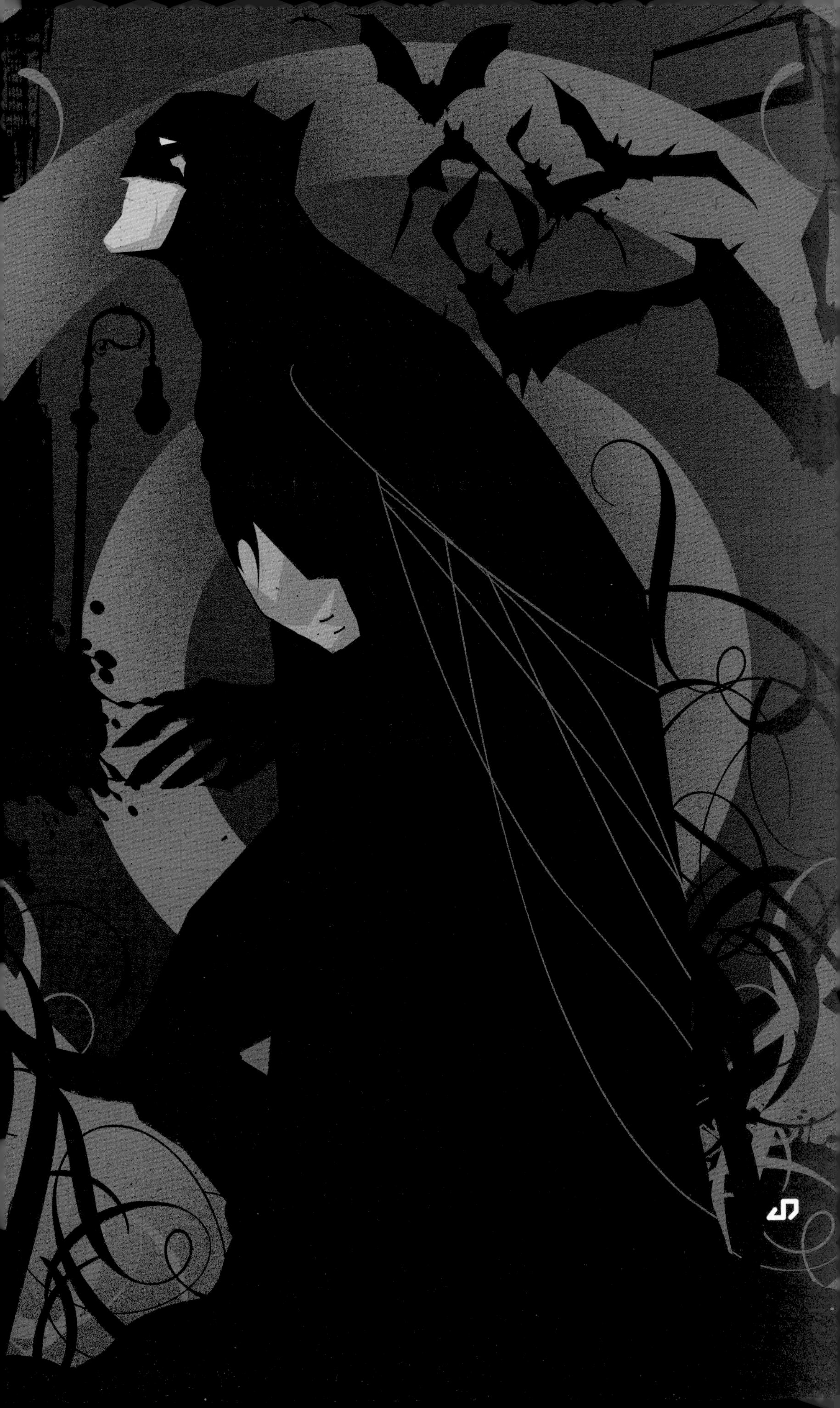

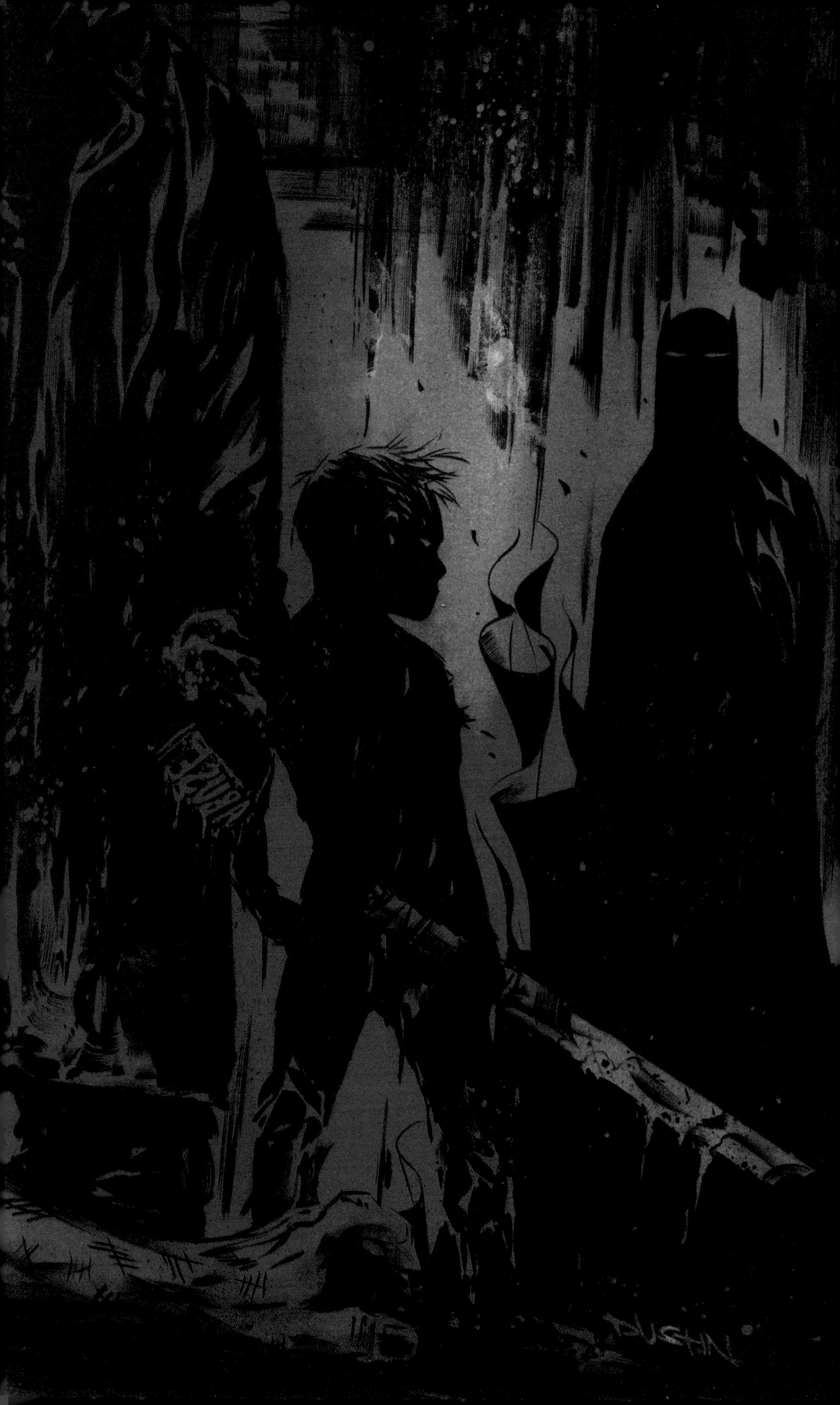

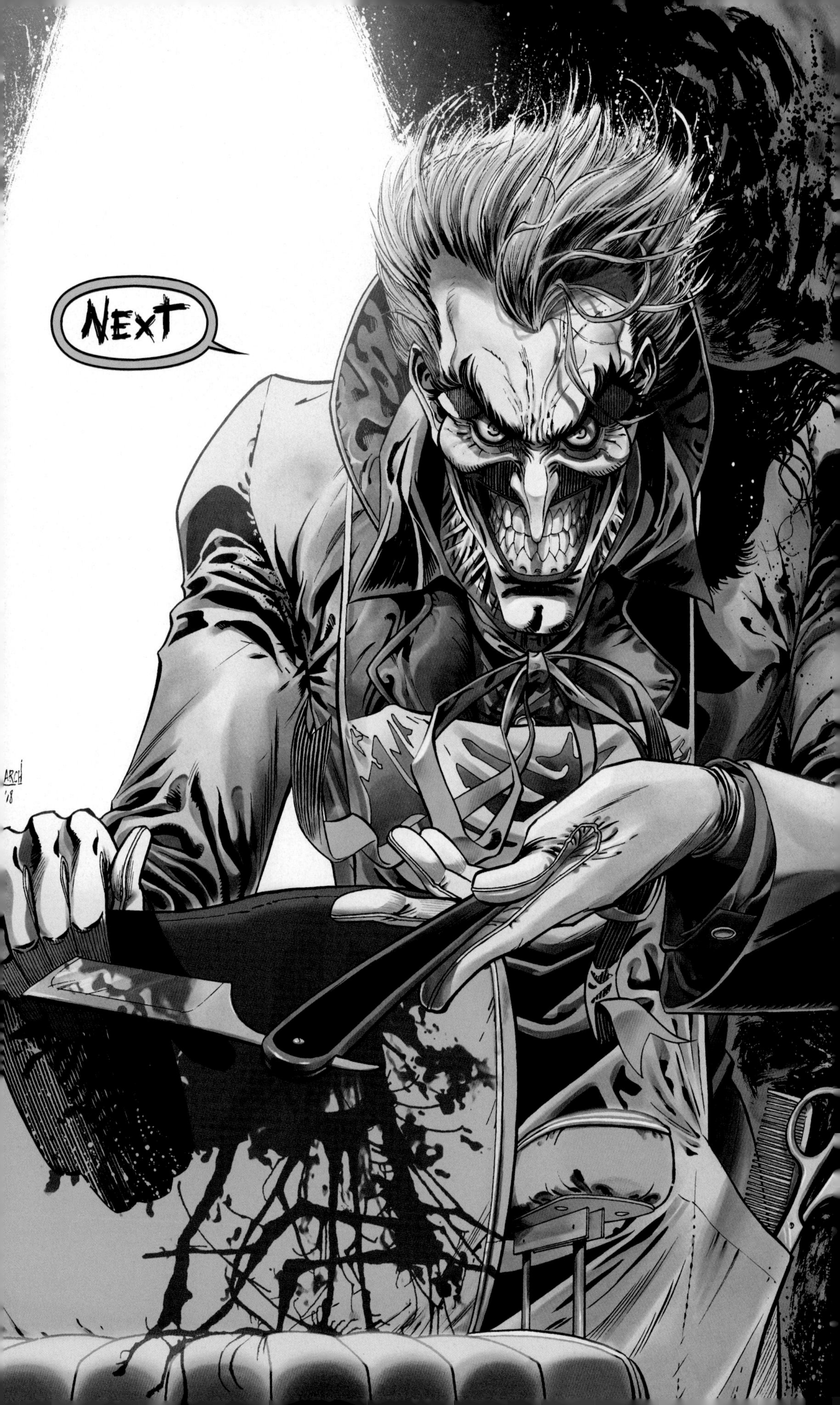
NEXT
ARCH '18

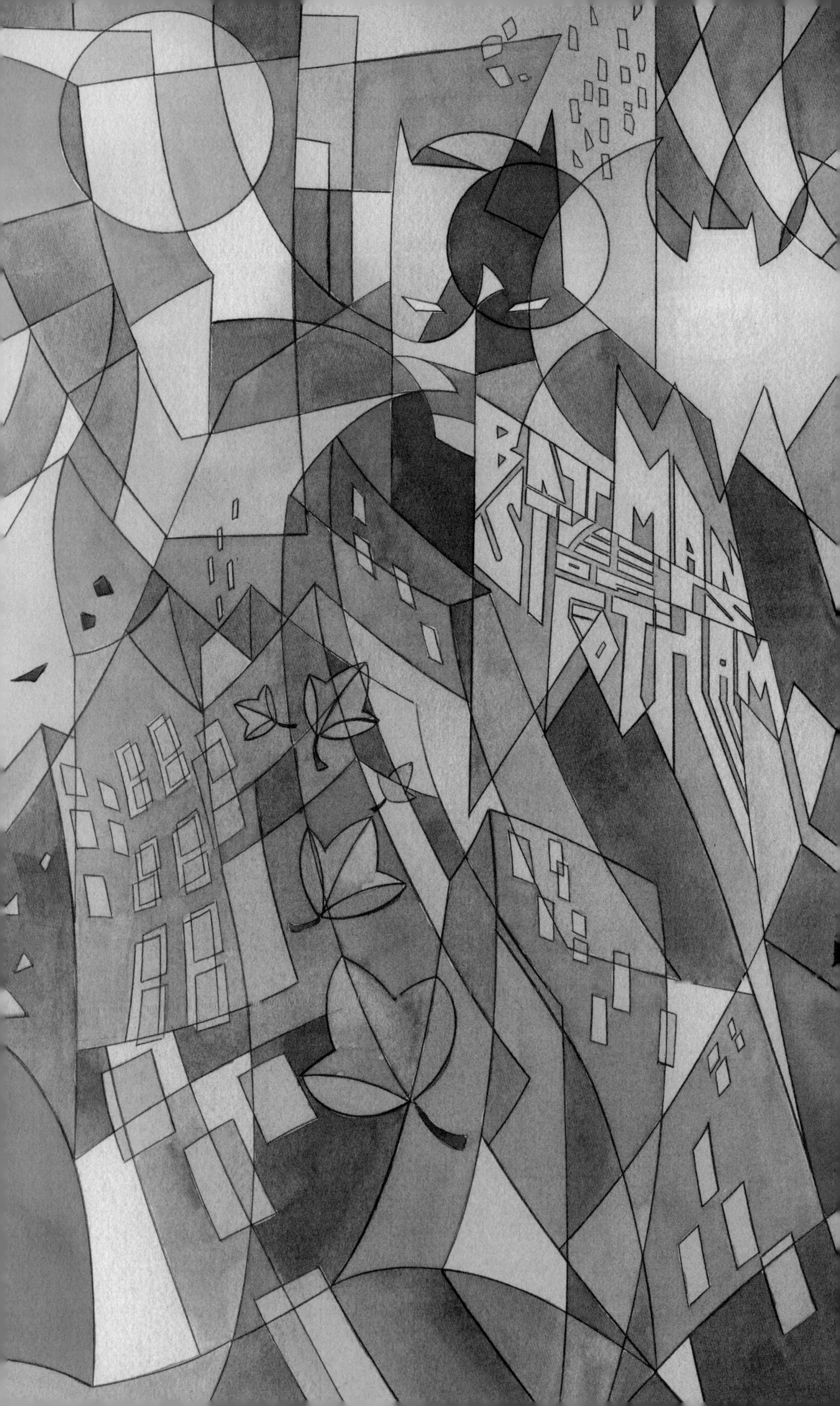
BATMAN
GOTHAM

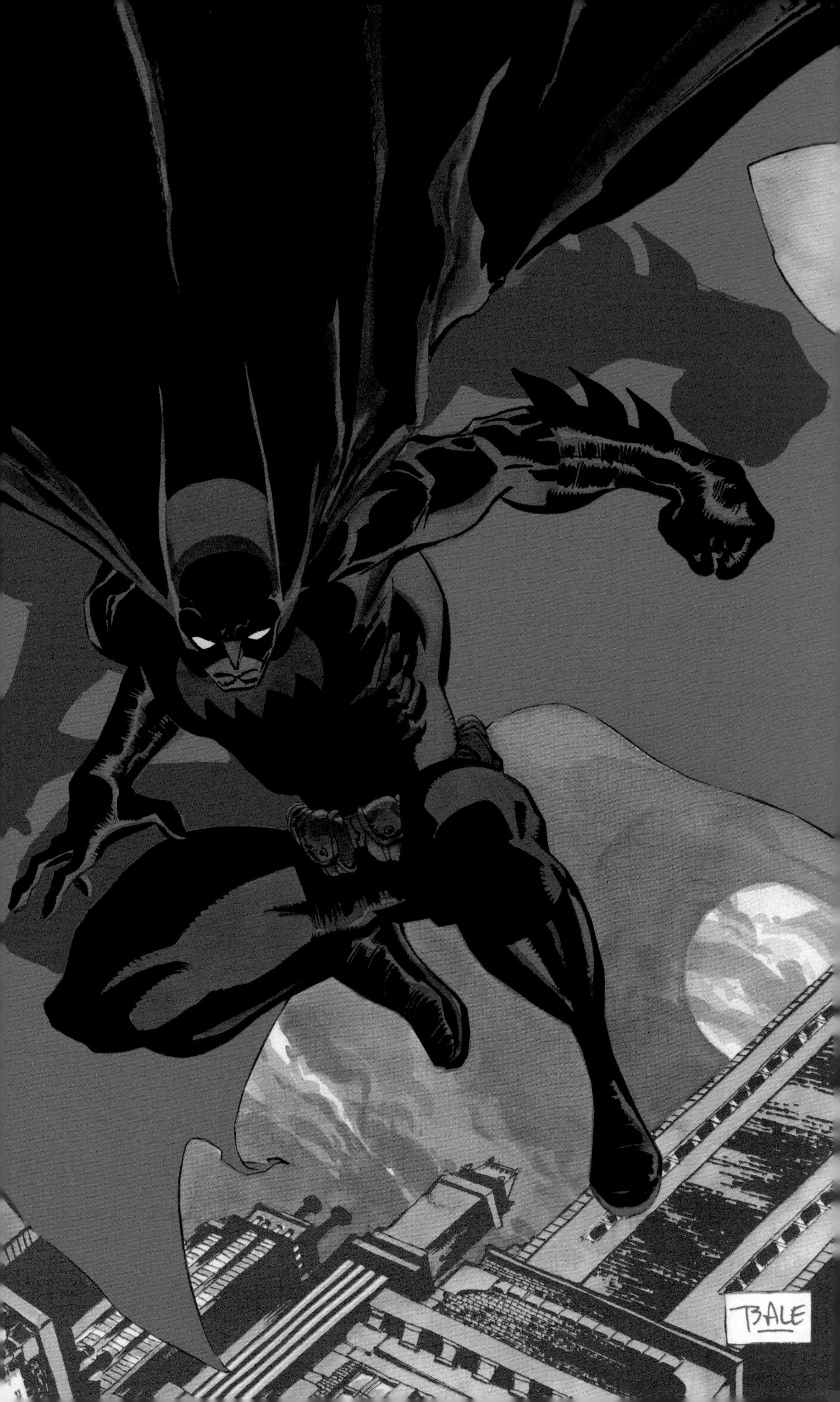
BALE

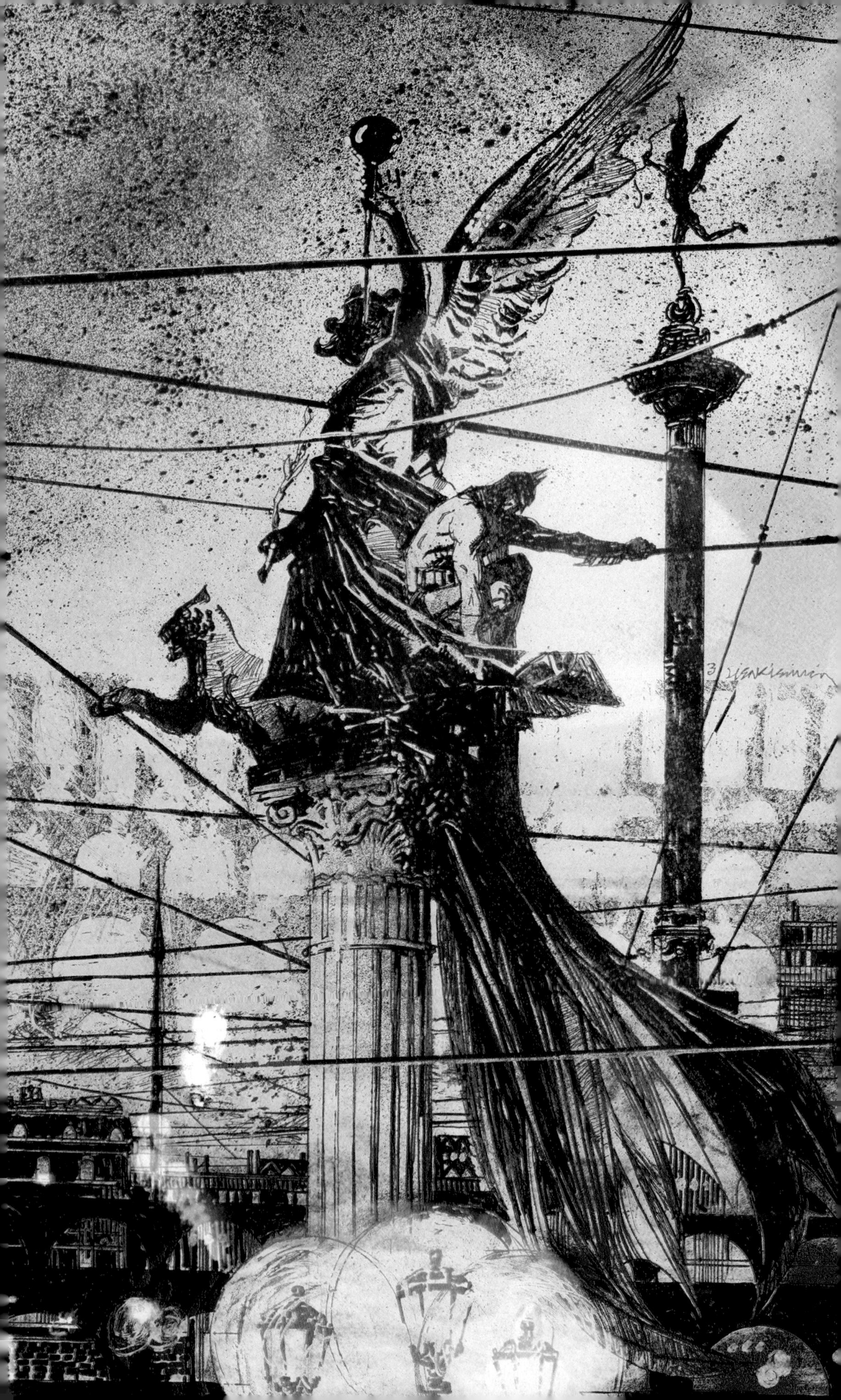

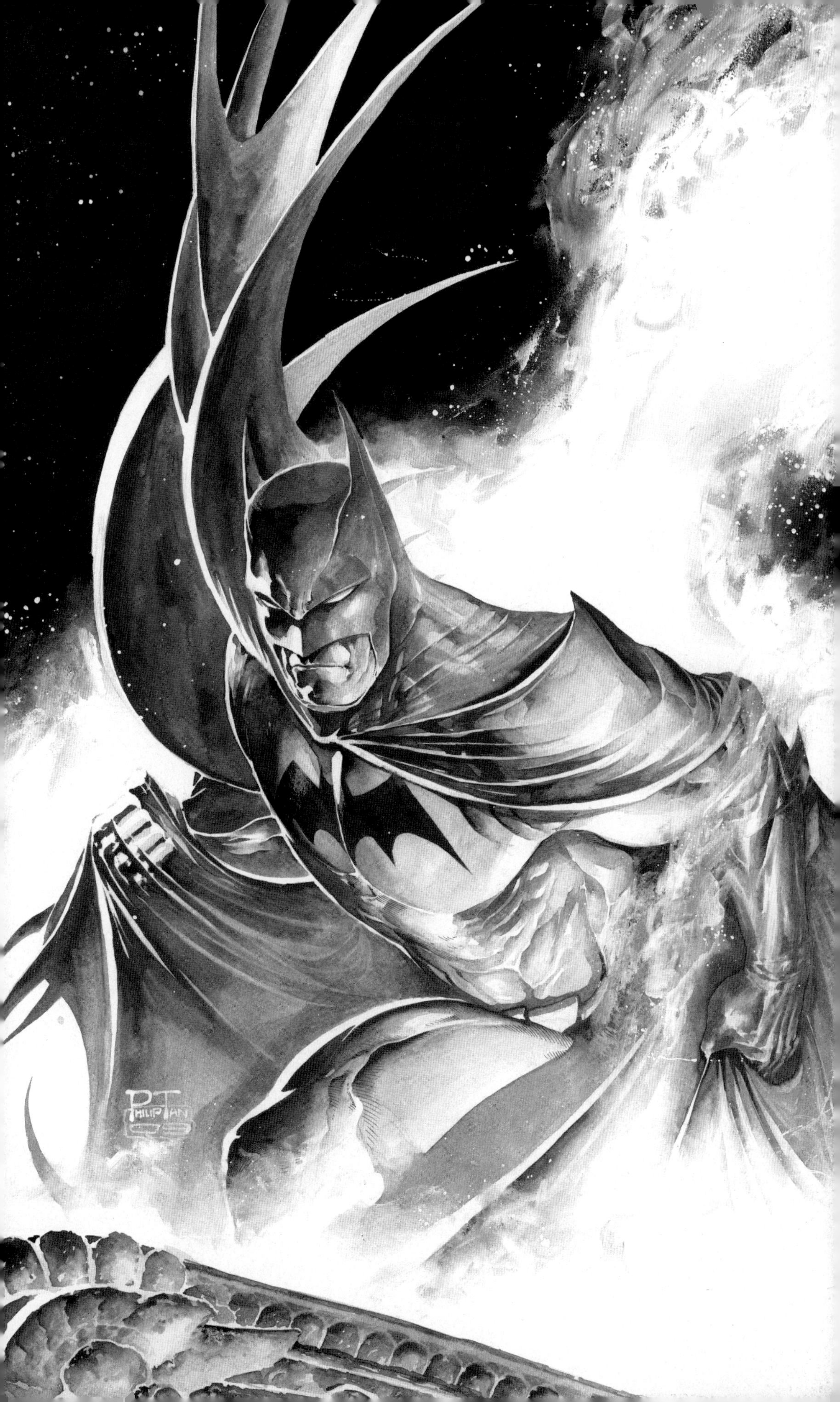
PHILIP TAN
09

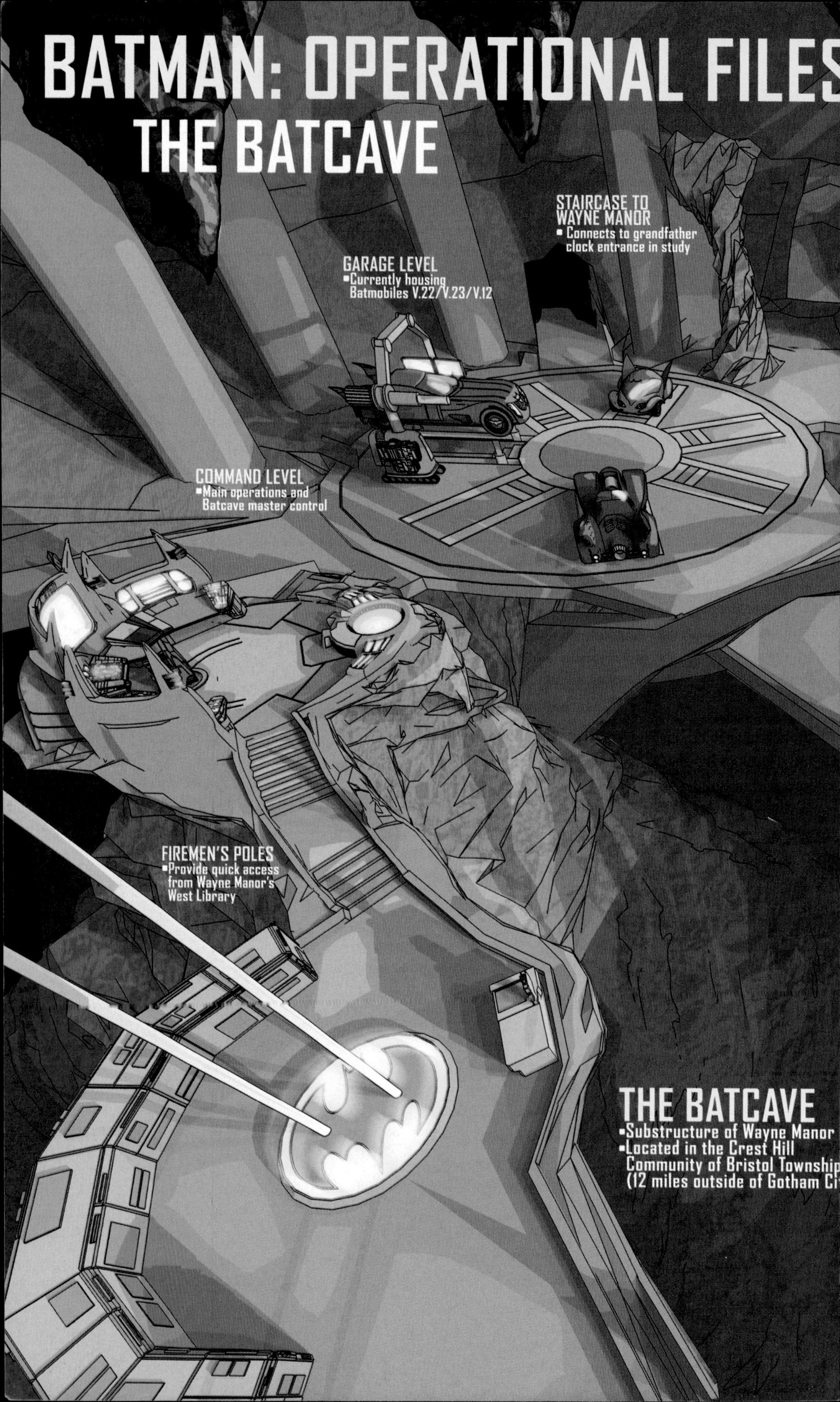
BATMAN: OPERATIONAL FILES
THE BATCAVE
STAIRCASE TO WAYNE MANOR
• Connects to grandfather clock entrance in study
GARAGE LEVEL
•Currently housing Batmobiles V.22/V.23/V.12
COMMAND LEVEL
•Main operations and Batcave master control
FIREMEN'S POLES
•Provide quick access from Wayne Manor's West Library
THE BATCAVE
•Substructure of Wayne Manor
•Located in the Crest Hill Community of Bristol Township
(12 miles outside of Gotham Ci

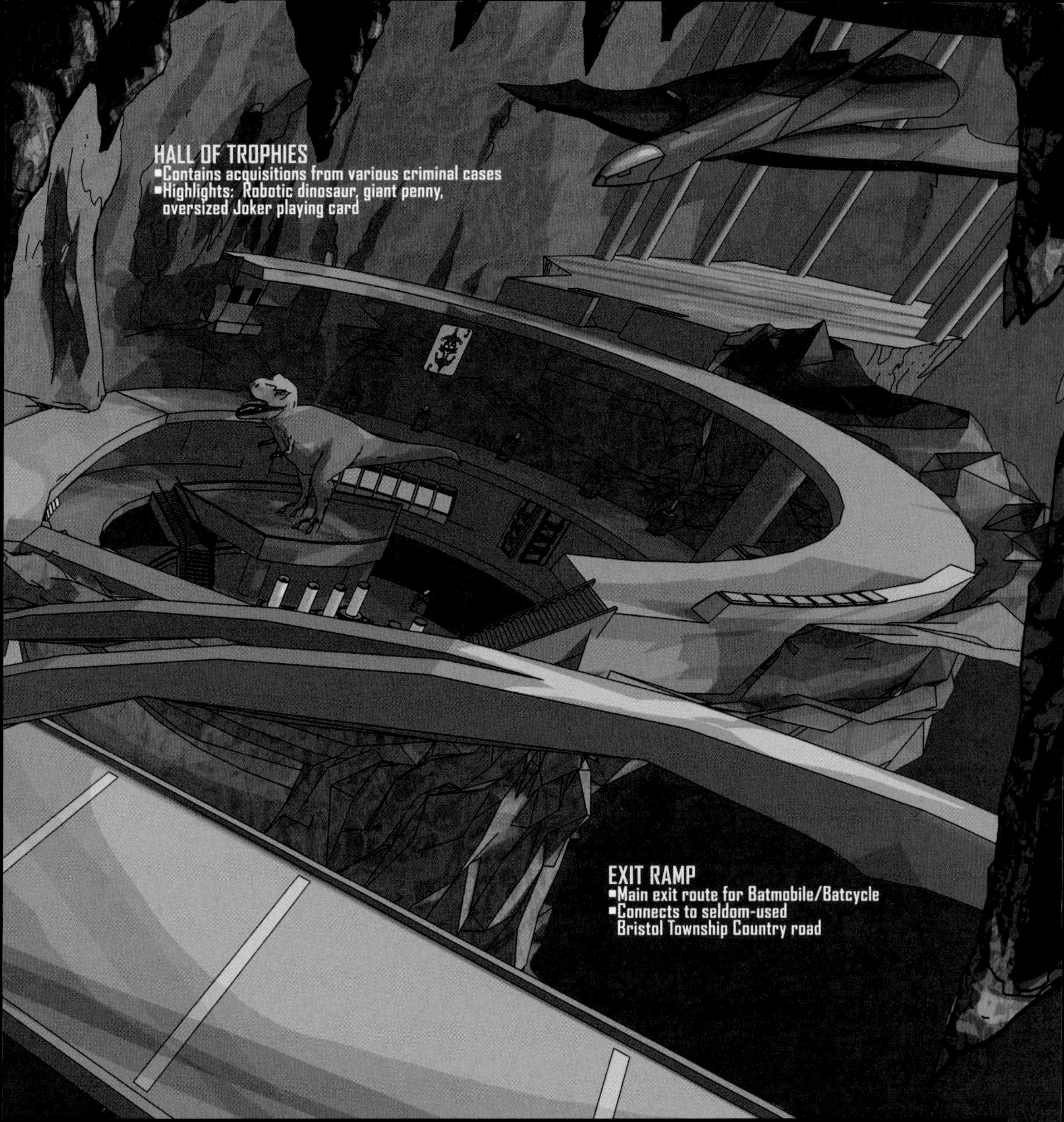
HALL OF TROPHIES
•Contains acquisitions from various criminal cases
•Highlights: Robotic dinosaur, giant penny, oversized Joker playing card
EXIT RAMP
•Main exit route for Batmobile/Batcycle
•Connects to seldom-used Bristol Township Country road

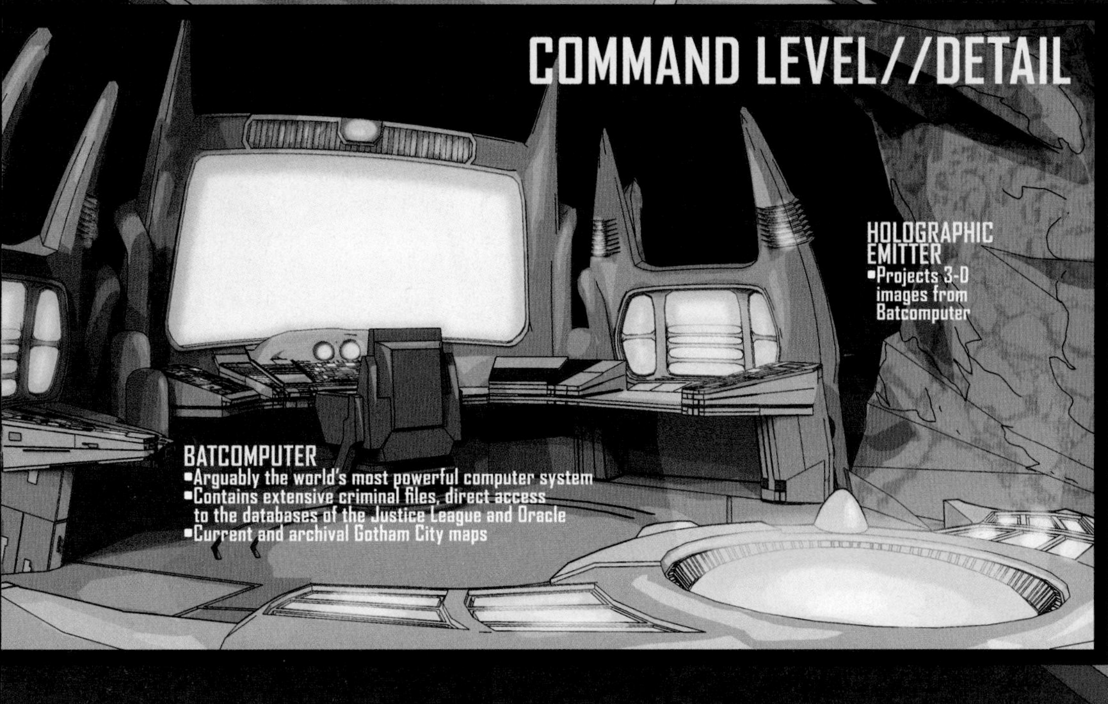
COMMAND LEVEL//DETAIL
HOLOGRAPHIC EMITTER
•Projects 3-D images from Batcomputer
BATCOMPUTER
•Arguably the world's most powerful computer system
•Contains extensive criminal files, direct access to the databases of the Justice League and Oracle
•Current and archival Gotham City maps

GARAGE LEVEL// DETAIL

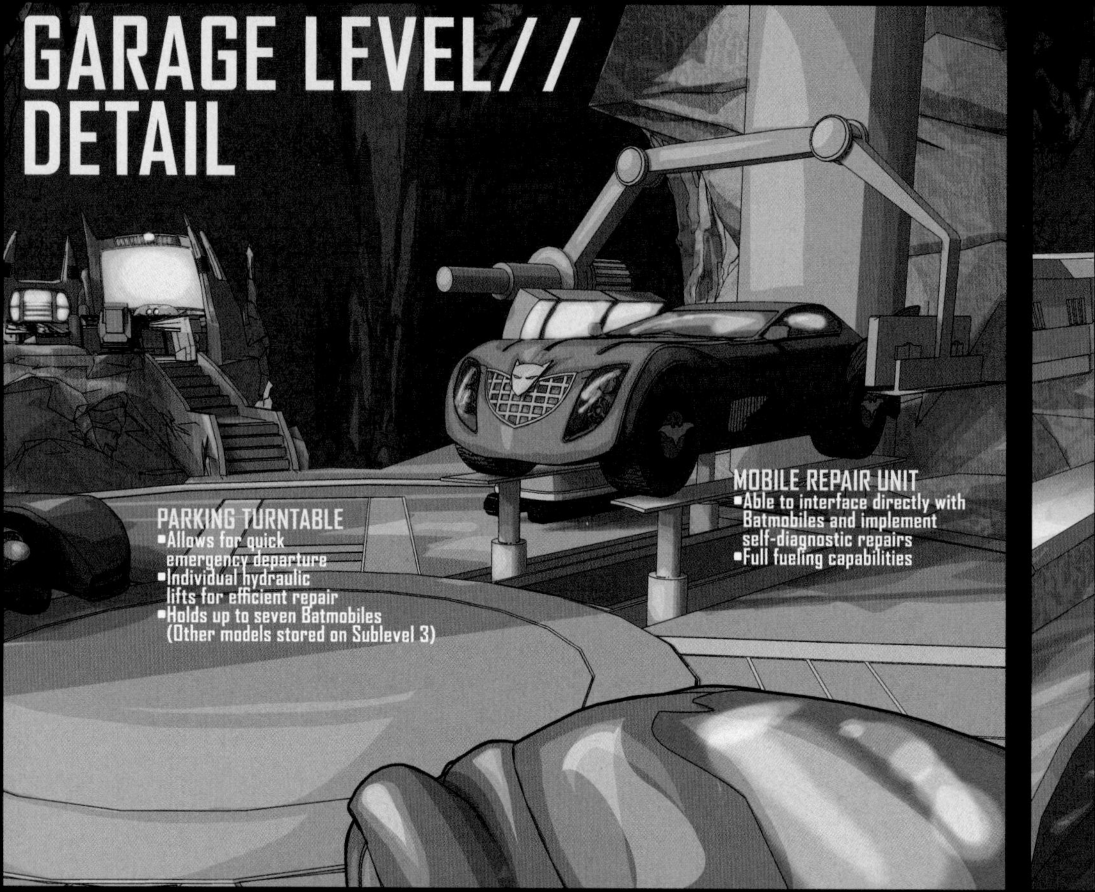
PARKING TURNTABLE
•Allows for quick emergency departure
•Individual hydraulic lifts for efficient repair
•Holds up to seven Batmobiles (Other models stored on Sublevel 3)
MOBILE REPAIR UNIT
•Able to interface directly with Batmobiles and implement self-diagnostic repairs
•Full fueling capabilities

SEA LEVEL A//DETAIL

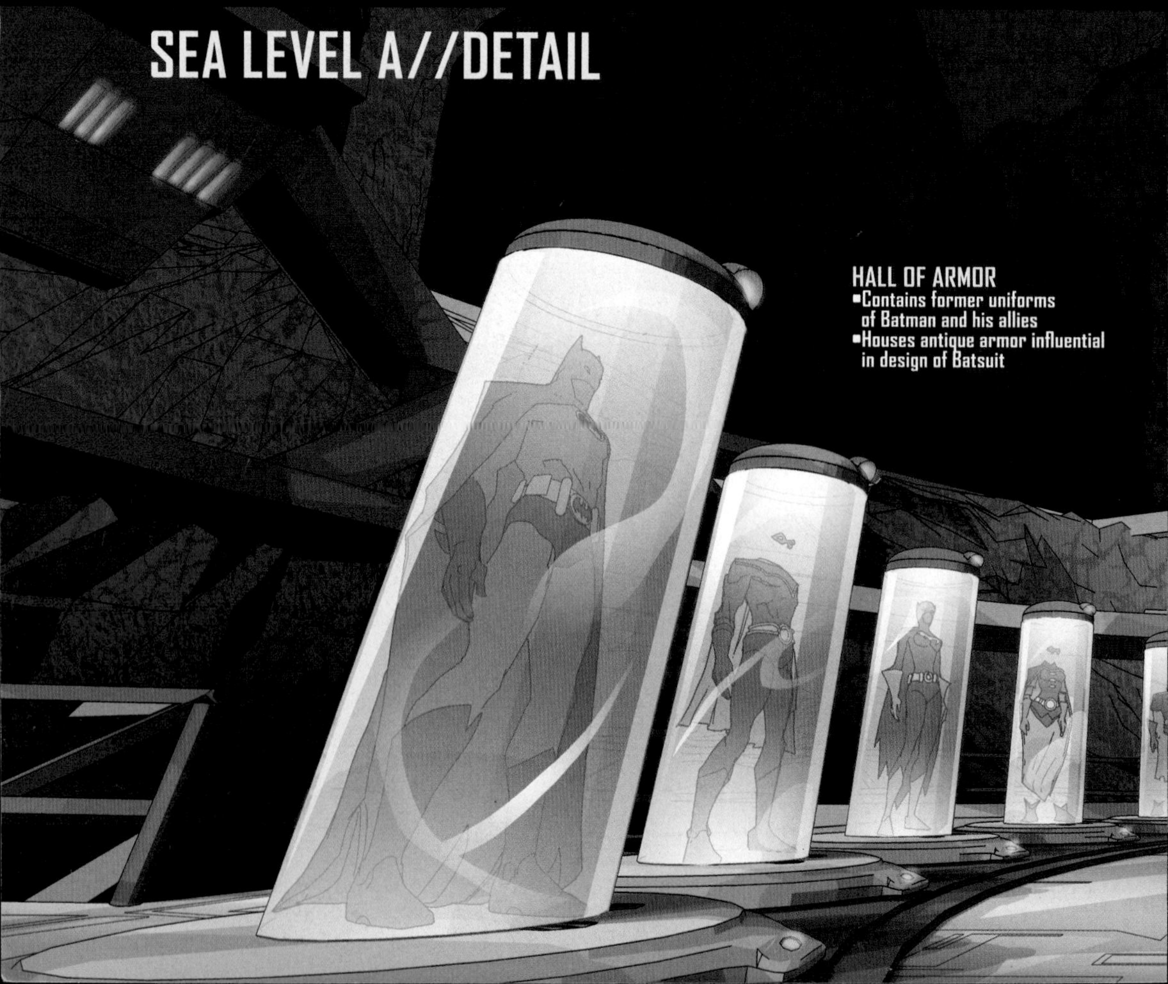
HALL OF ARMOR
•Contains former uniforms of Batman and his allies
•Houses antique armor influential in design of Batsuit

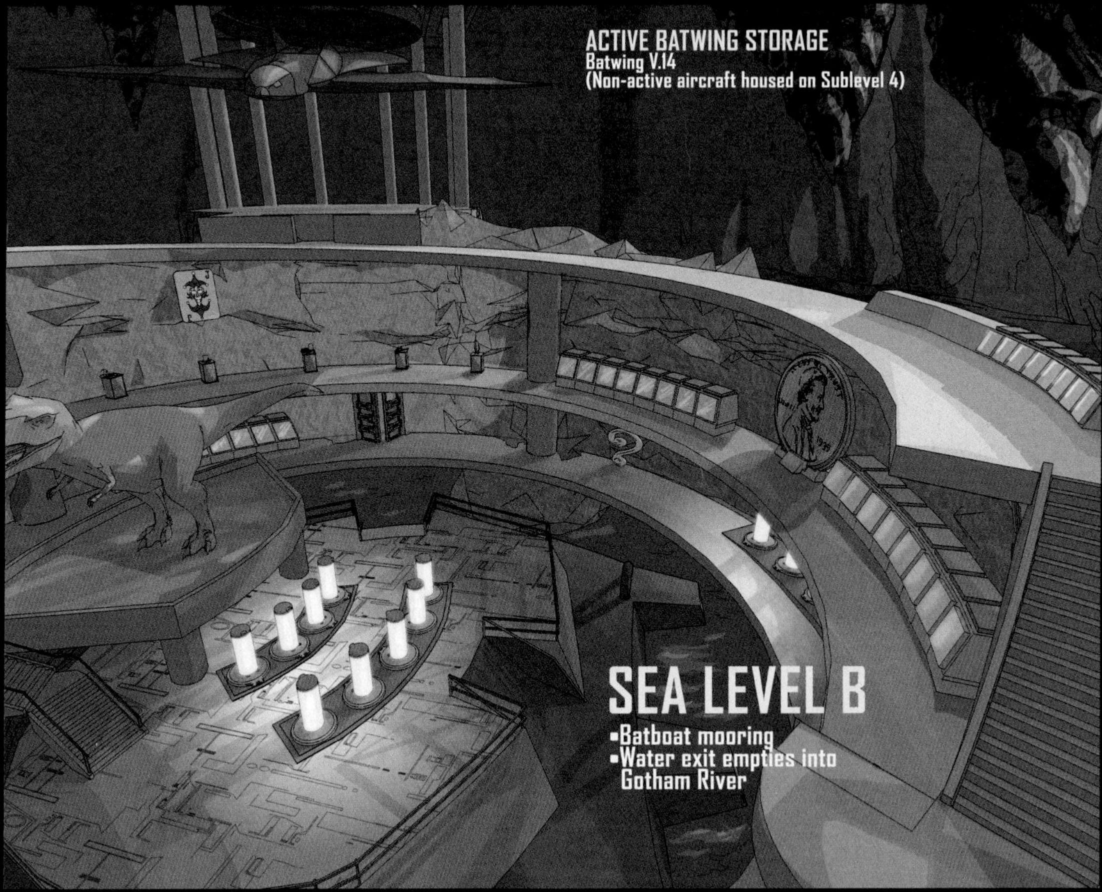
ACTIVE BATWING STORAGE
Batwing V.14
(Non-active aircraft housed on Sublevel 4)
SEA LEVEL B
▪Batboat mooring
▪Water exit empties into Gotham River

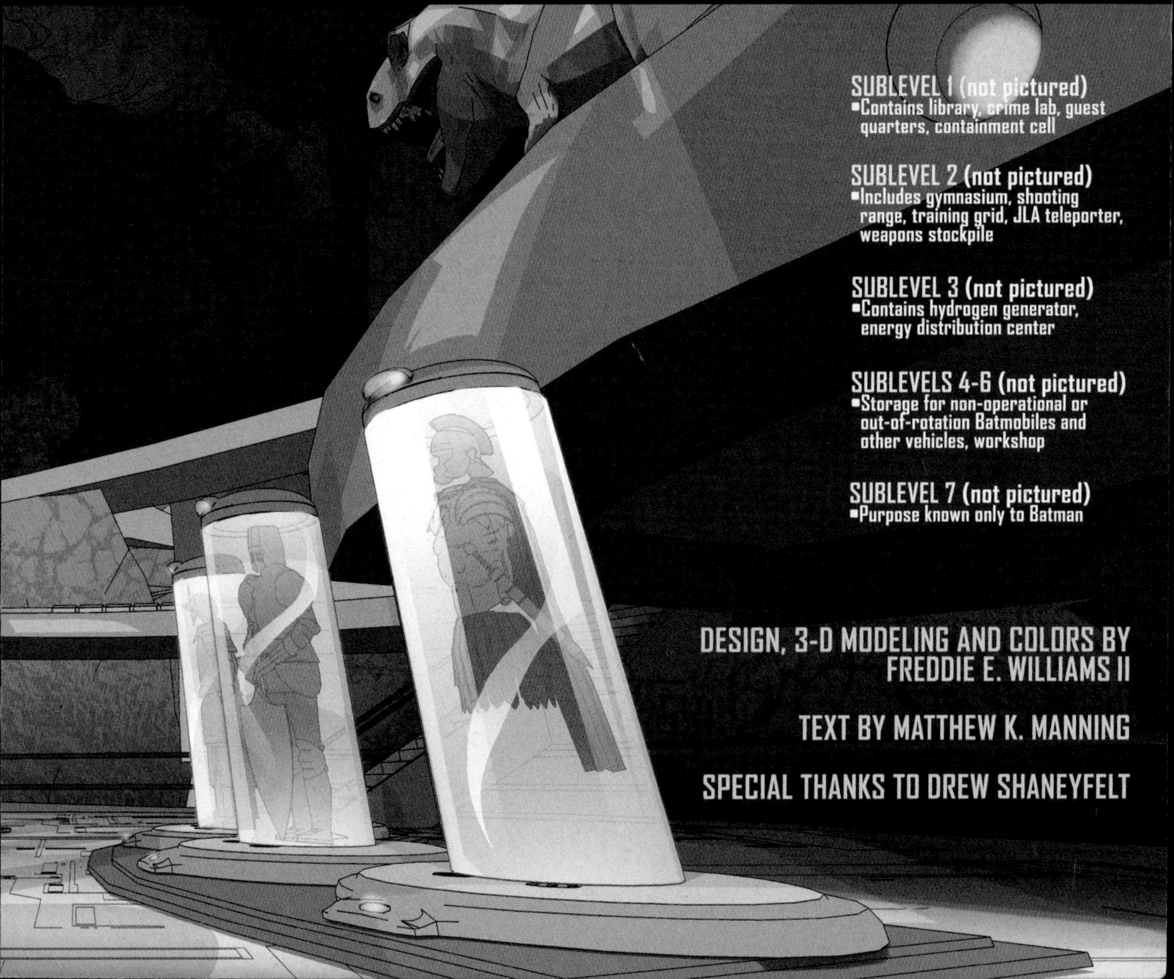
SUBLEVEL 1 (not pictured)
▪Contains library, crime lab, guest quarters, containment cell
SUBLEVEL 2 (not pictured)
▪Includes gymnasium, shooting range, training grid, JLA teleporter, weapons stockpile
SUBLEVEL 3 (not pictured)
▪Contains hydrogen generator, energy distribution center
SUBLEVELS 4-6 (not pictured)
▪Storage for non-operational or out-of-rotation Batmobiles and other vehicles, workshop
SUBLEVEL 7 (not pictured)
▪Purpose known only to Batman
DESIGN, 3-D MODELING AND COLORS BY FREDDIE E. WILLIAMS II
TEXT BY MATTHEW K. MANNING
SPECIAL THANKS TO DREW SHANEYFELT

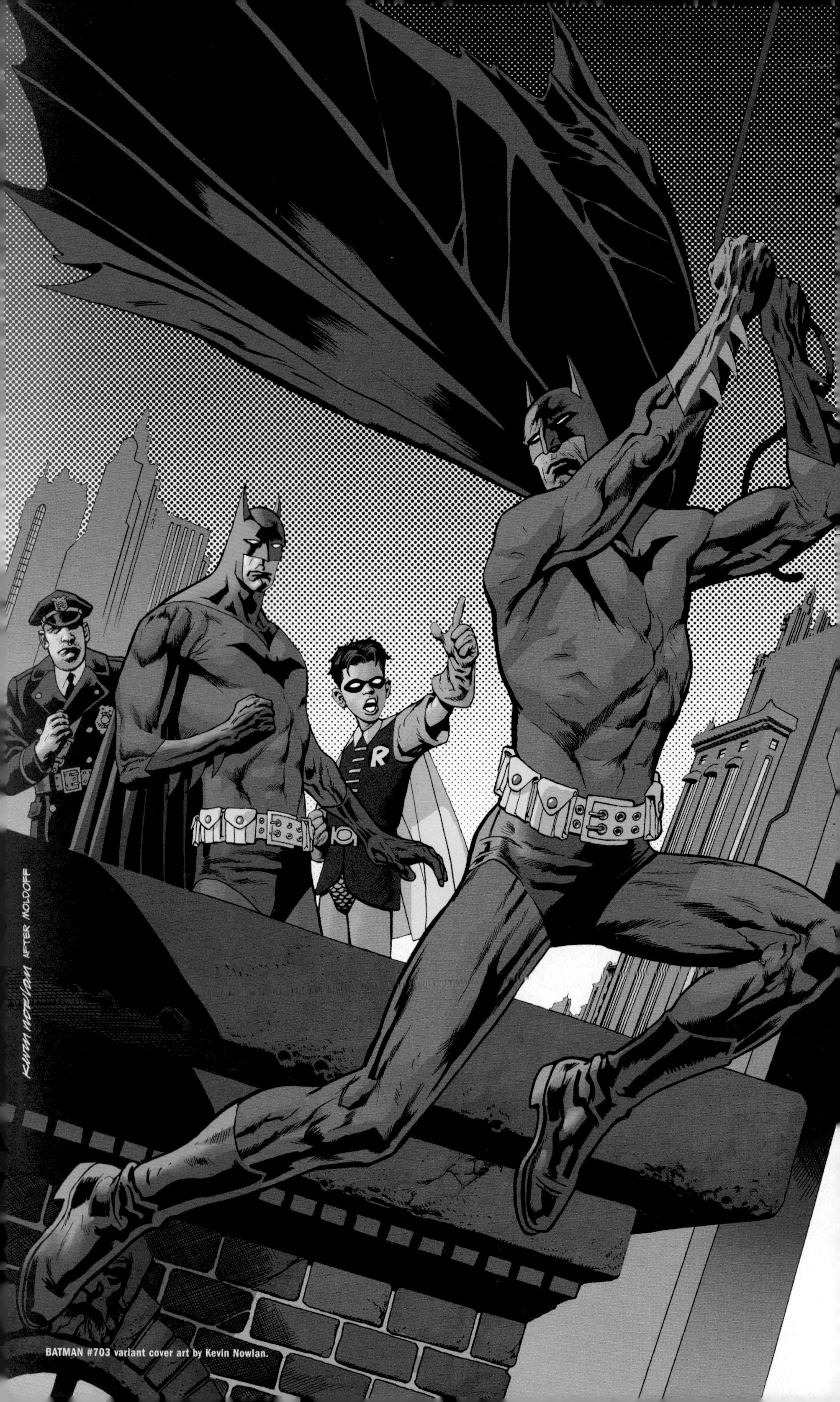
AFTER MOLDOFF

BATMAN #703 variant cover art by Kevin Nowlan.

FROM *NEW YORK TIMES* #1 BEST-SELLING WRITER

GRANT MORRISON

with ANDY KUBERT

BATMAN:
THE BLACK GLOVE

with J.H. WILLIAMS III
and TONY S. DANIEL

BATMAN: R.I.P.

with TONY S. DANIEL

BATMAN: THE RETURN
OF BRUCE WAYNE

with FRAZER IRVING,
RYAN SOOK and other top
talent

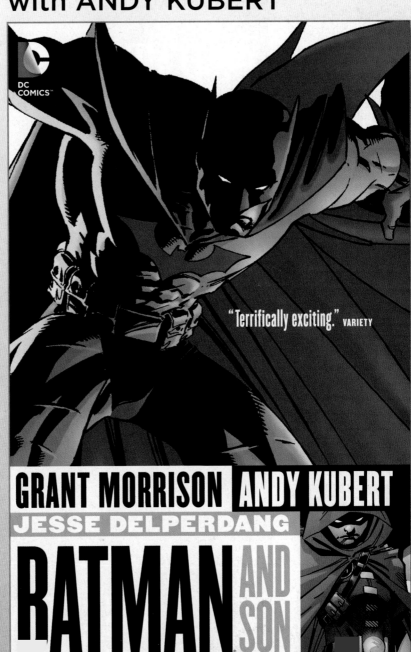

GRANT MORRISON   ANDY KUBERT
JESSE DELPERDANG
BATMAN AND SON

DC COMICS™

From the WRITER/ARTIST of *DETECTIVE COMICS*

TONY S. DANIEL
BATMAN: EYE OF THE BEHOLDER

BATMAN: R.I.P.

with GRANT MORRISON

**BATMAN:
LIFE AFTER DEATH**

**BATMAN: BATTLE FOR
THE COWL**